TRUE TO FORM

A Celebration of the Art of the Chinese Craftsman • LYNN PAN •

FormAsia

TRUETOFORM
Published 1995
ISBN: 962-7283-16-0

Registered address:
Coopers & Lybrand
Caroline Centre, 10th Floor,
28 Yun Yang Road,
Causeway Bay, Hong Kong

Written by Lynn Pan
Designed by Lilian Tang Design Limited, Hong Kong
Photography by Kwan Kwong Chung

Proofread by Geraldine Moor
Colour separations by Lau Wing Chung
Printed in Hong Kong by Leefung-Asco Printers Trading Limited

CONTENTS

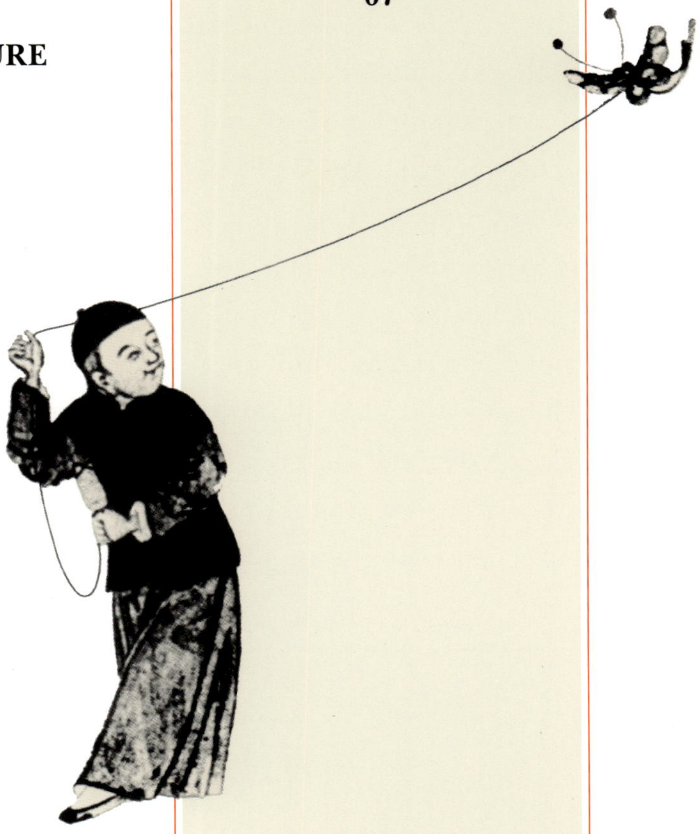

PREFACE

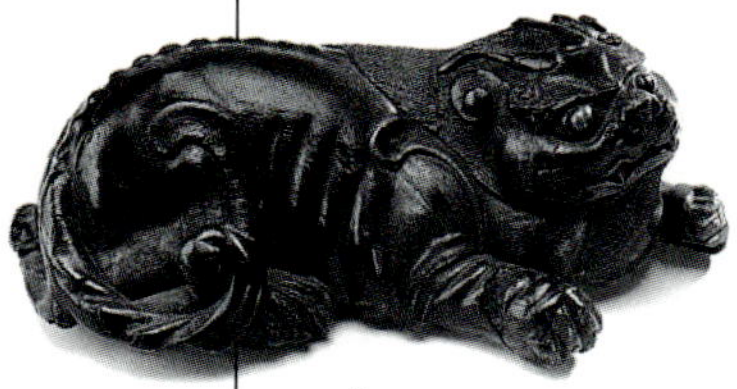

WHEN ONE LOOKS AT A BEAUTIFUL WORK OF CHINESE CRAFT, one's feeling is that the form which the craftsman has created is a *natural* form - a form which has emerged inevitably out of the movement of the maker's hands. It is as though the creator was being faithful to the essential nature of things, and instinctively harmonizing his work with it. If one theme in this book is to stand out in higher relief than any other, it is that something is pleasing to the eye because it is true to form. No matter how utilitarian or workaday, every one of the objects pictured within conveys that sense of visual fitness.

There are as many ways of seeing an object as there are pairs of eyes to see it. Some eyes may respond most intensely to form or colour; others may focus on function or physical texture. Perspective, sequence, the change of light and shade or of mood and setting - all can influence the observing eye. And it may take a frame to concentrate a painting's power of revelation.

The objects whose images make up this book have been "framed" not only by the page itself but by their grouping. The two halves into which they fall mirror a bifurcation in both Chinese life and art. There were the men of letters, and there was the rest of humanity: this was the grand canyon in the life of traditional China. Of course the two worlds, the lettered and unlettered, intersected at some points, but nevertheless the art which took its place in the one and that which belonged to the other were divided by more than the blink of an eye.

Within each of the two groupings, the objects have been arranged according to whether they relate to daily living, to calling, or to recreation.

LIVING

LIVING

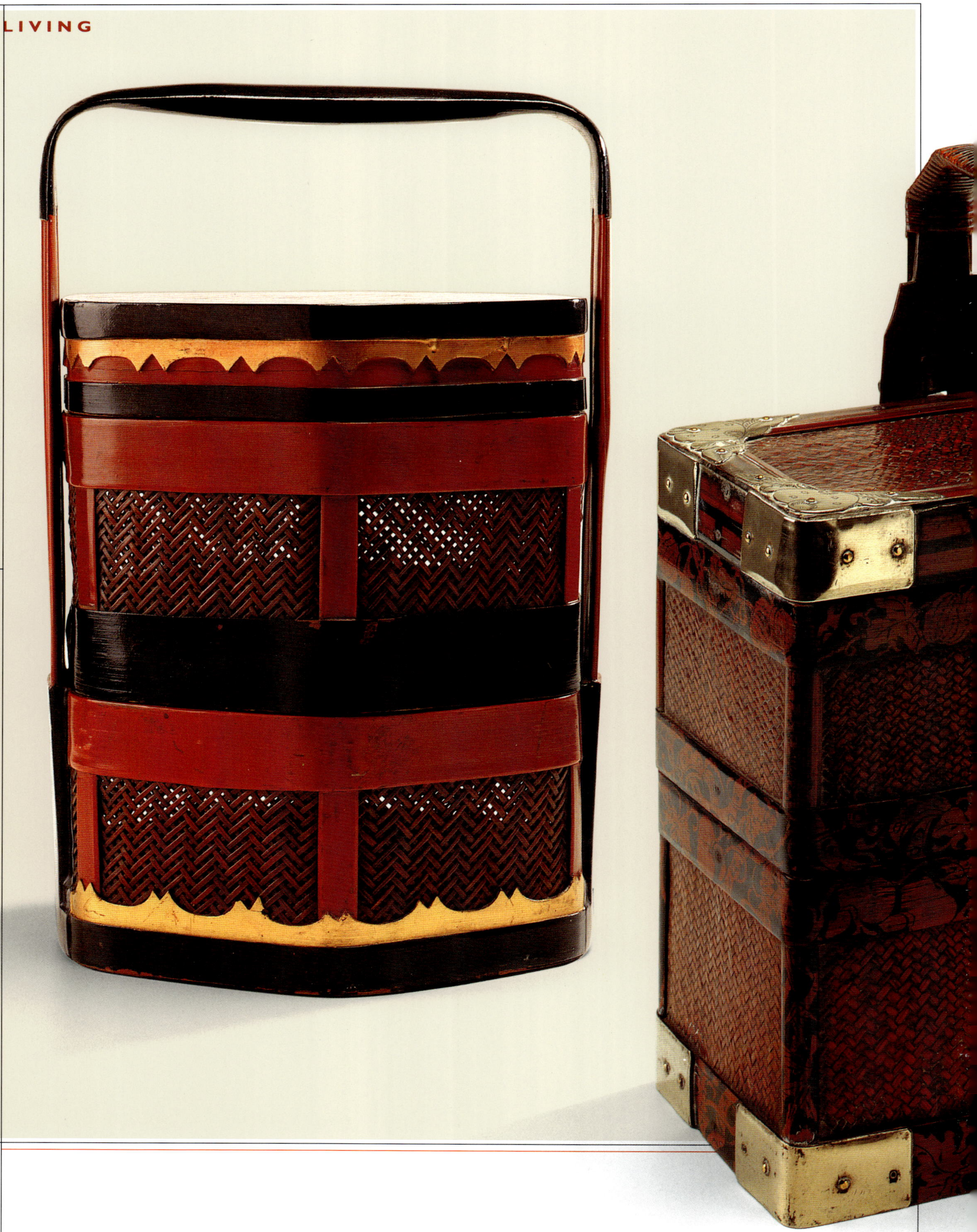

Two-tiered carrying basket in loosely woven bamboo with lacquered cover, handle and trimmings, height 60 cm.

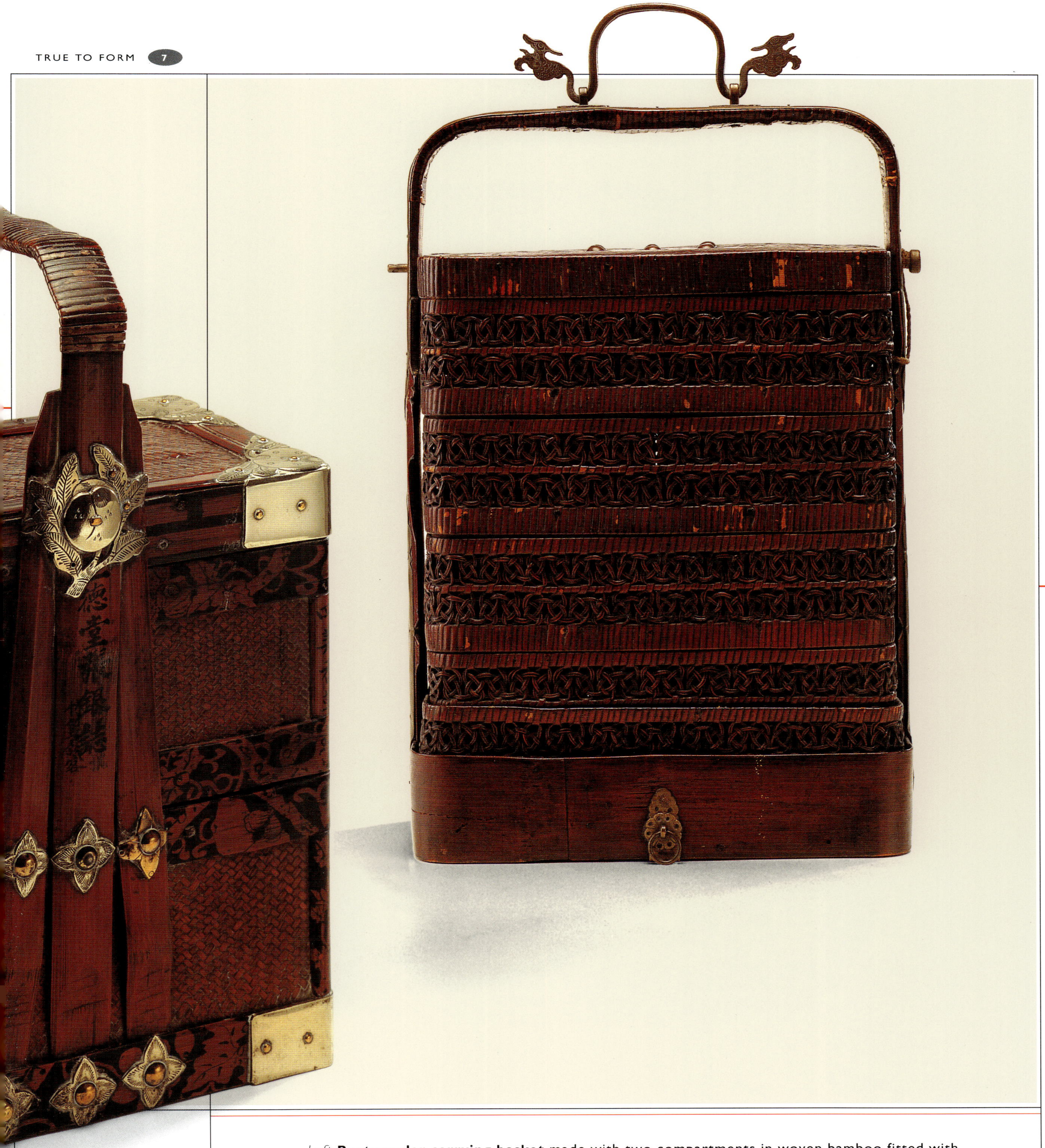

Left **Rectangular carrying basket** made with two compartments in woven bamboo fitted with metal trimmings, height 45 cm. *Right* Four-tiered **picnic bamboo basket** with metal hoop atop handle, height 45 cm.

LIVING

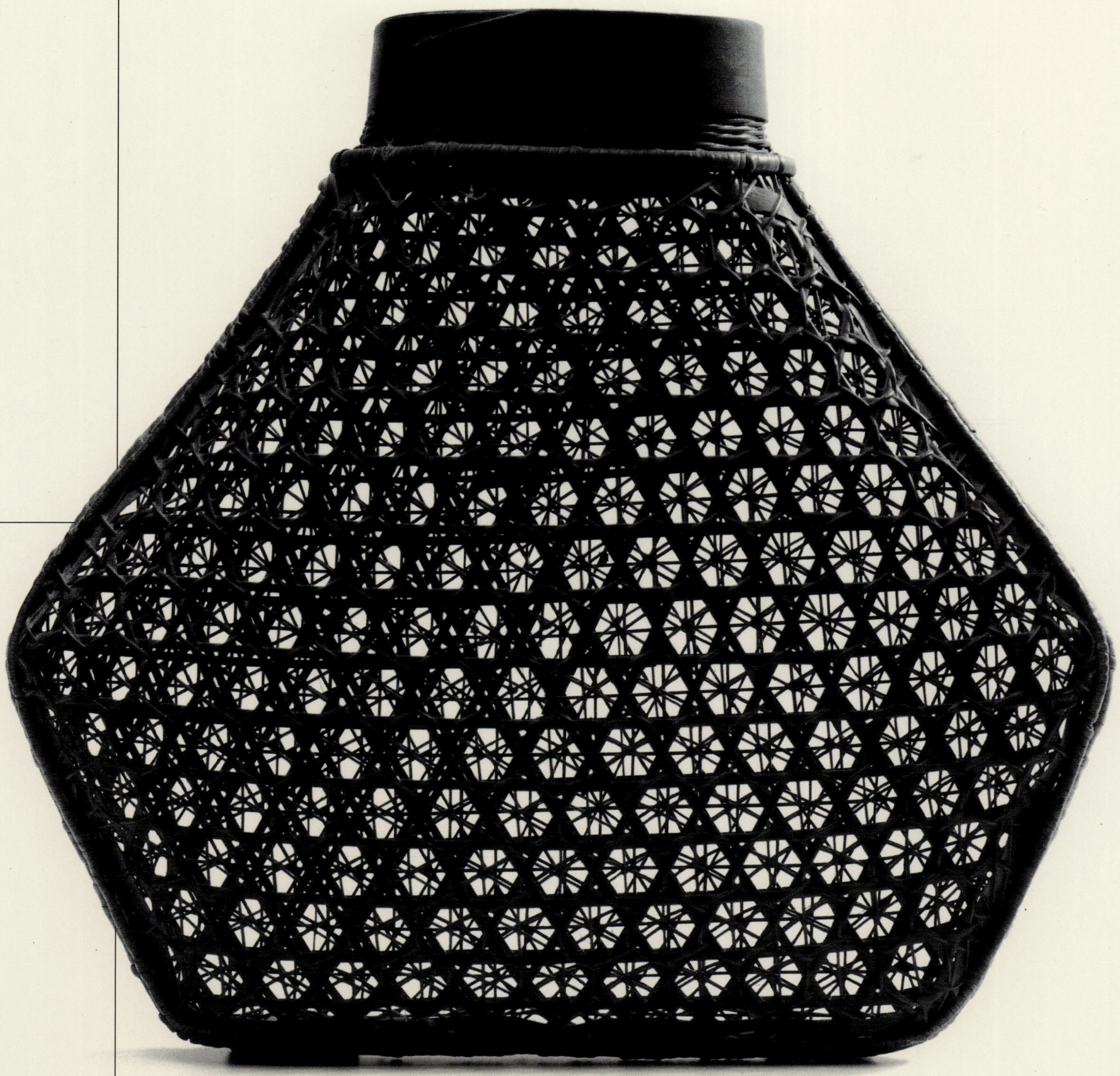

Flask in open rattan weaving used by women for keeping strands of hair detached during combing. The hair was saved for use as switches or hairpieces, height 20 cm.

Round basket of woven bamboo with dipped handle and wooden base carved in the "key pattern" seen in the most ancient sacrificial bronze vessels, height 35 cm.

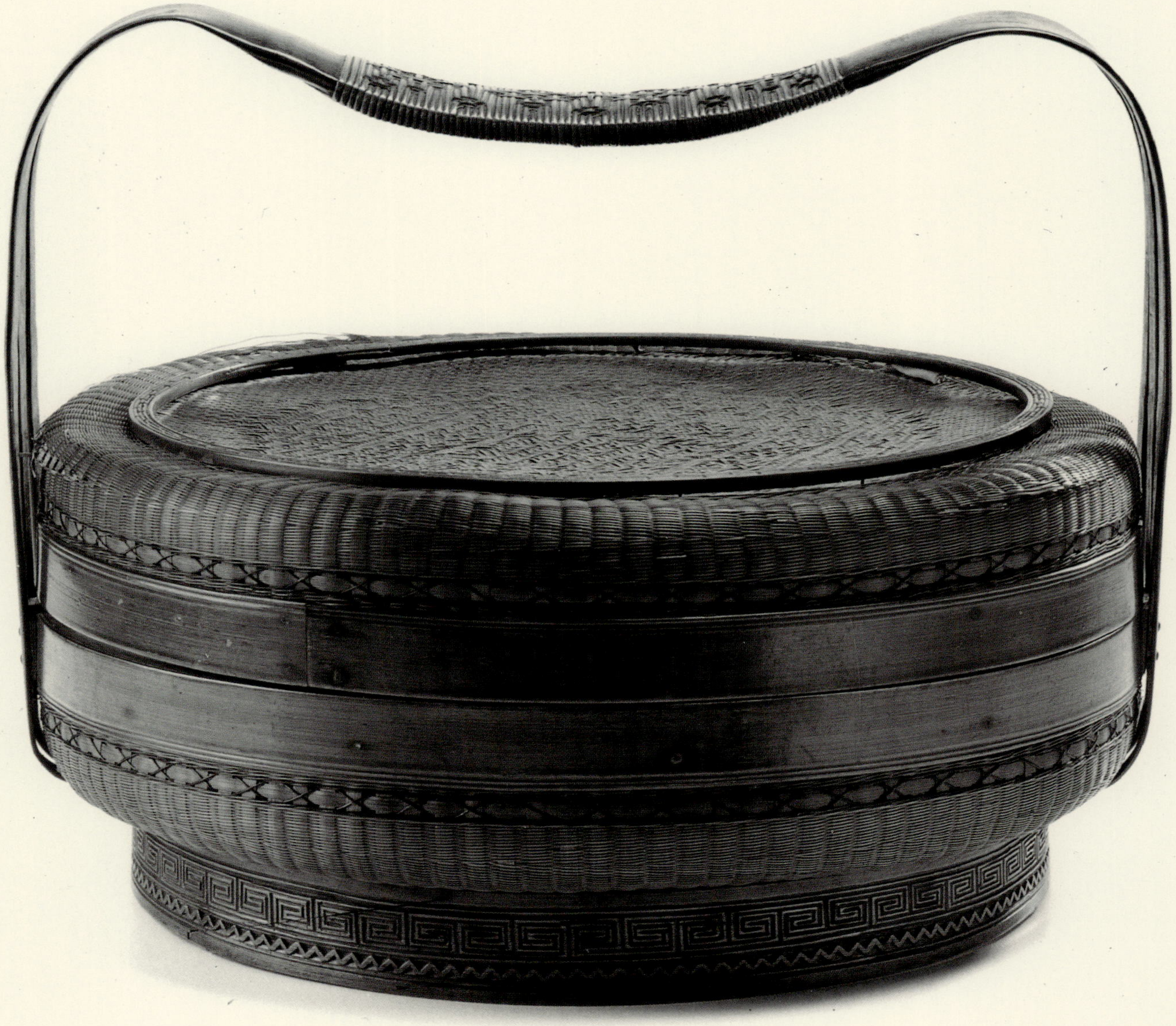

LIVING

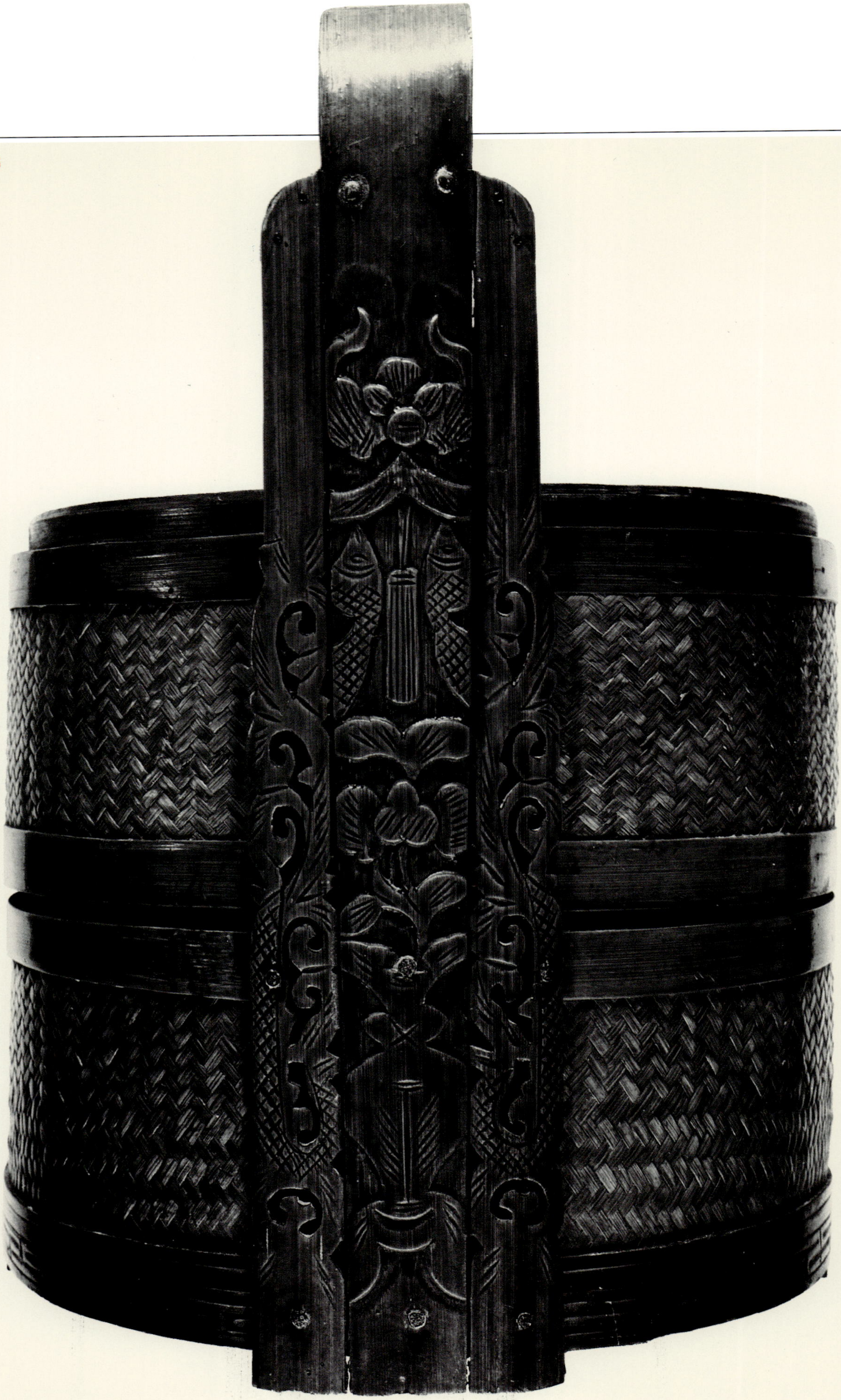

Carrying basket in braid-patterned bamboo weaving made in two compartments, with handle carved in fish and floral design, height 50 cm.

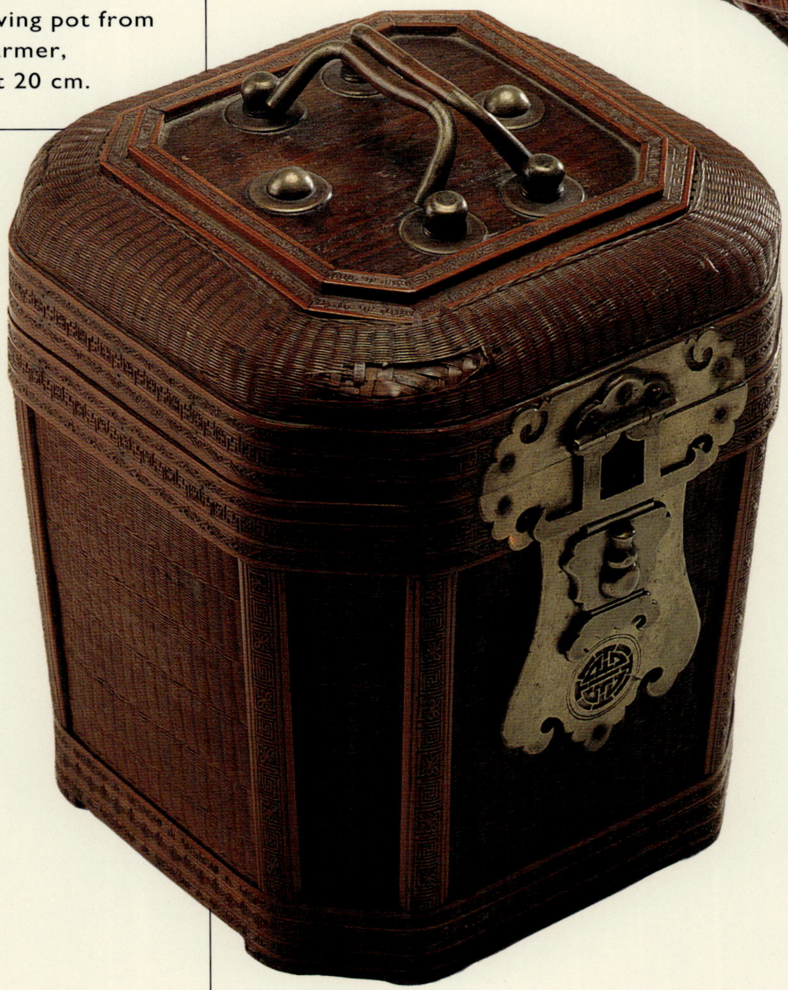

Wickerware tea cosy with metal handles and perforation in the lock through which spout of teapot projects, making it possible to pour without removing pot from its warmer, height 20 cm.

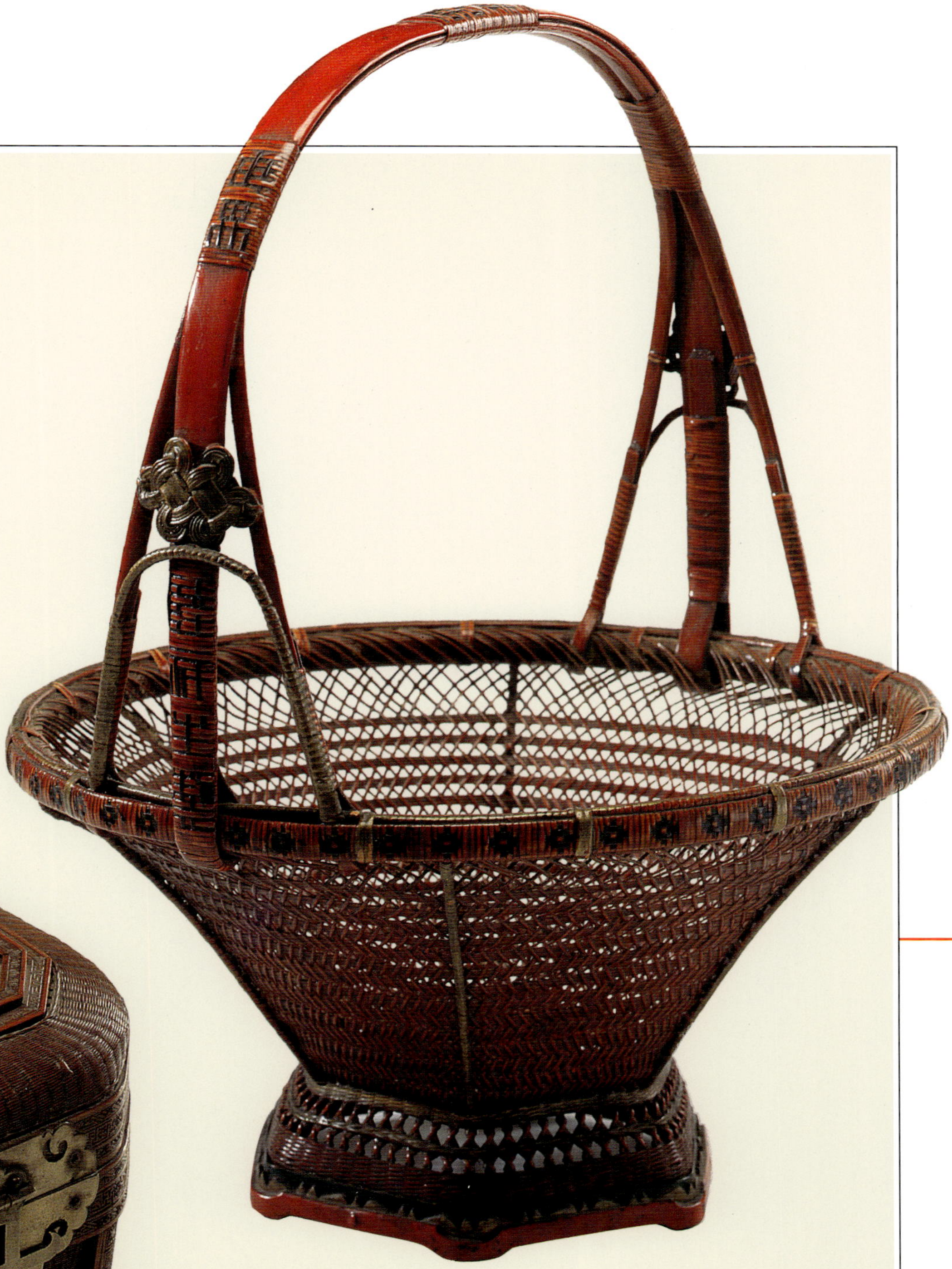

Bamboo flower basket in open weave with hexagonal base and coil handle of three strips, height 50 cm.

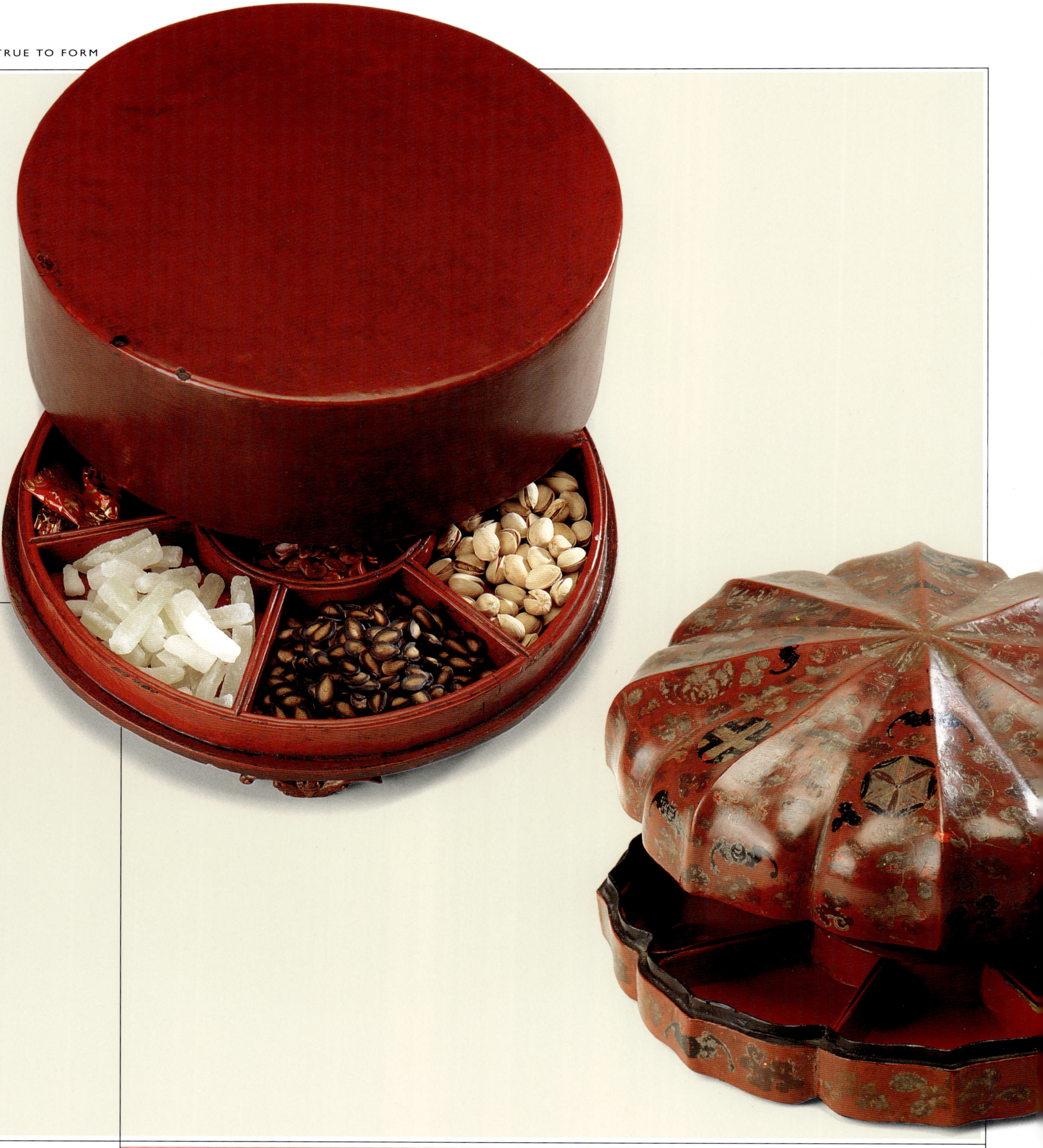

Lacquered boxes for sweetmeats with trays divided into compartments for melon seeds, nuts, crystallized fruit and other kinds of confectionary traditionally offered to those who come to pay Lunar New Year calls, diameters 33 cm.

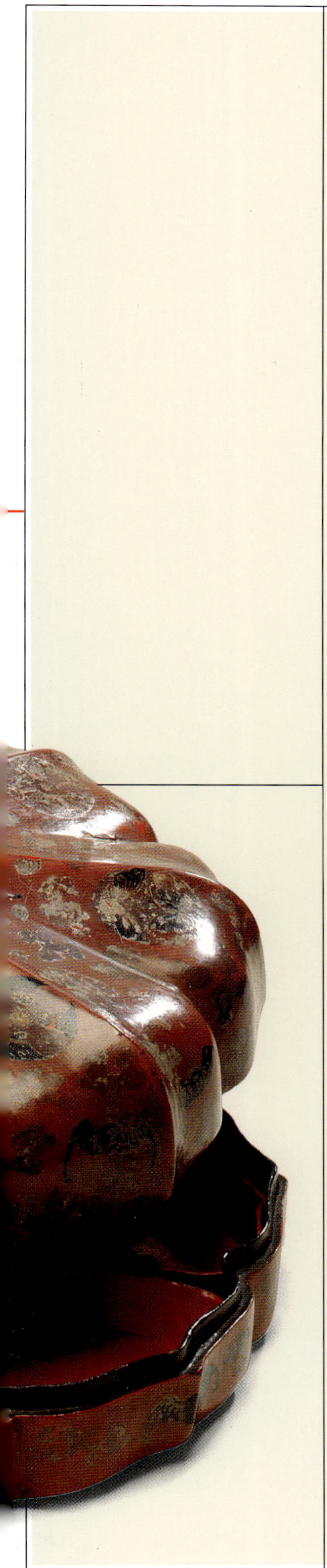

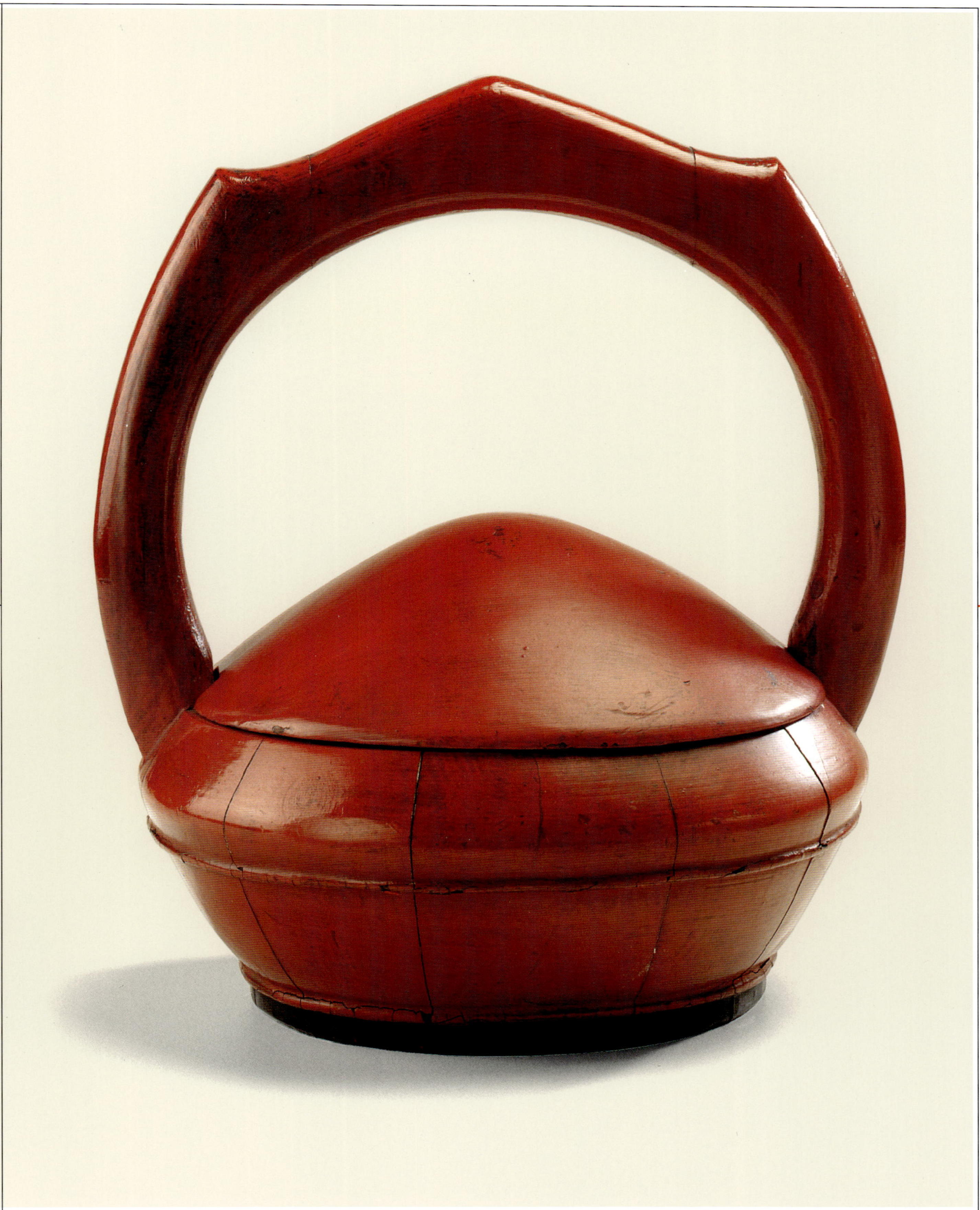

Container with handle in red lacquered wood with two twisted wires serving as braces round body and at foot, height 36 cm.

LIVING

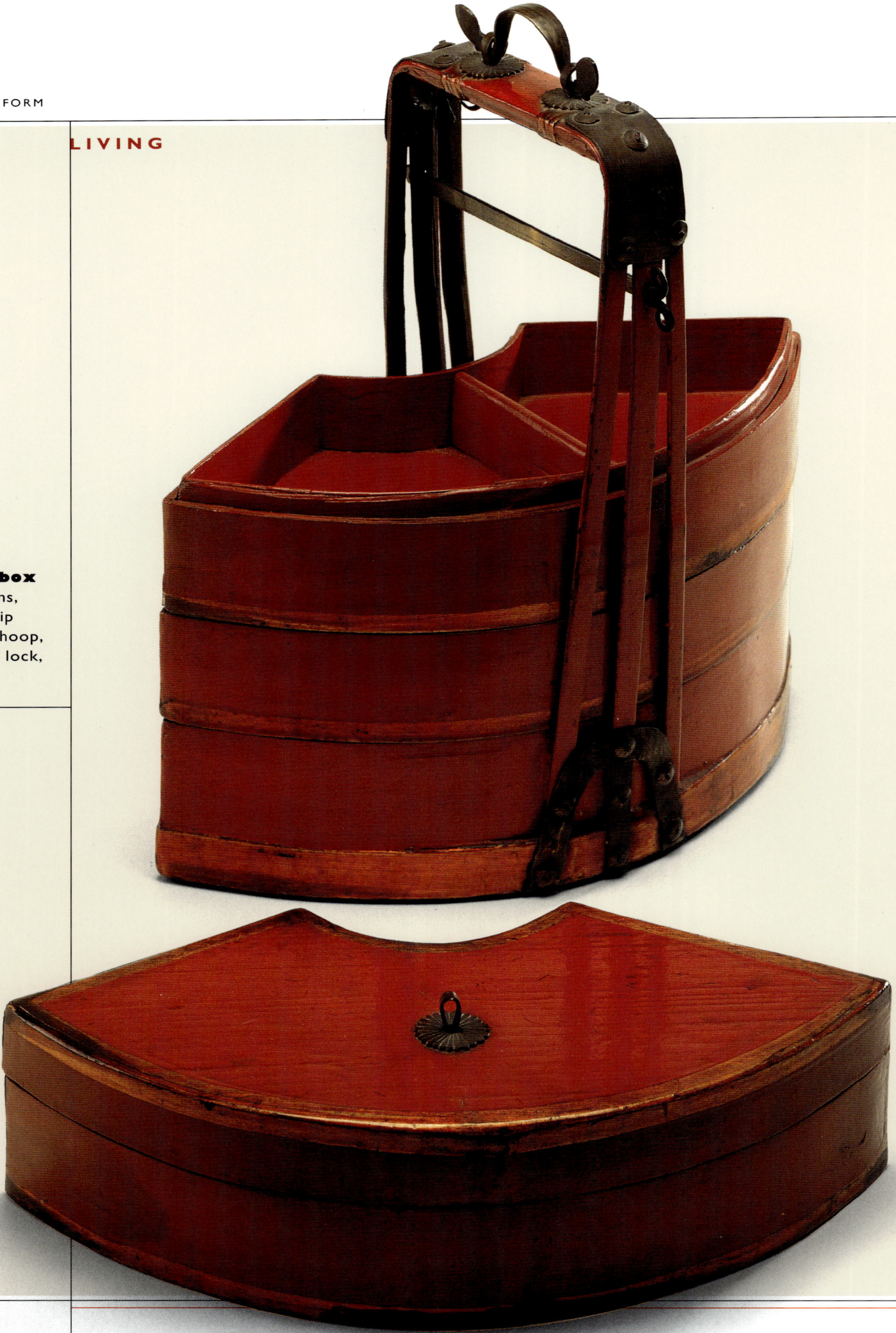

Tiered lacquered box for keeping fans, with three-strip handle, metal hoop, trimmings and lock, height 40 cm.

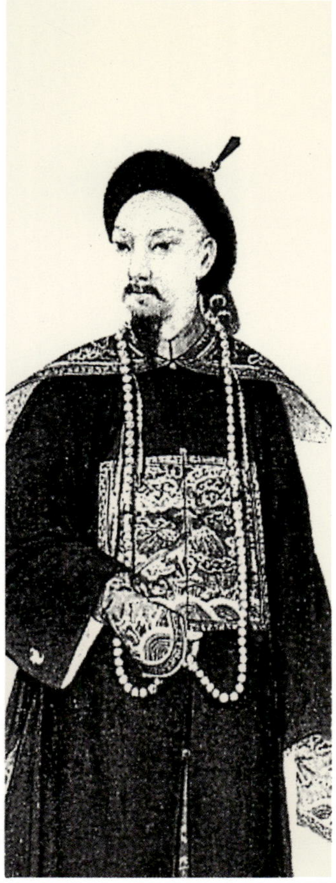

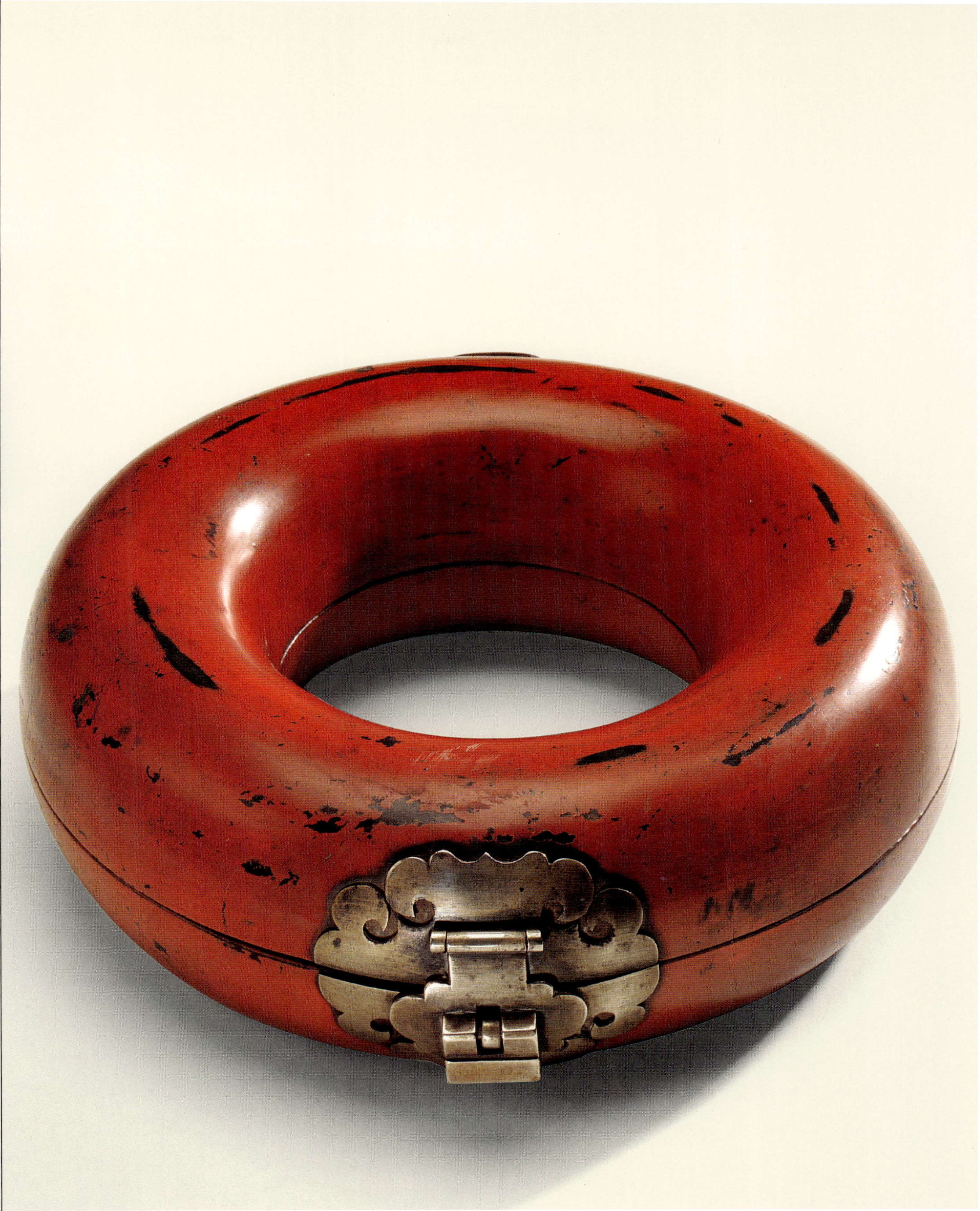

Doughnut-shaped box in lacquer with brass lock for keeping *chaozhu,* court necklace, the string of beads made of coral, amber and other stones worn by officials of the Qing dynasty, diameter 22 cm.

LIVING

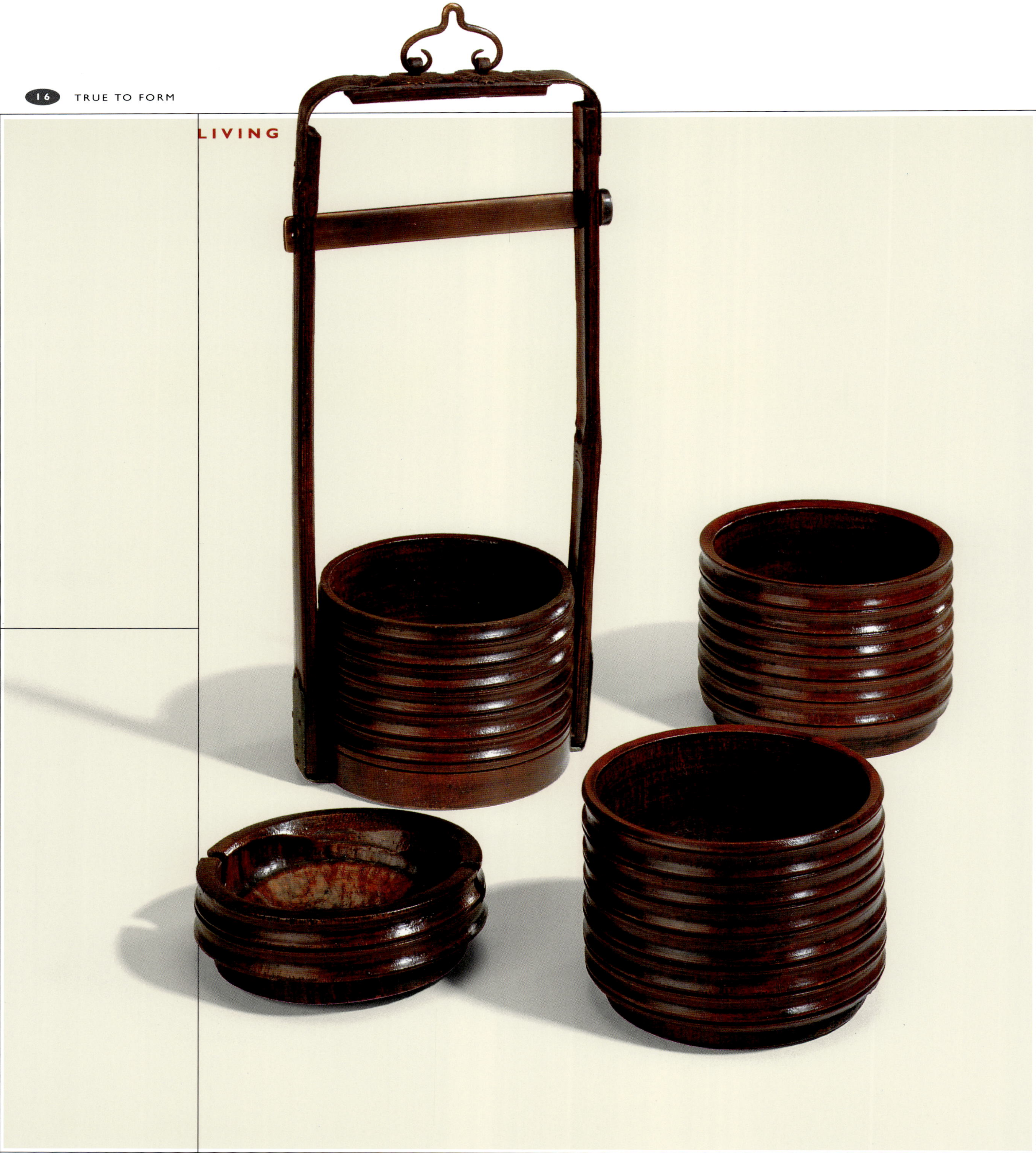

Tiered lunch box in lacquered bamboo with brass handle, height 35 cm.

Pair of *renmian* ("human face") **bamboo sections** cultivated to achieve required shape for decorative purpose, height 40 cm.

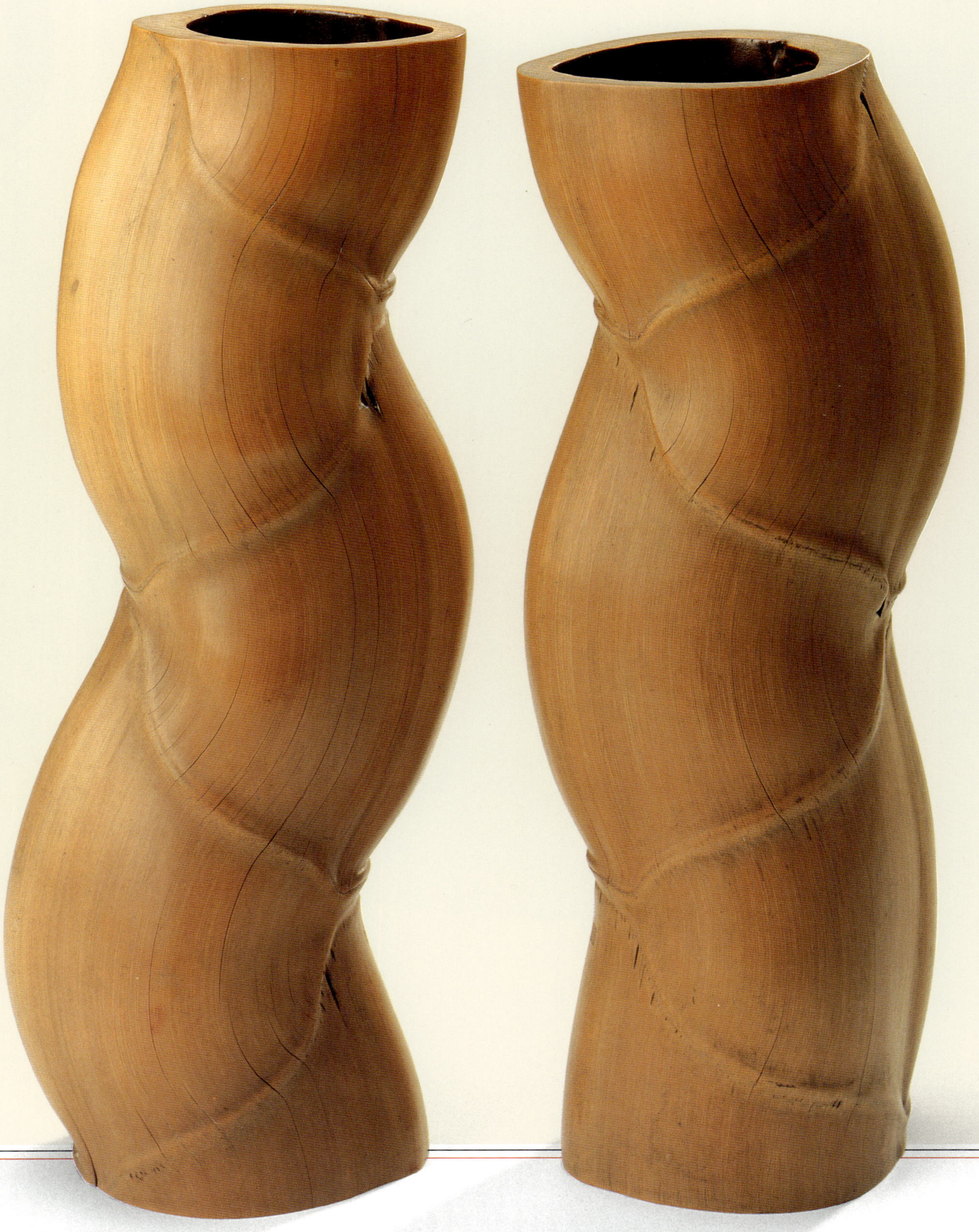

LIVING

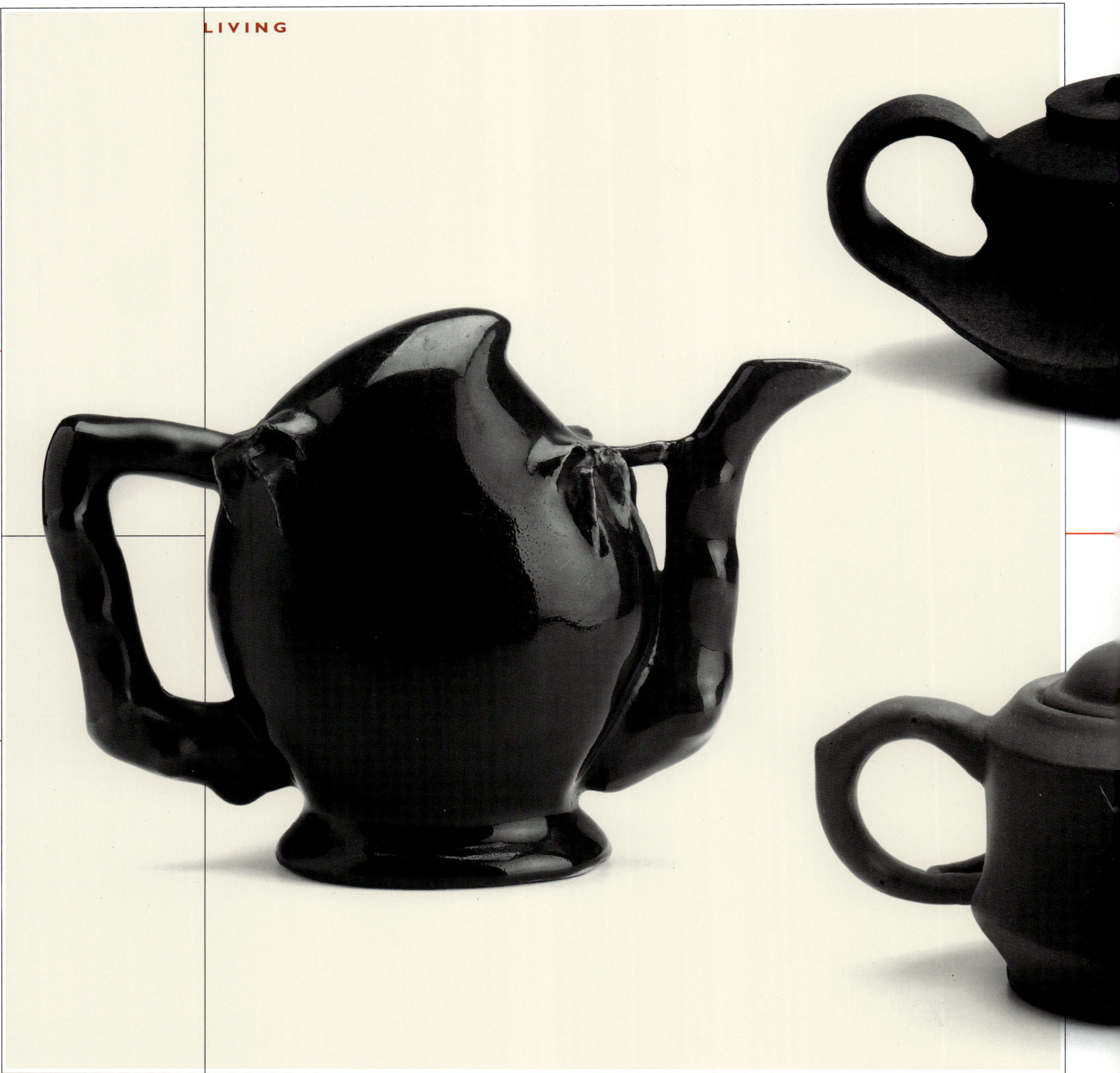

Above **Peach-shaped wine pot** without opening for lid used at wedding banquets. The pot, filled through a hole at the bottom, has double communicating pipes inside and was made by a craftsman who lived during the time of the Qianlong Emperor (1736-1795) and who died with the secret of how it was made, height, 22 cm.

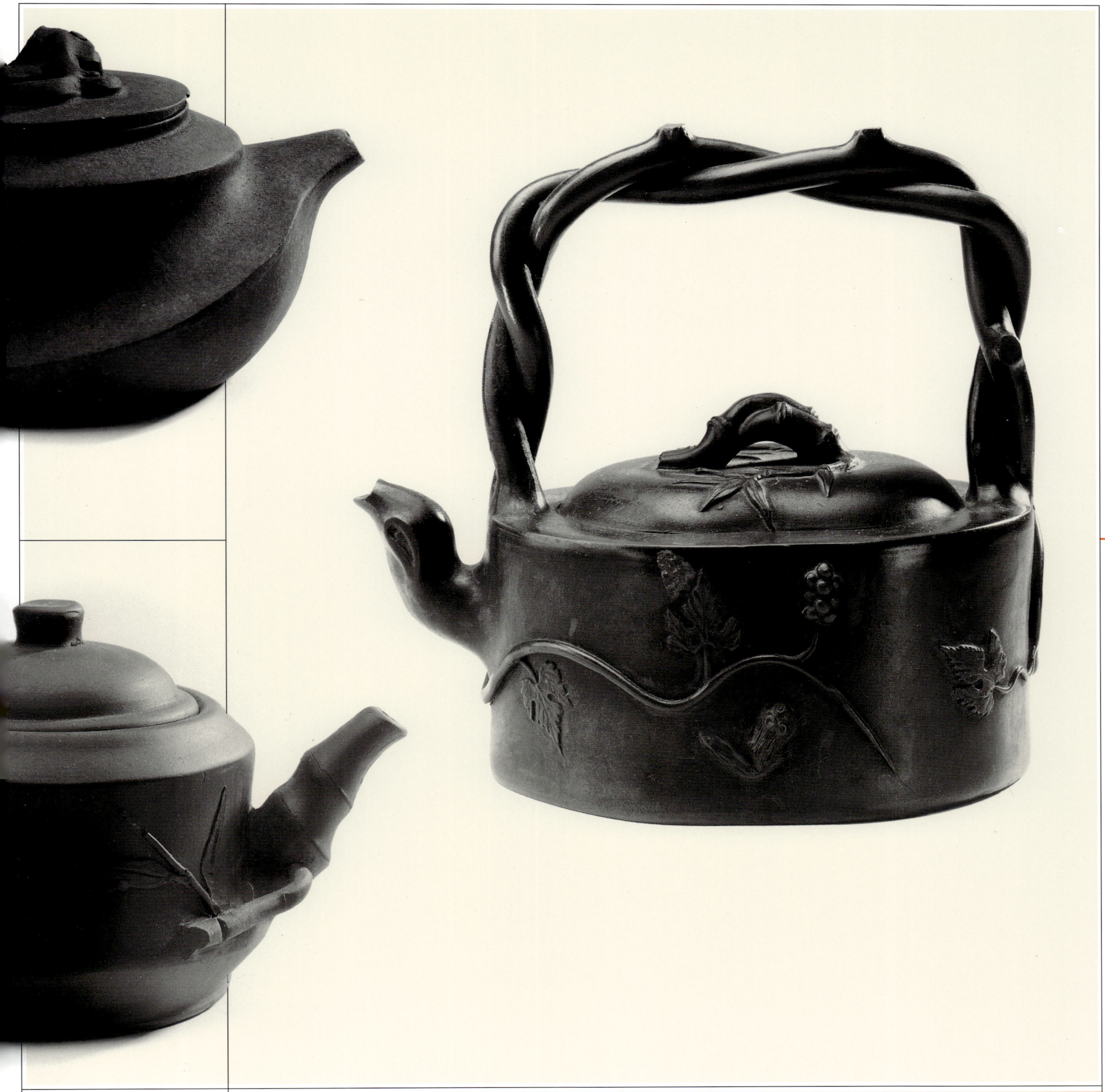

Three clay teapots traditional to Yixing, in Jiangsu province, whose potteries are famous for their "purple sand" wares.

LIVING

Chopsticks
for all occasions.

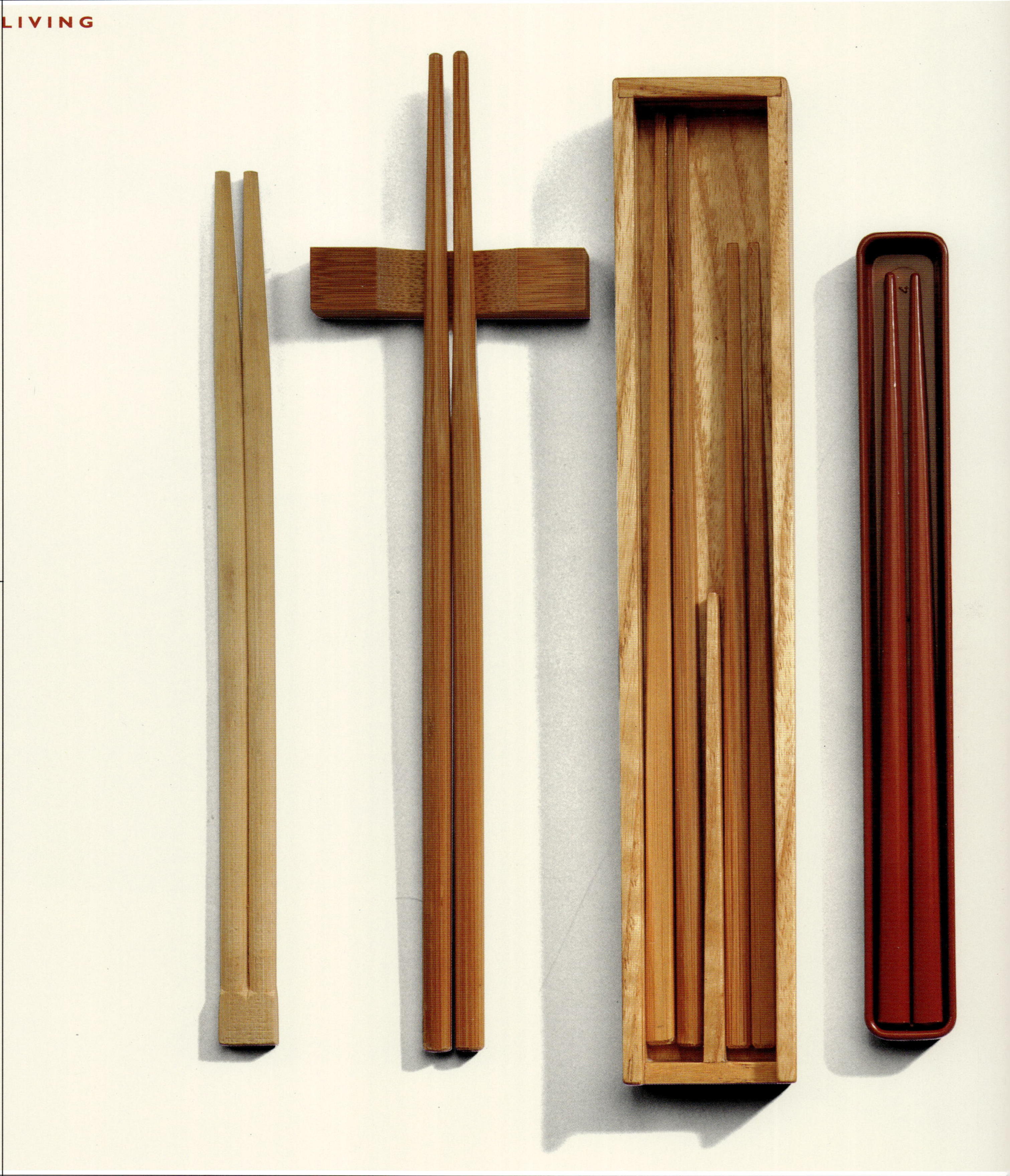

Joined pair
to be pulled apart
upon use

Wooden pair
on wooden rest for
everyday use

His and hers pairs
in box

Pair in box
for travelling

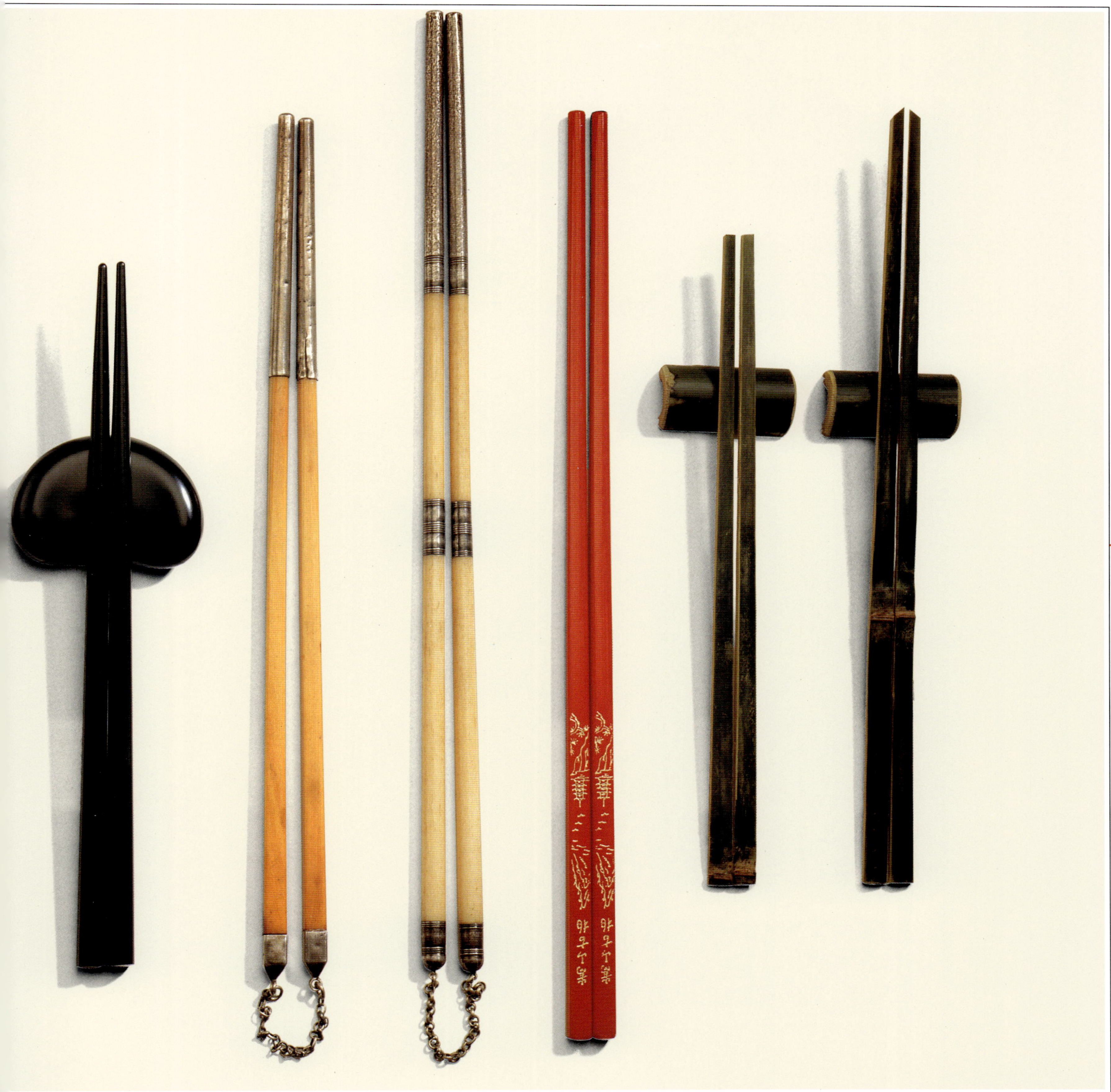

Pair in lacquered wood

Two pairs in ivory topped, tipped and looped in silver

Pair in auspicious red for celebrations, inscribed with "ancient cypress of lofty mountains"

Two pairs in green bamboo to mark a crossing of such thresholds as going to school, or becoming employed, for the first time.

LIVING

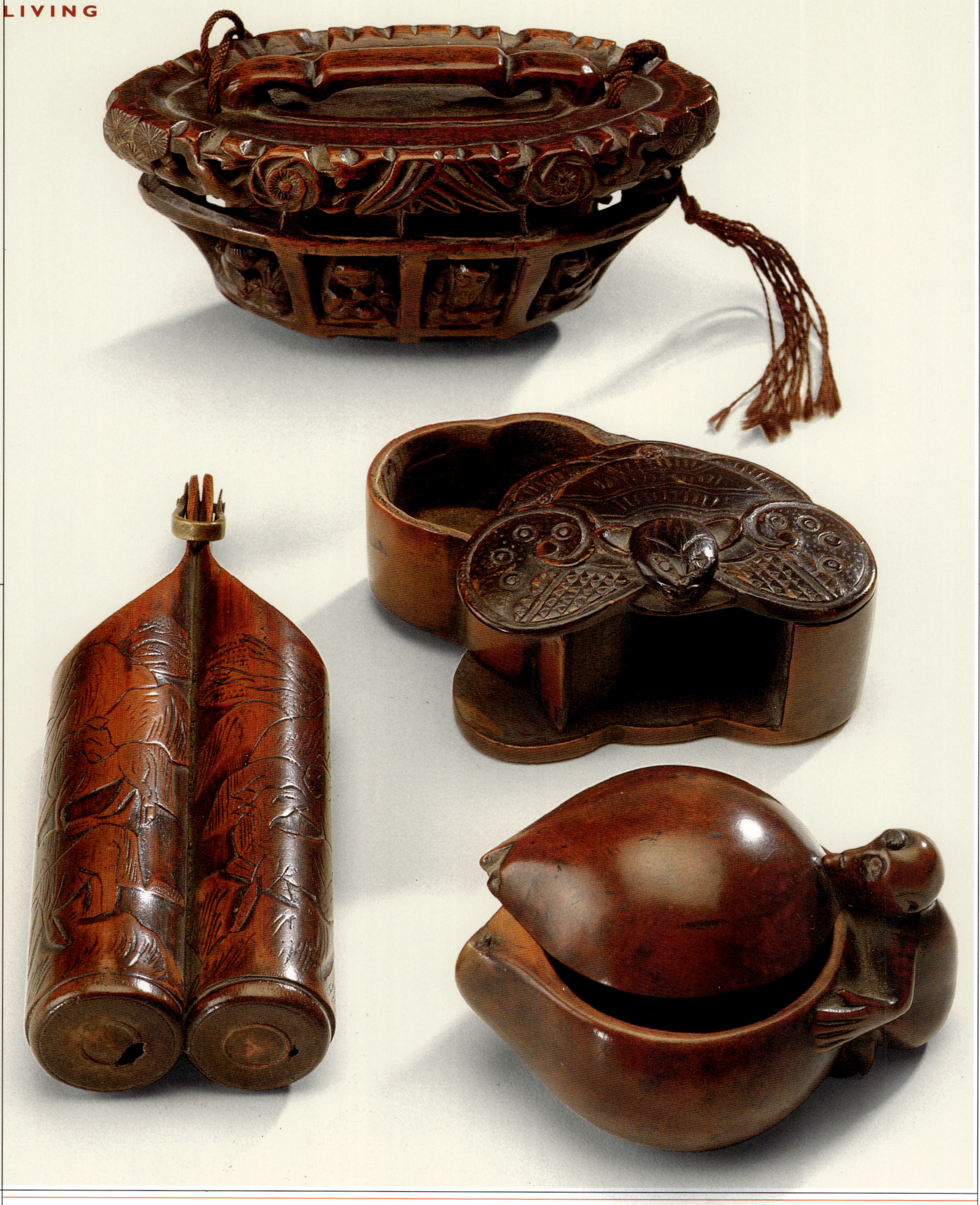

Clockwise **Tobacco boxes** in wood, 19th century, carved in shape of tub, butterfly and monkey holding peach, diameter 12 cm; *Left* What is thought to be a **carrier for a barber's razor.**

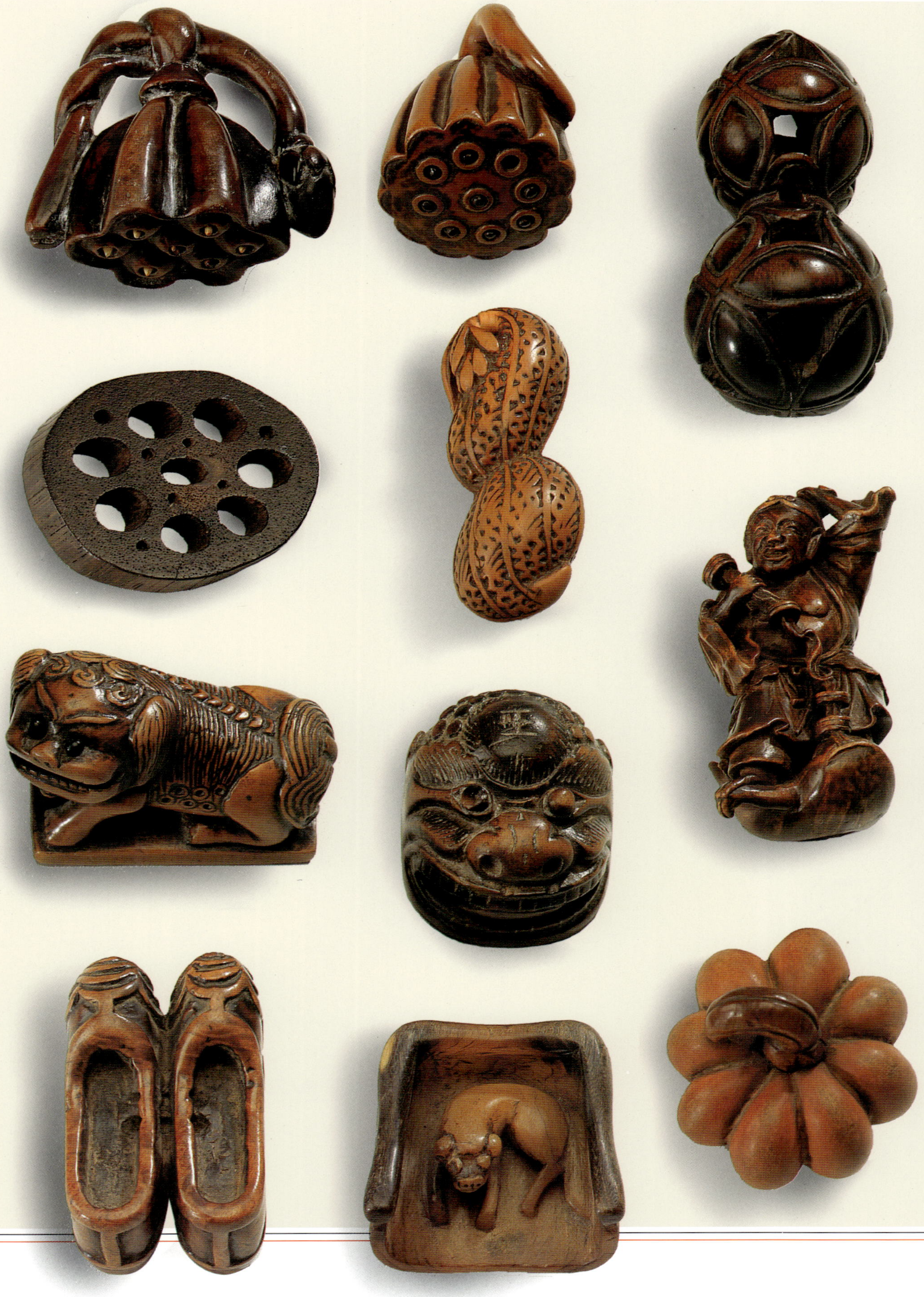

Toggles, called *chui'er* in northern China and the progenitor of Japanese *netsuke*, were fastened to the end of a cord for attaching purses, pouches, pipes and so on to the belt. Carved mostly from boxwood, toggles come in such shapes of old Chinese symbolism as double bottle gourd, lotus seed pod and pumpkin, diameters 6 cm.

LIVING

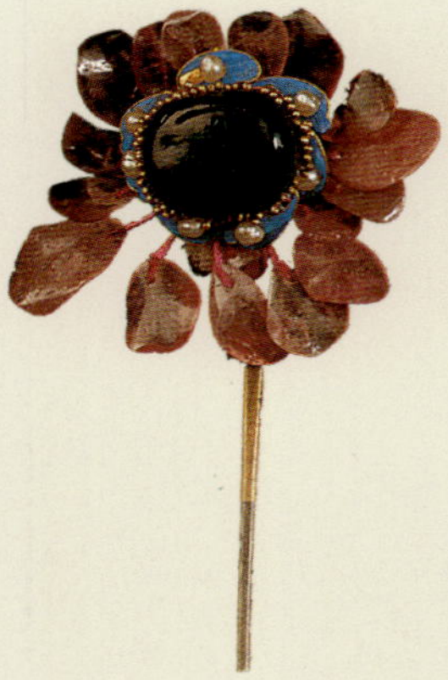

Hairpins of floral pattern in kingfisher-feather inlay decorated with ruby *(top)* and tourmaline *(bottom)*.

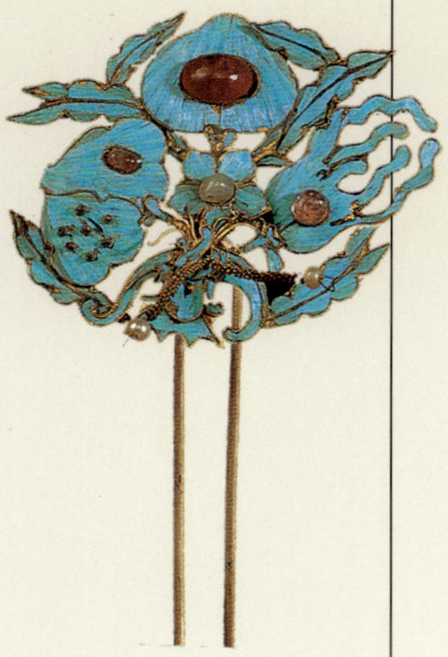

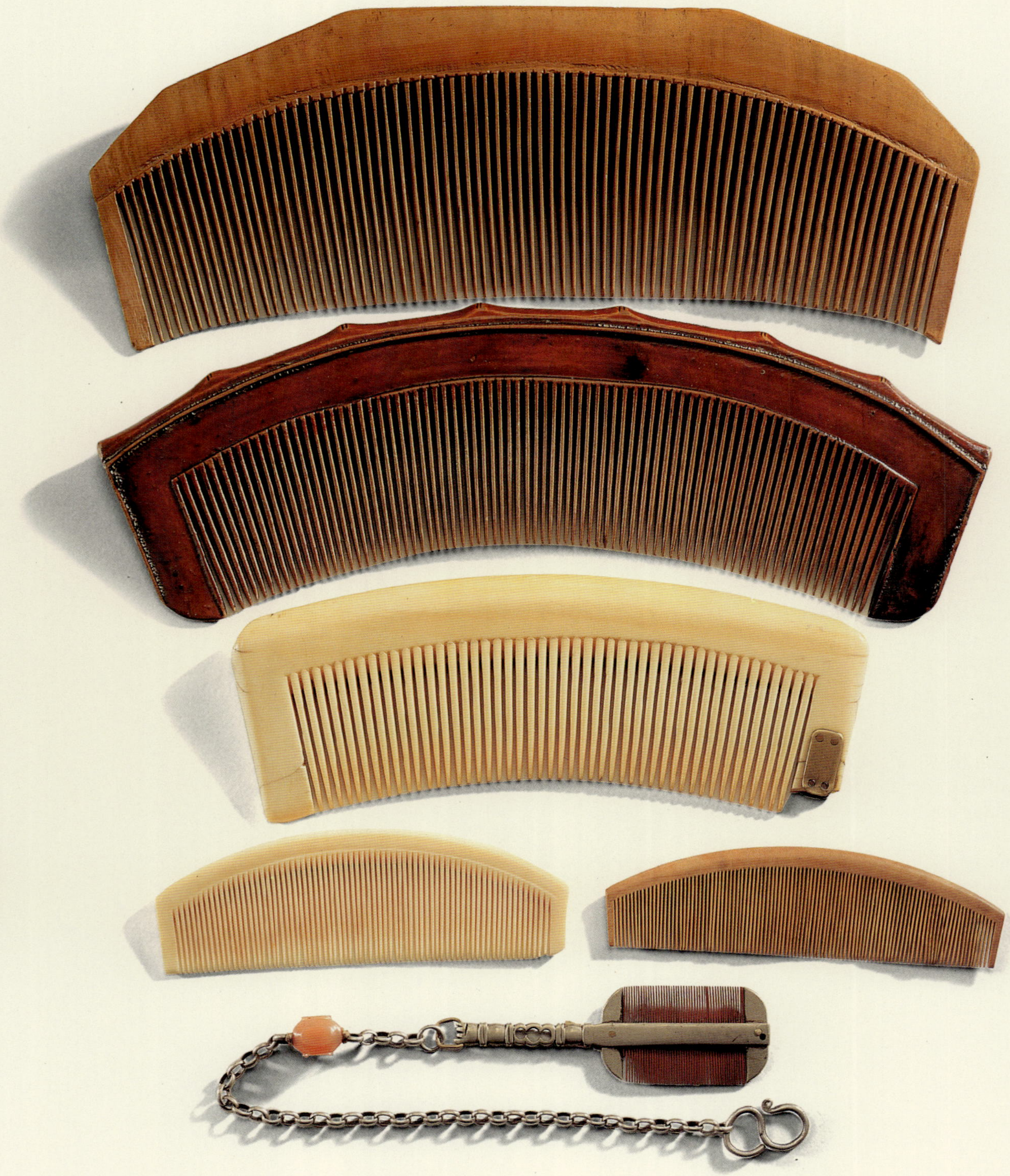

Above **Handmade hair combs** of lacquered wood and ivory. The bottom one, made of wood and *paktong* and trailing a silver chain decorated with coral bead, is the fine-toothed, double-edged kind called *bizi* used for combing beards.

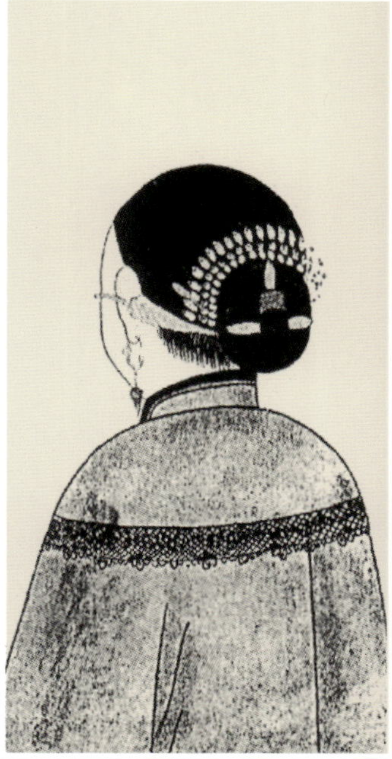

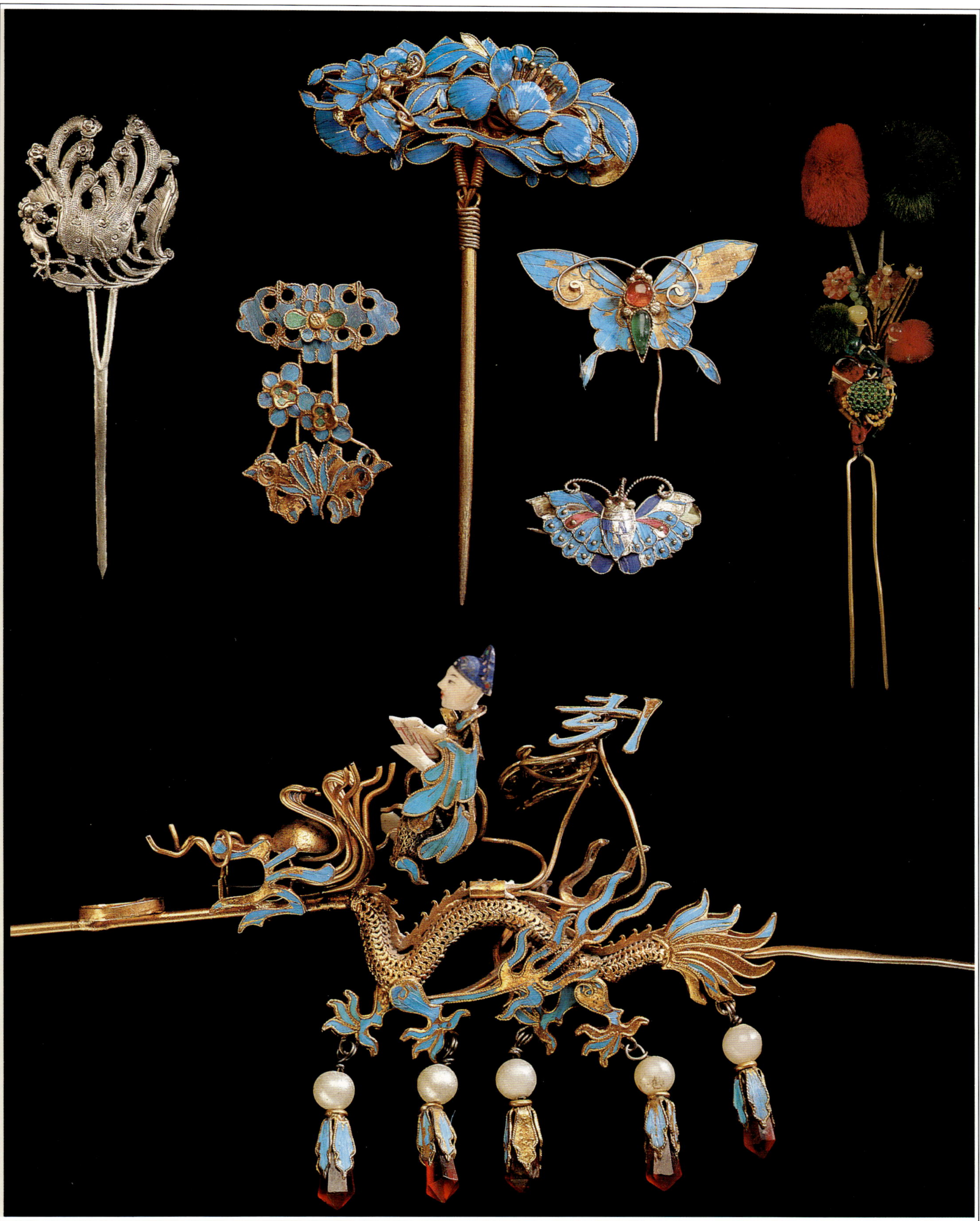

Hairpins in kingfisher-feather inlay with one shaft, called *zan*; two shafts, called *chai*; and hairpins with dangling pendants that wobbled when the wearer moved.

LIVING

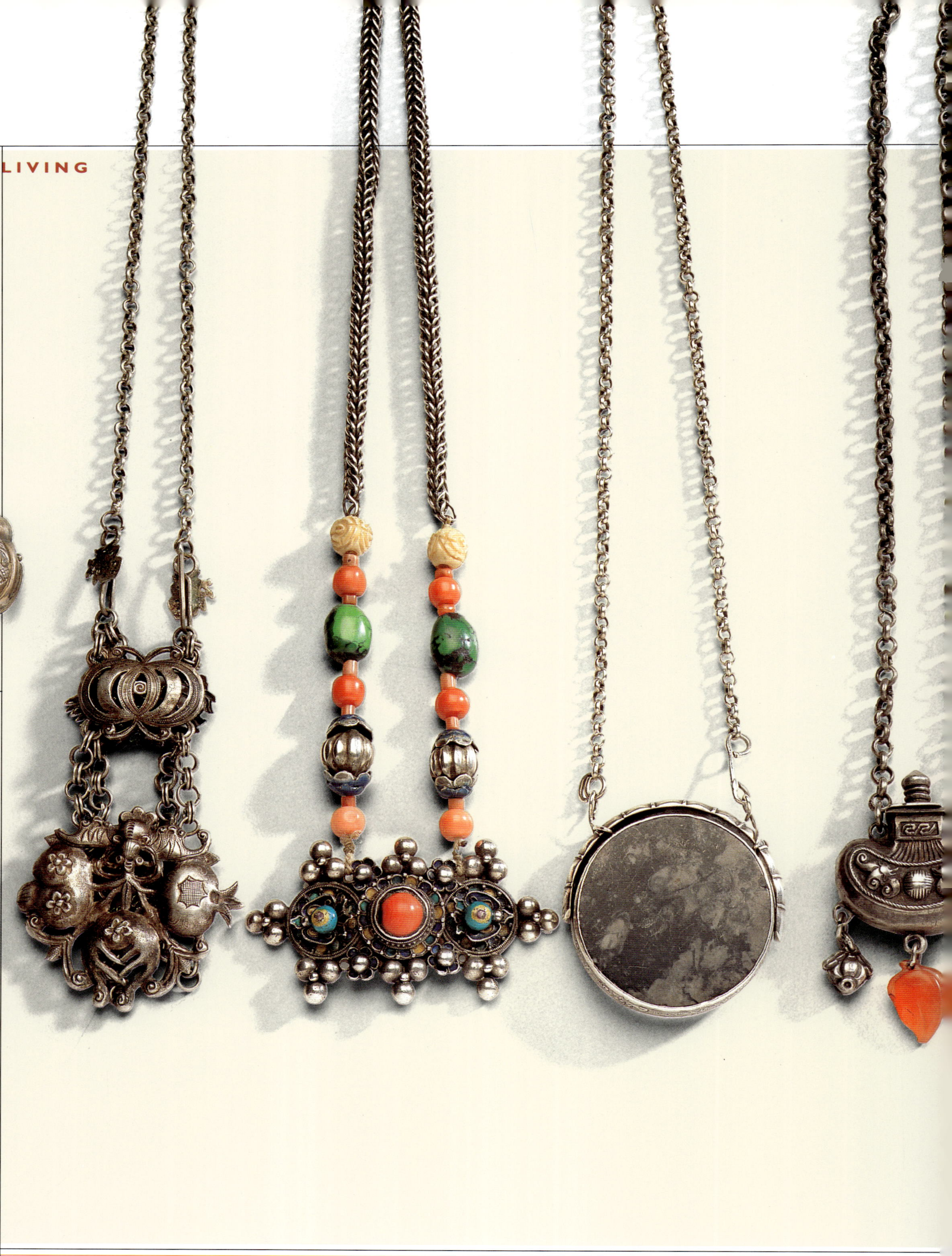

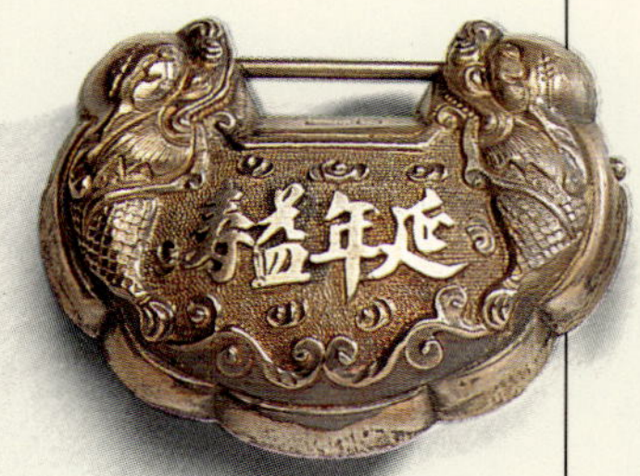

Above **Hollowed silver padlock** with moulded fish design and inscription reading "lengthen his life" intended to be hung from a child's neck to "lock" him to life. *Below* **Lady's ornament** with coral.

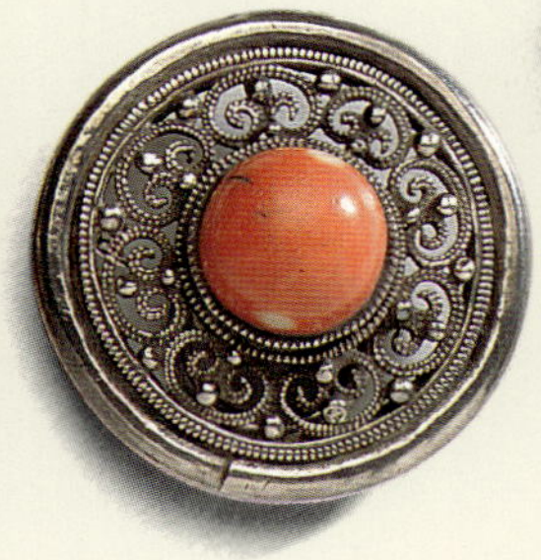

Above **Necklaces and lockets** decorated with precious stones. *Right* **Silver bracelet and bangles,** and ball-shaped silver **fragrance locket** with floral pattern in openwork.

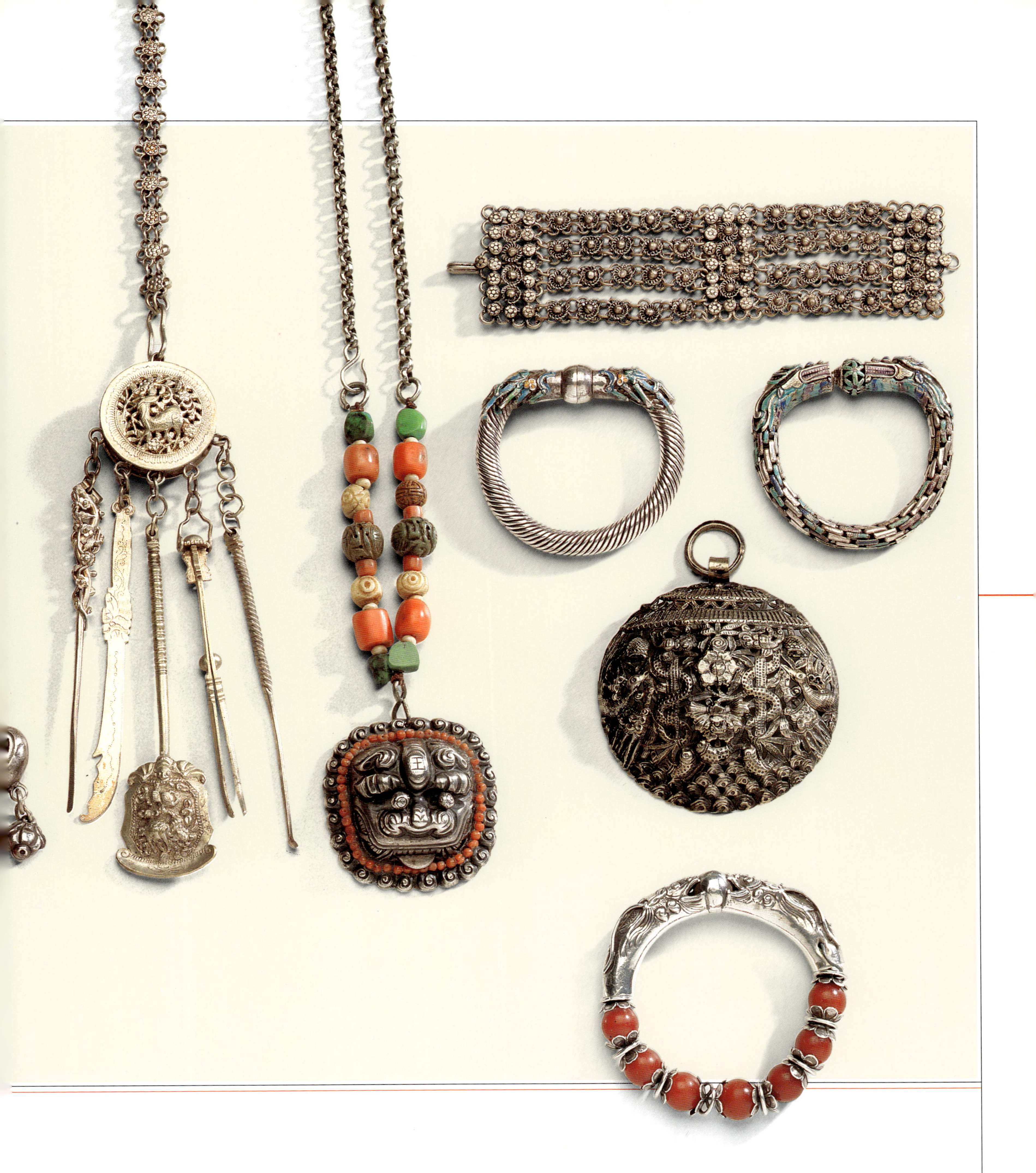

LIVING

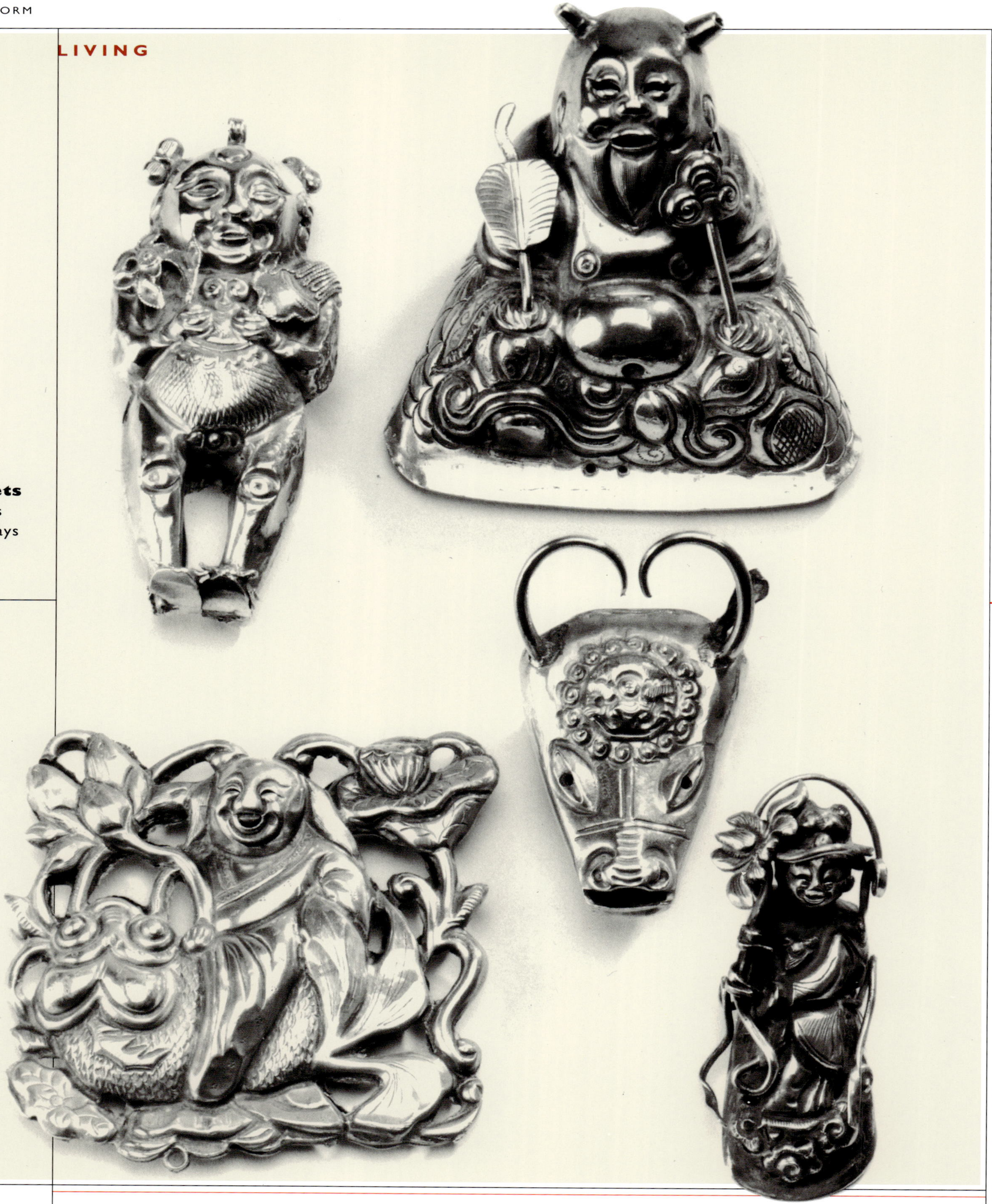

Felicitous silver amulets sewn on to caps worn on birthdays or festivals by little boys.

These charms, thought to have protective powers, normally depict favourite Chinese figures like the God of Longevity *(bottom row, second from right)*, and the legendary Liu Hai with a blossoming lotus on his head and riding a toad that could spit gold coins *(bottom left)*.

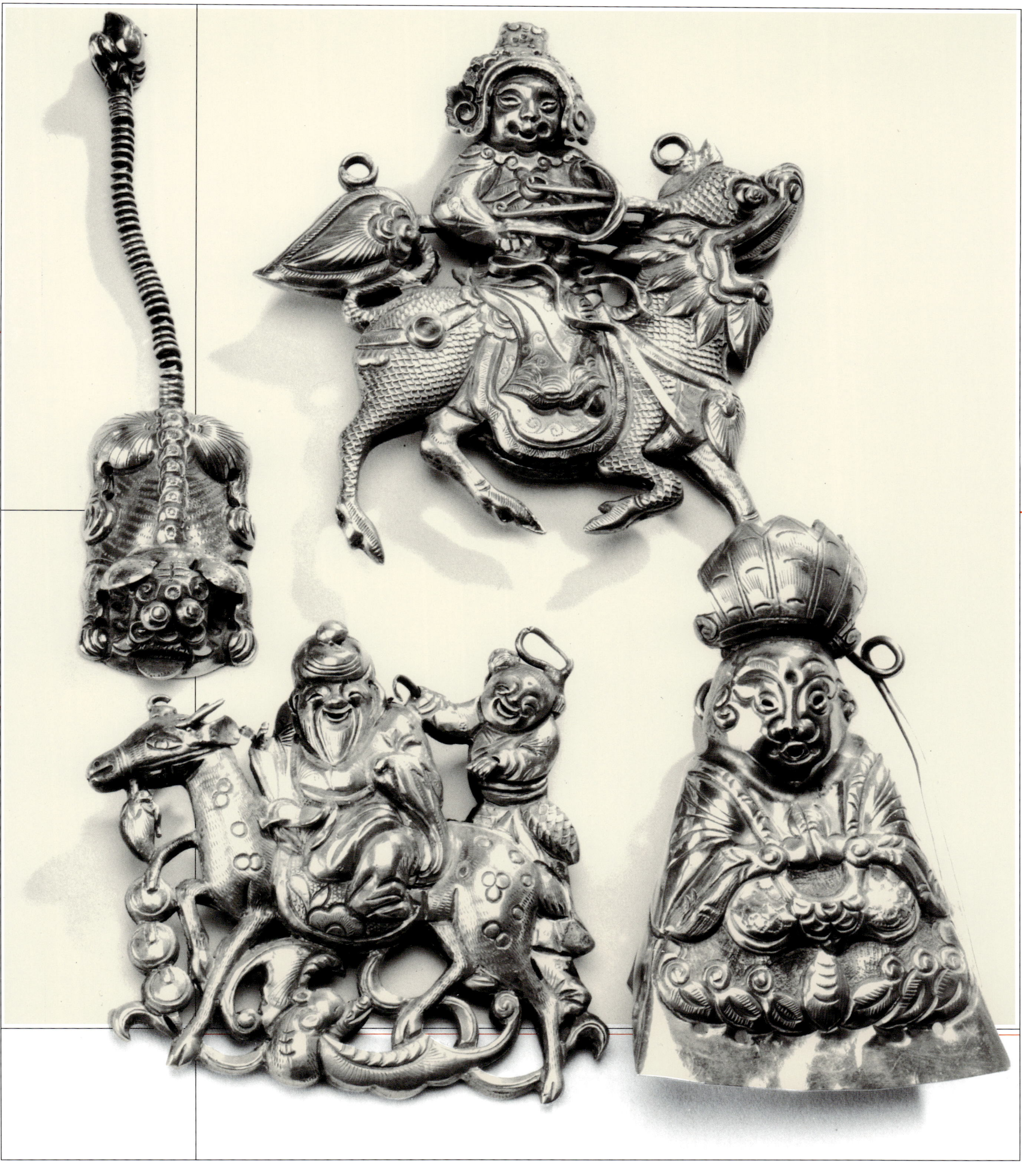

LIVING

Centre **Central panel,** outlined and densely embroidered in multicoloured floss silk thread, of woman's pleated skirt worn wrap-around style. The swing of such skirts was accentuated by the gait forced on the wearer by footbinding.

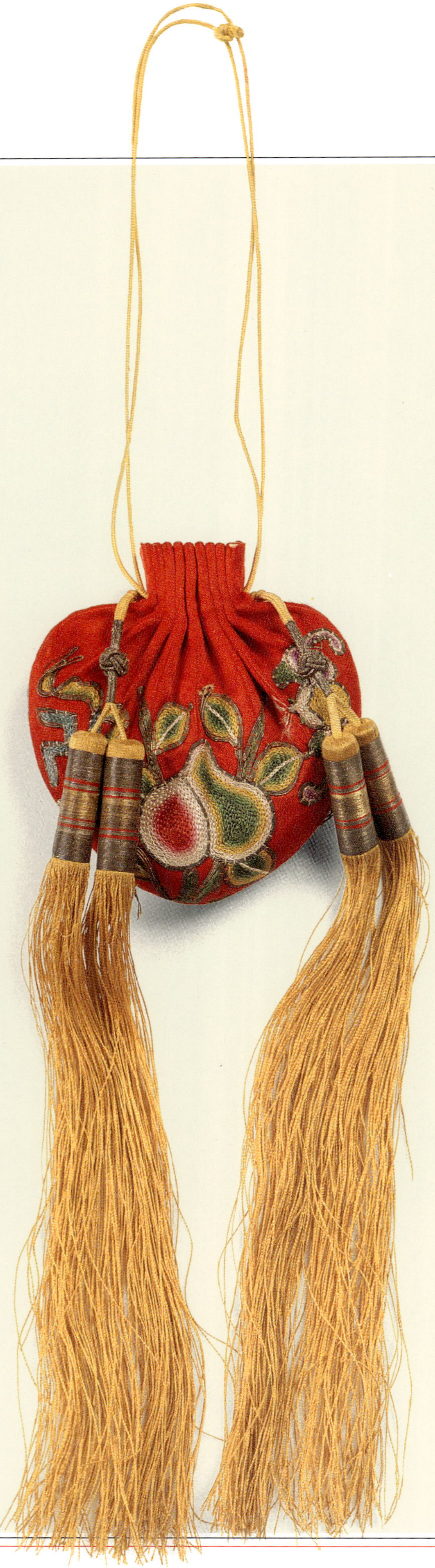

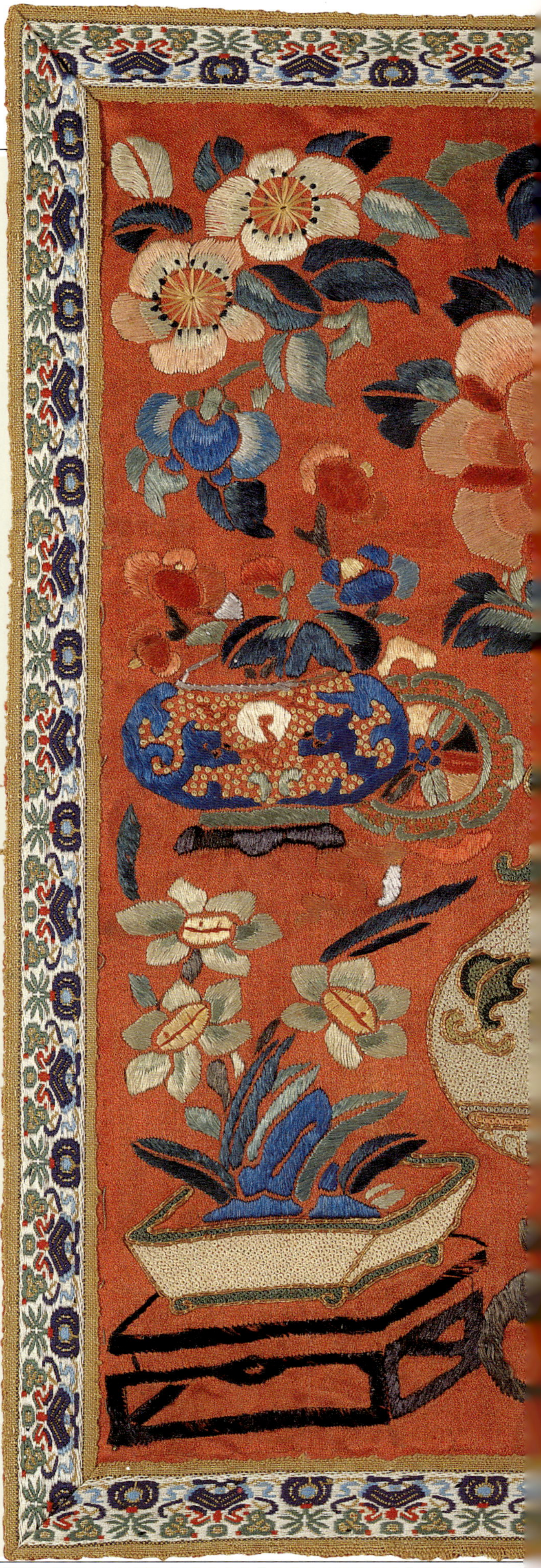

Left and right **Kidney-shaped scent pouches** and **gourd-shaped purse**, probably all made as part of a wedding trousseau.

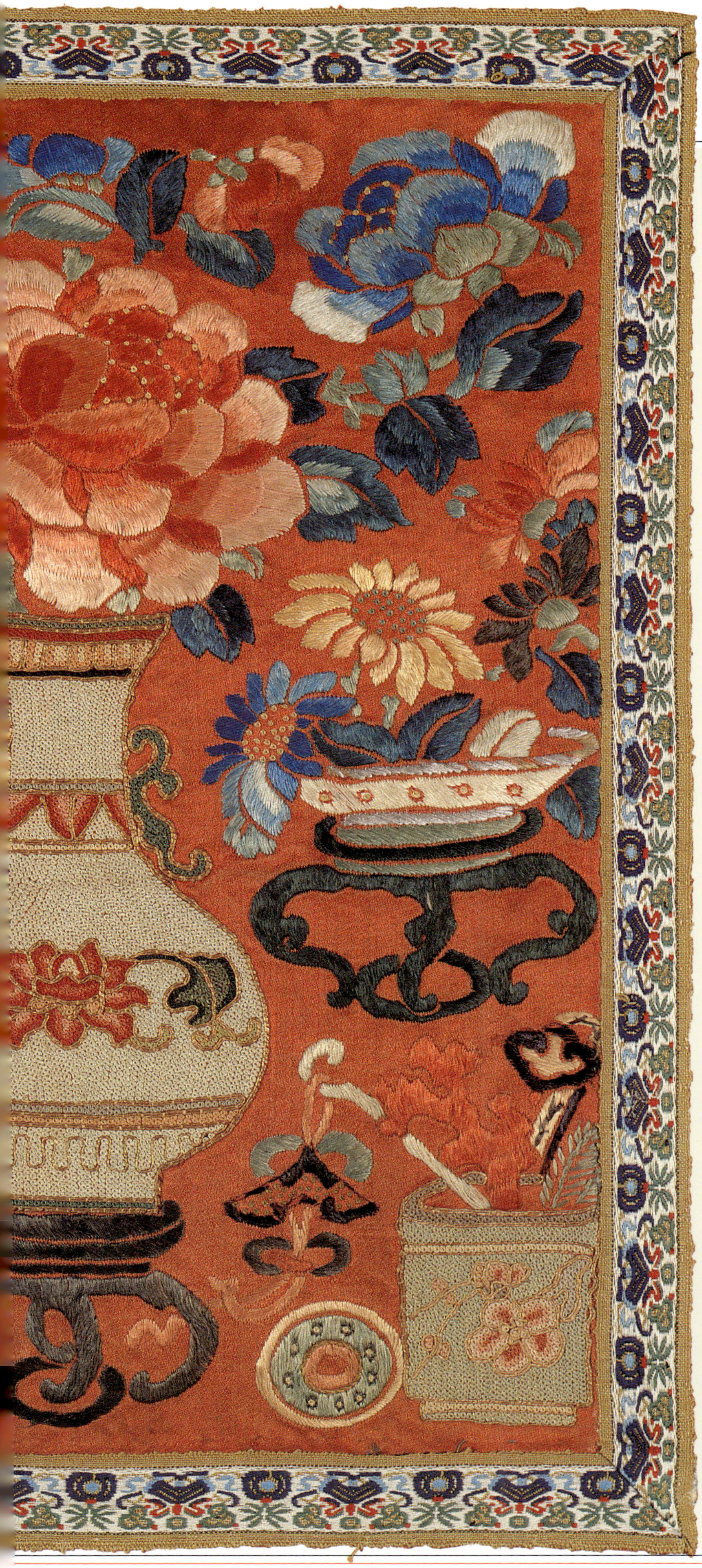
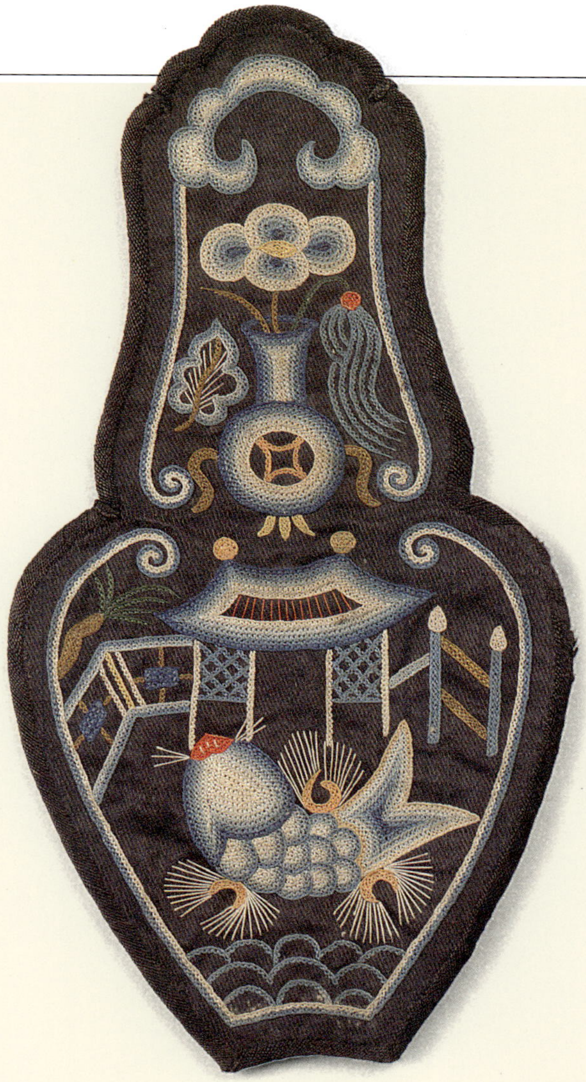
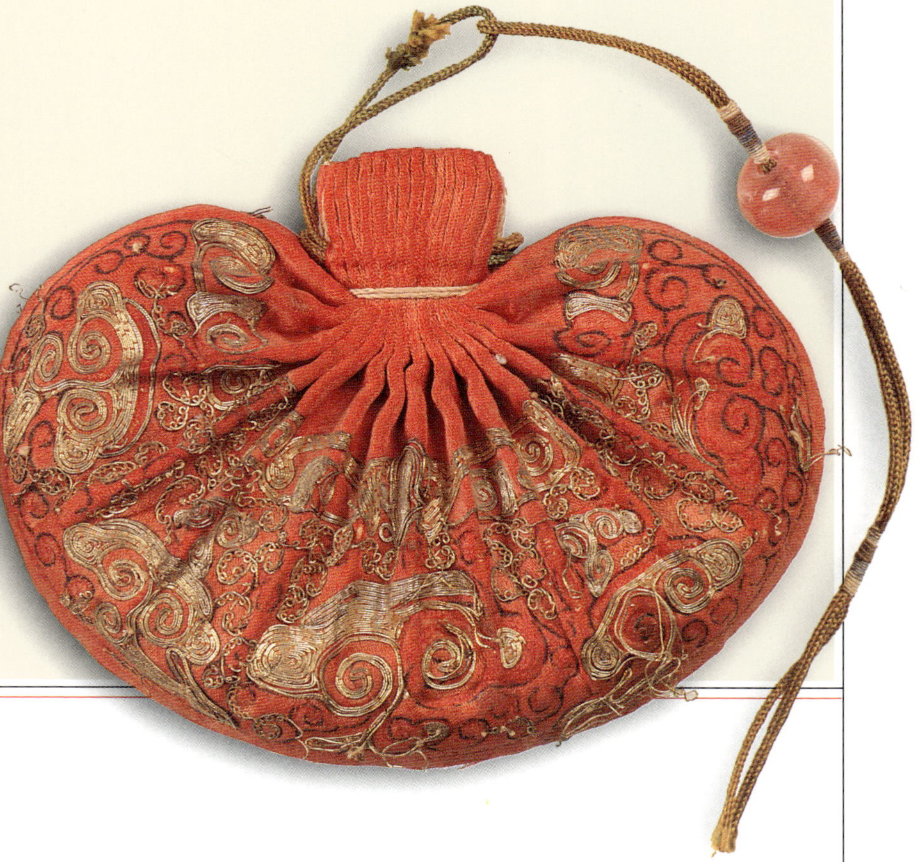

LIVING

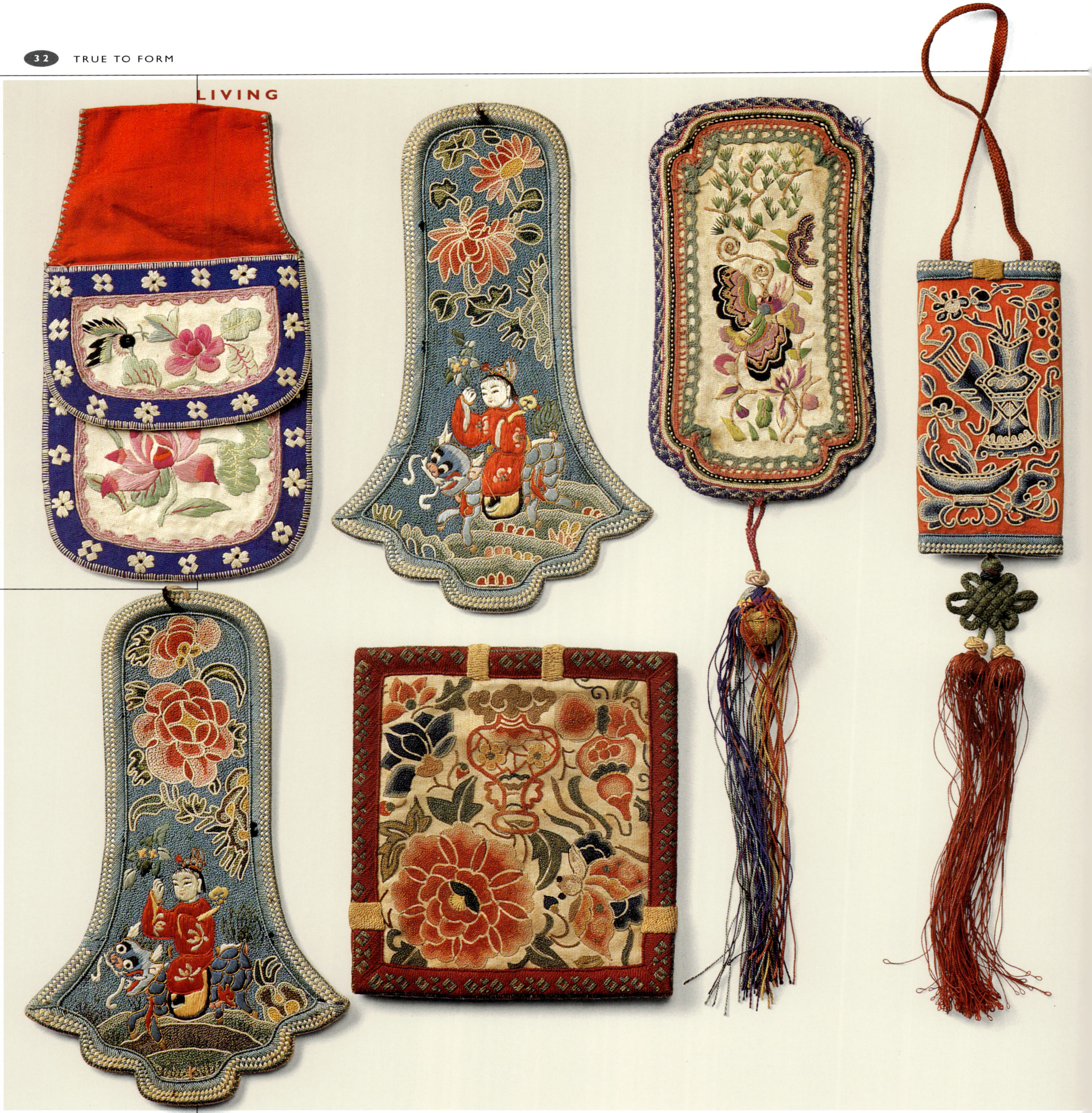

Left to right **Silk embroidered waist purse** *(top)*, **bell-shaped key holder** *(bottom)*, **key holder** *(top)*, **purse** *(bottom)*, **spectacle case**, **pouch for name cards or trinkets**. *Next page* **Purses** and one of a pair of **women's ankle wraps**, worn like a bow tie over matching silk embroidered shoes.

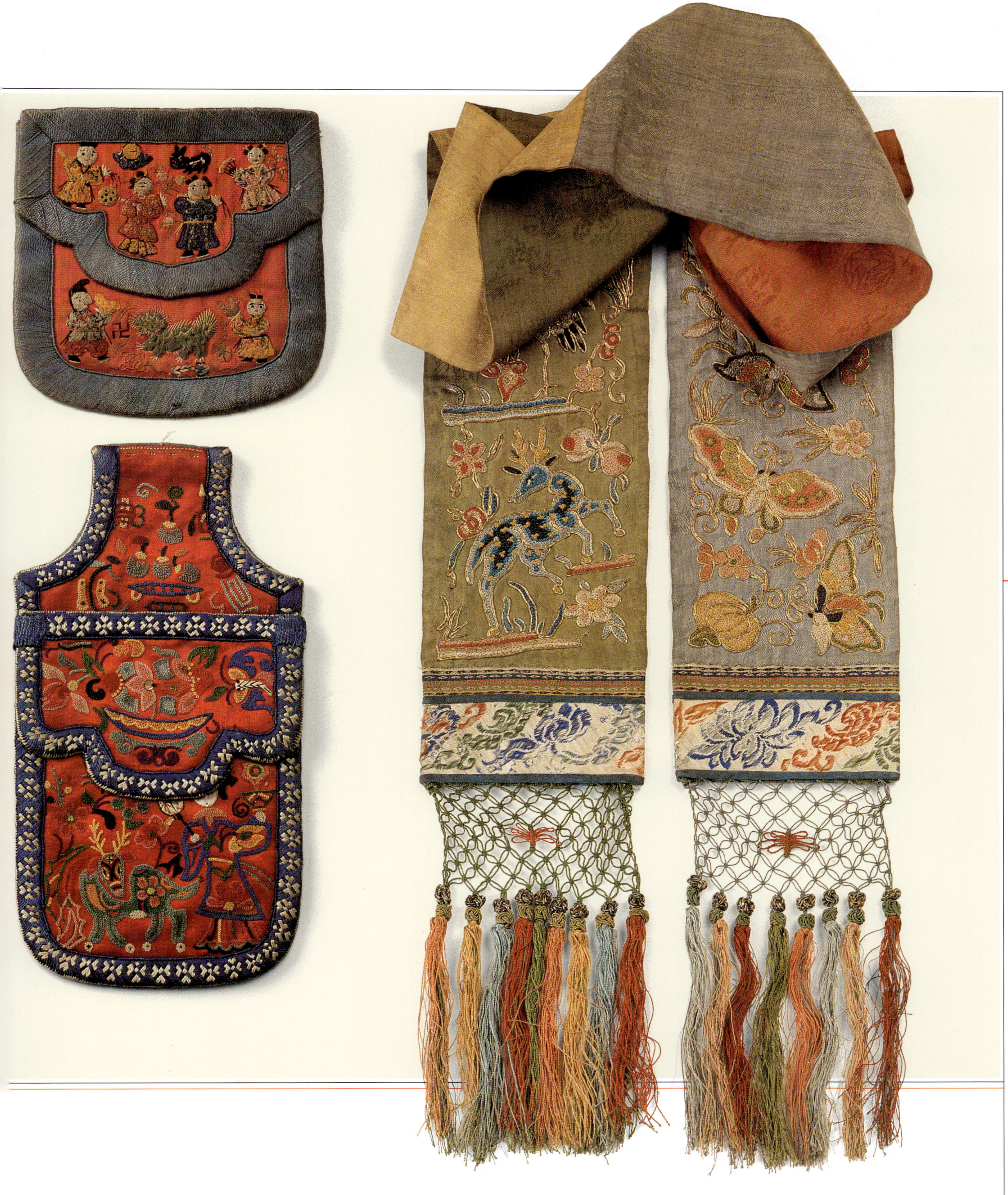

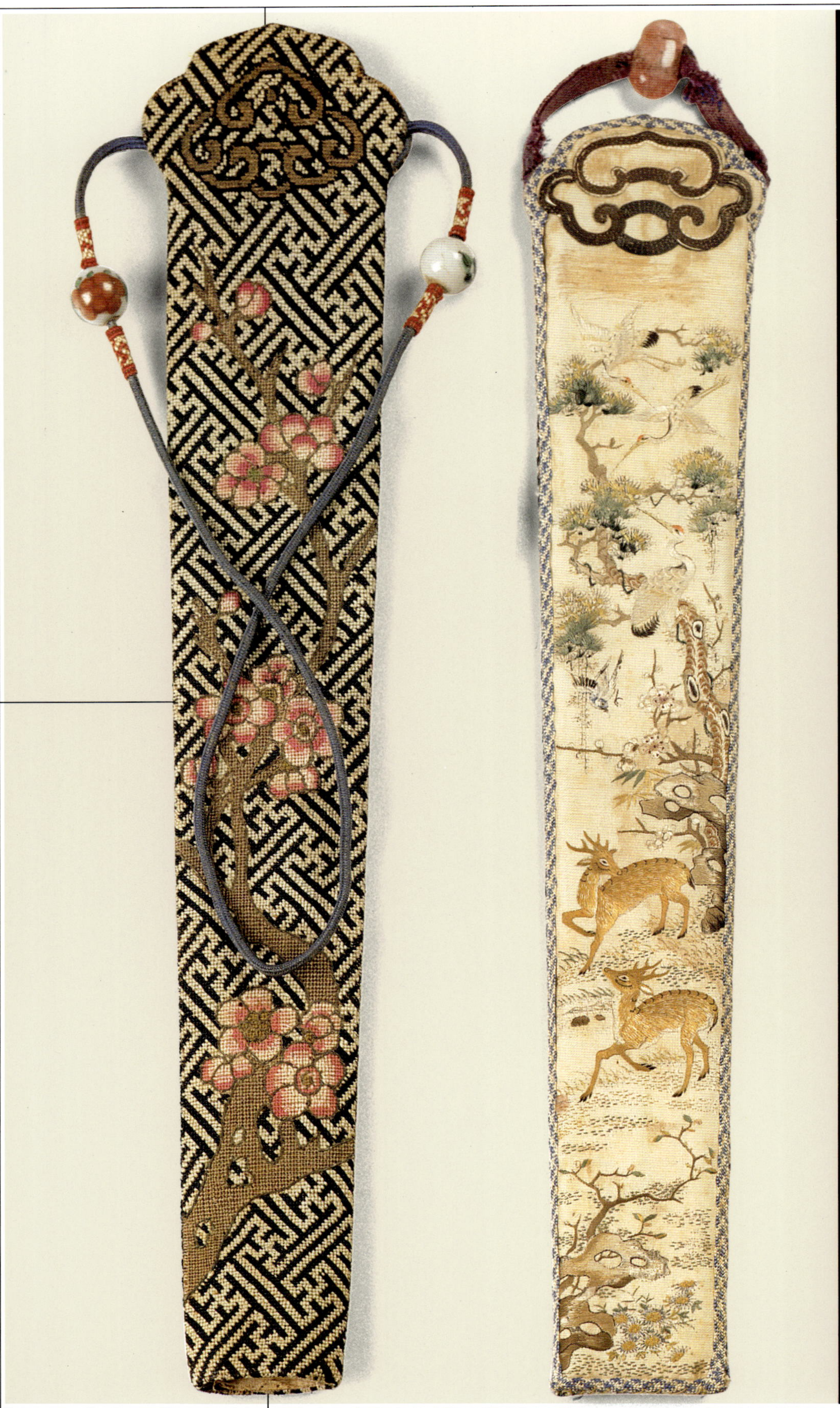

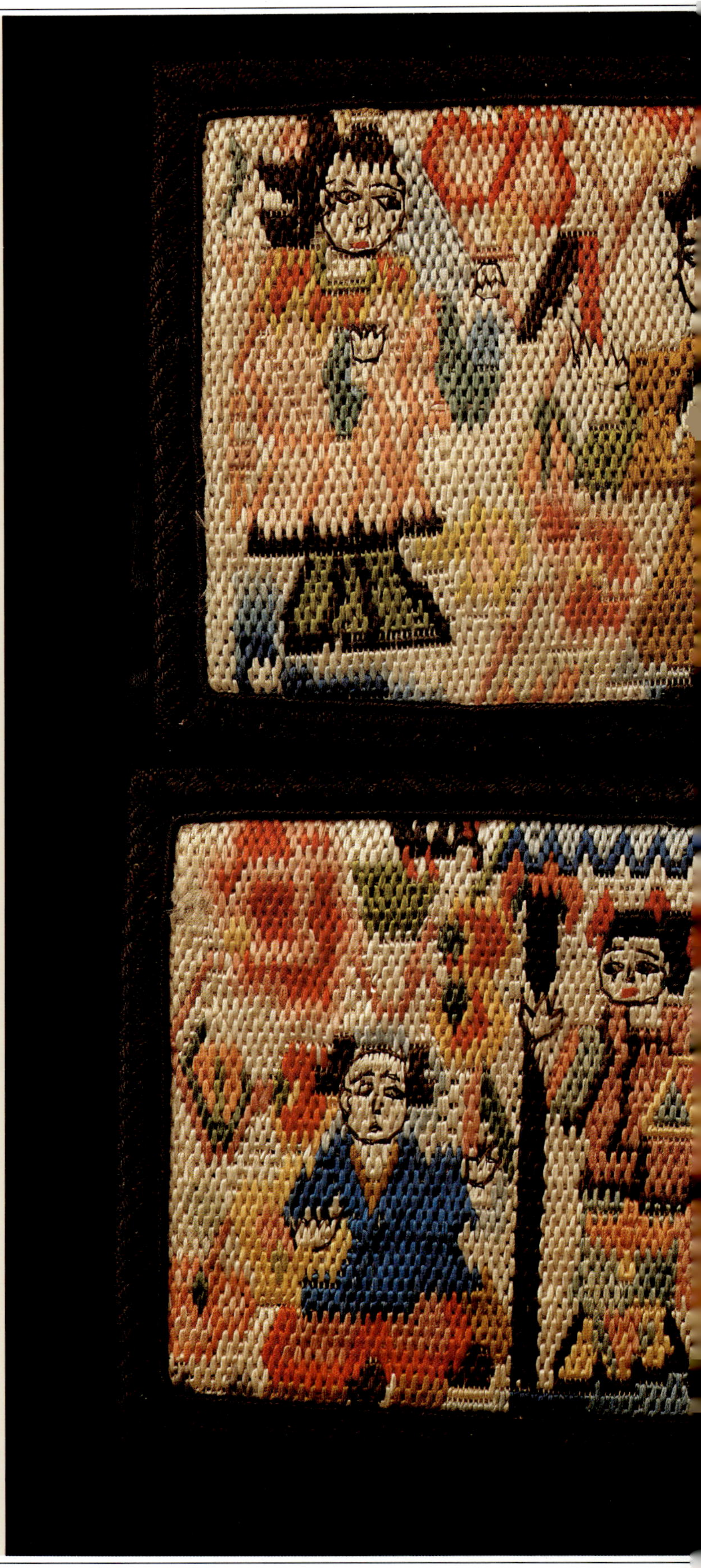

Left **Two silk fan holders**. Such holders were probably secreted in ladies' sleeves. *Right* Detail from **embroidered purses.**

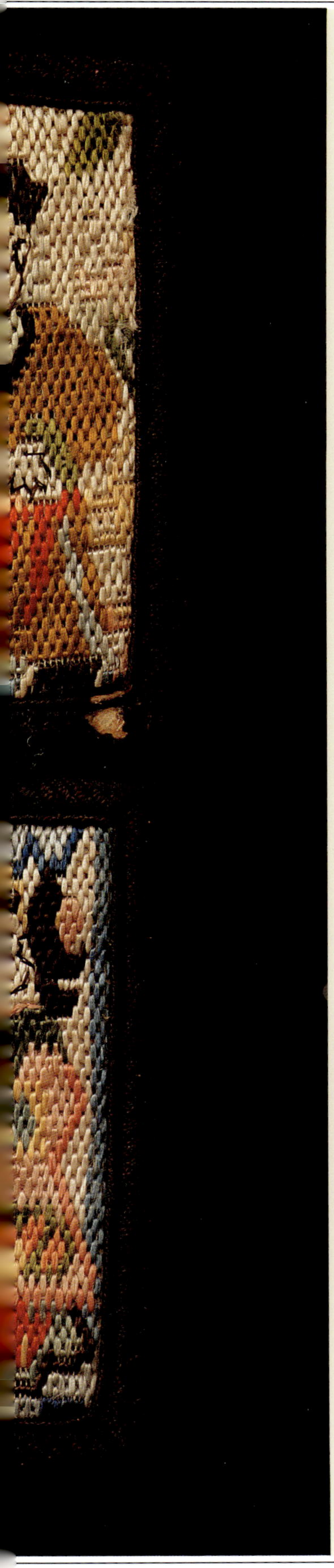

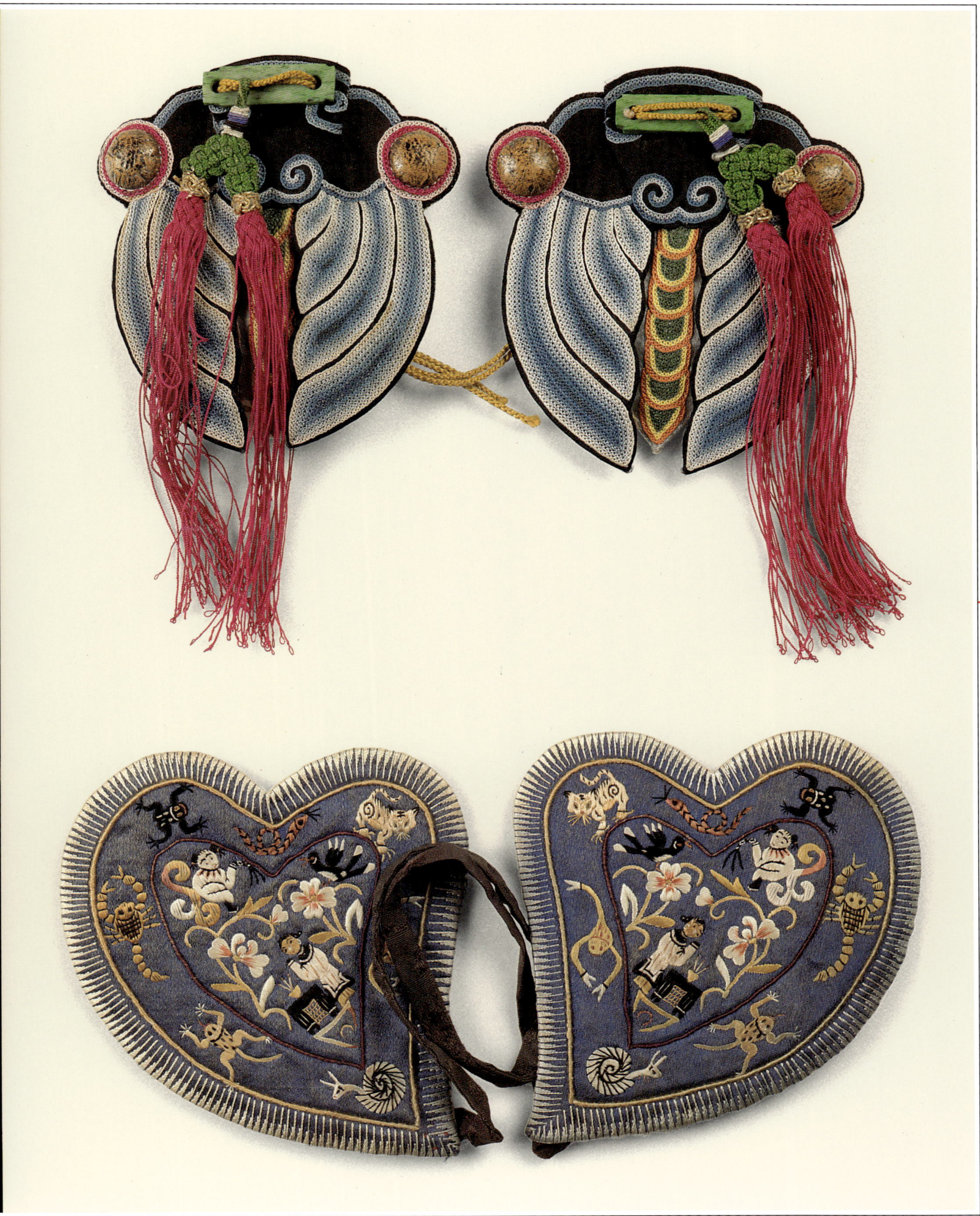

Pairs of ear muffs in embroidered silk.

LIVING

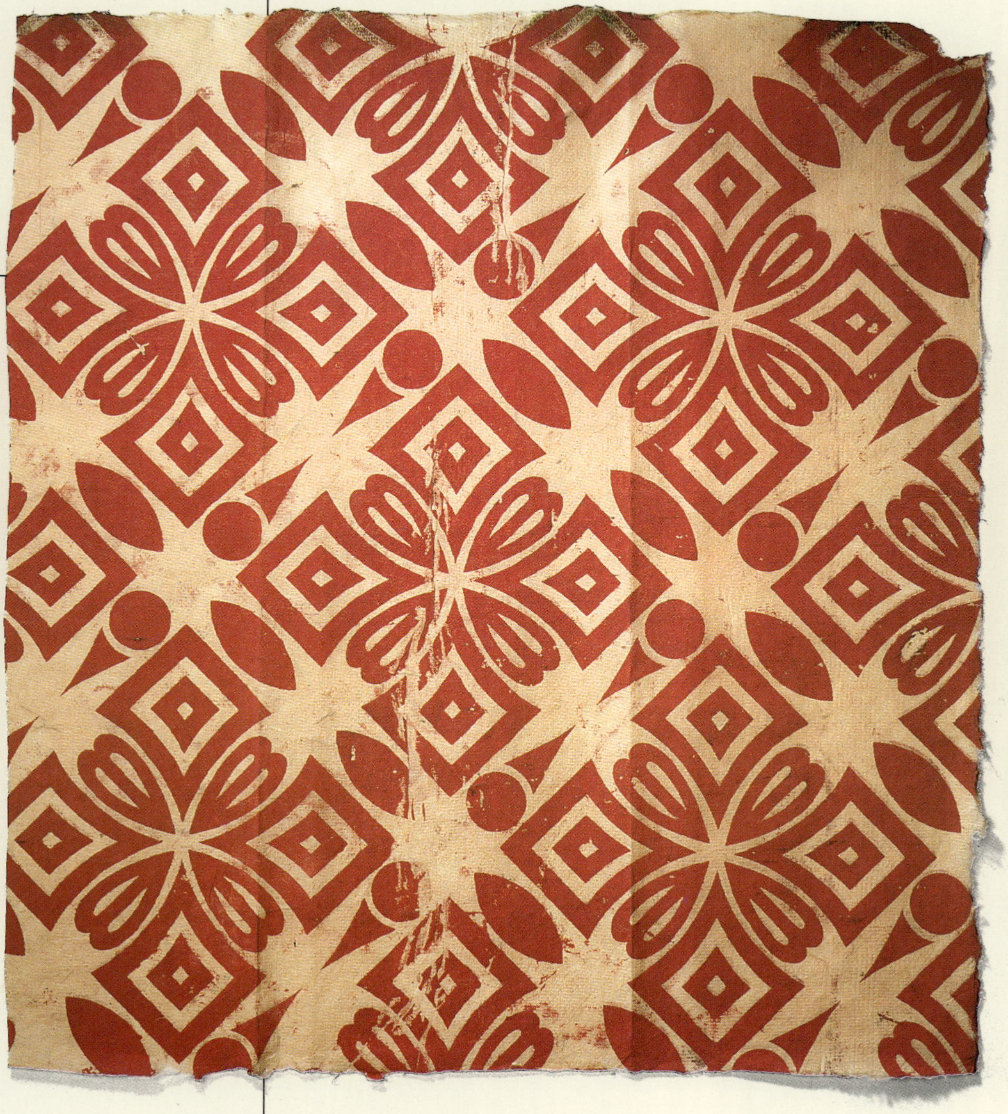

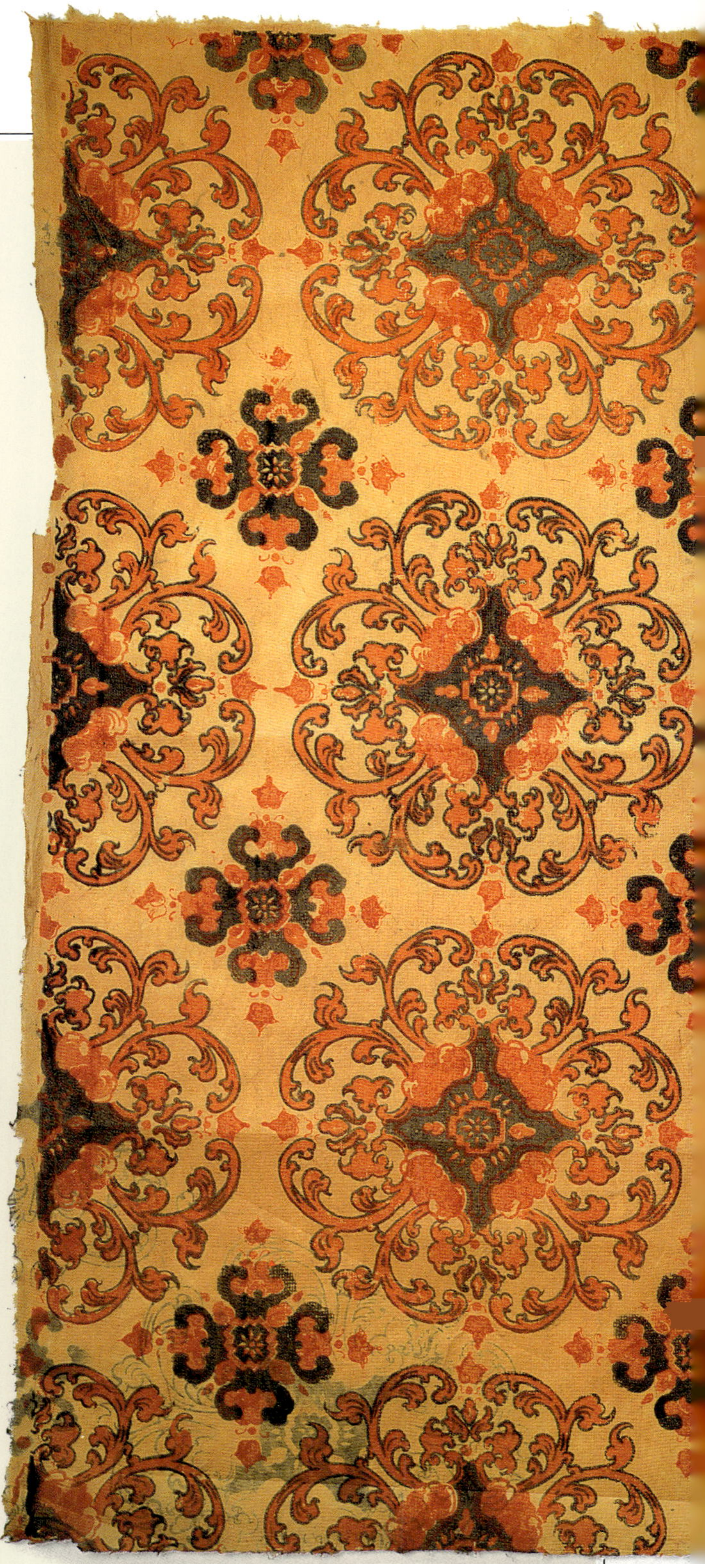

First and second left **Paper** from Xin Yuanfa ("New Yuanfa"), the last wood block printing house in Hong Kong. The original Yuanfa was in Shunde, in Guangdong province. *Right* **Wrapping paper**, printed for shops in Hong Kong in the 1920s.

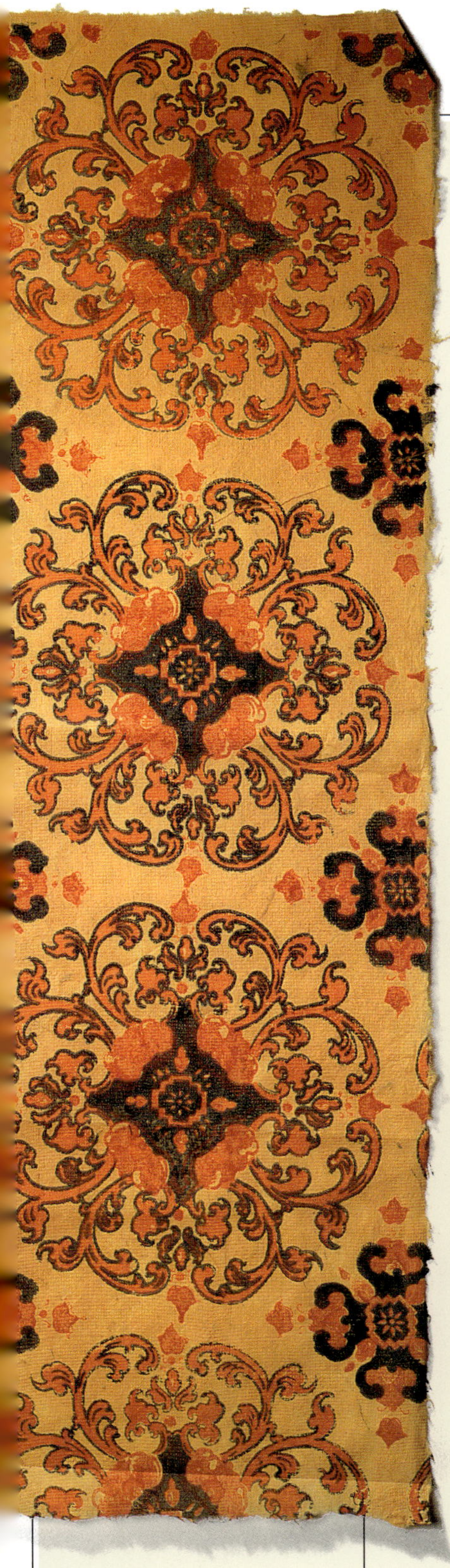

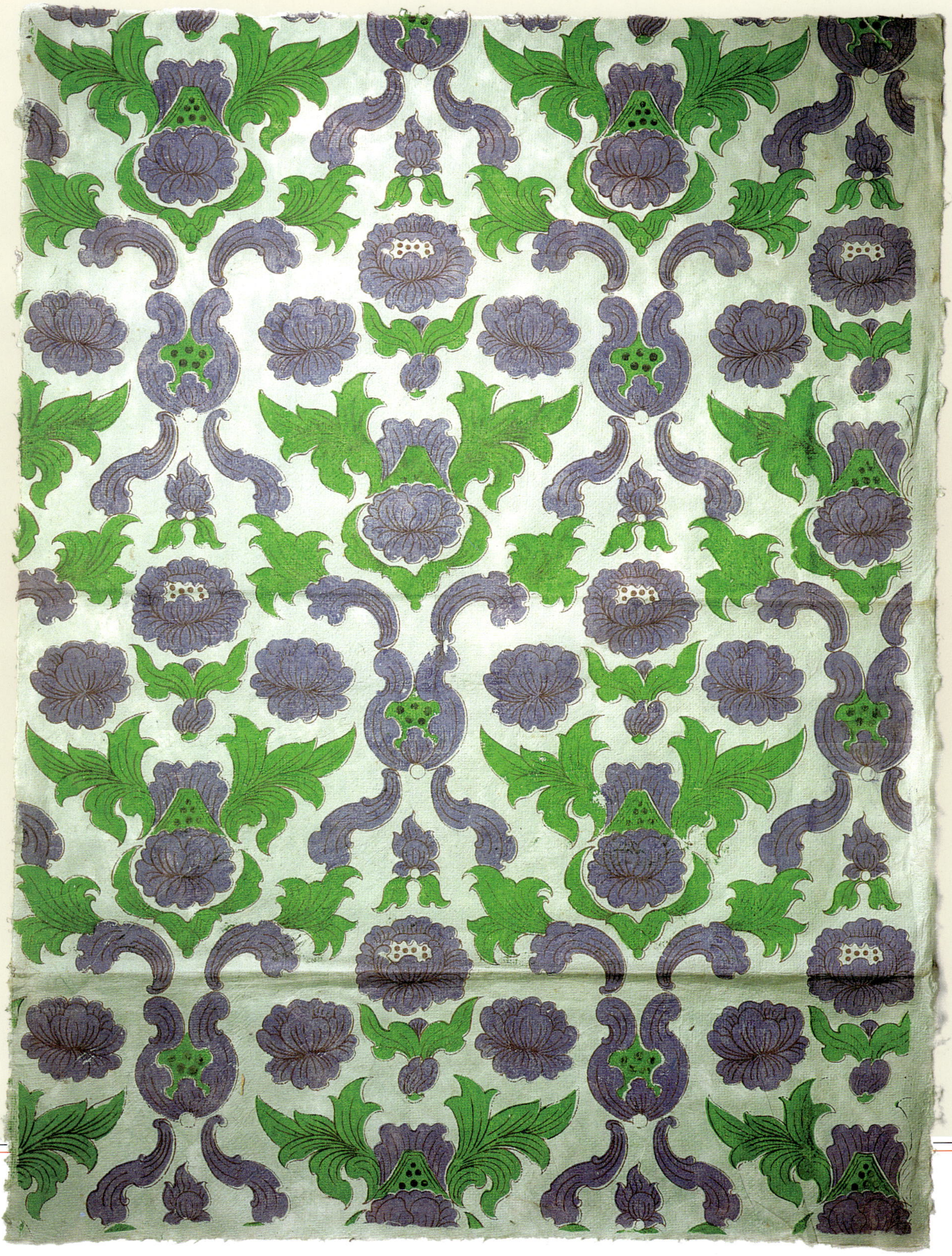

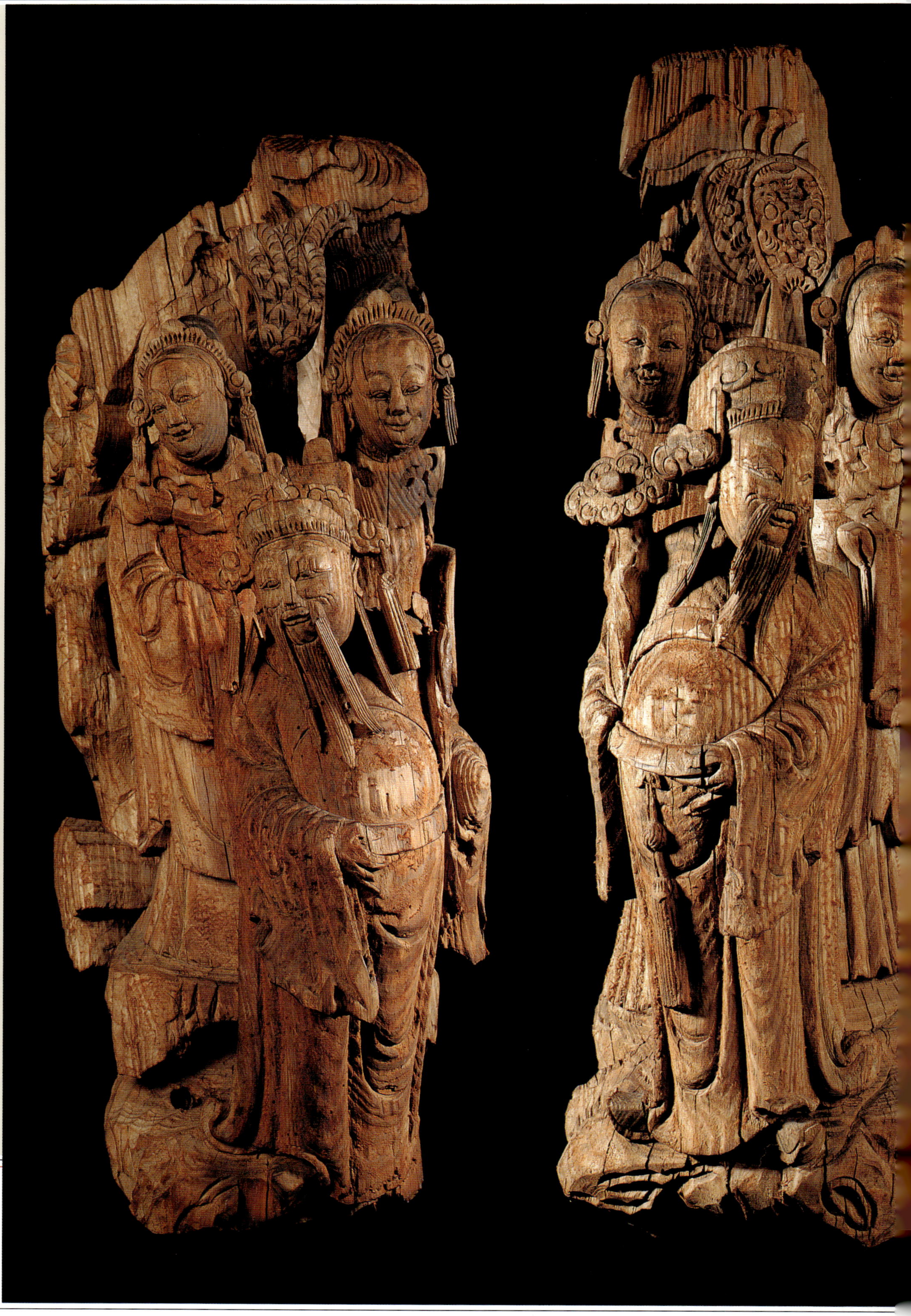

Pair of elm wood carvings, once adorning pillars of north China building, of God of Wealth and his attendants.

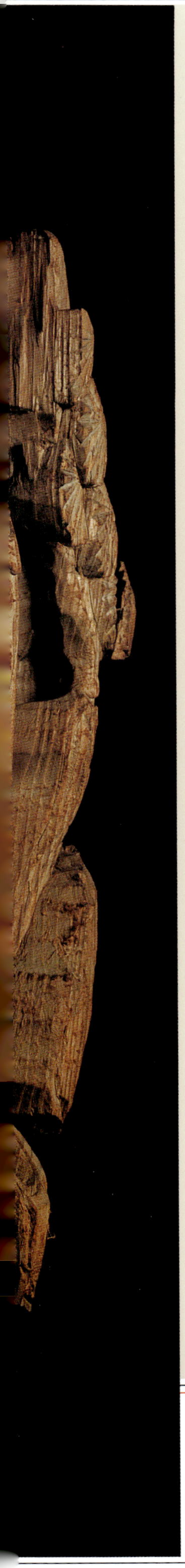

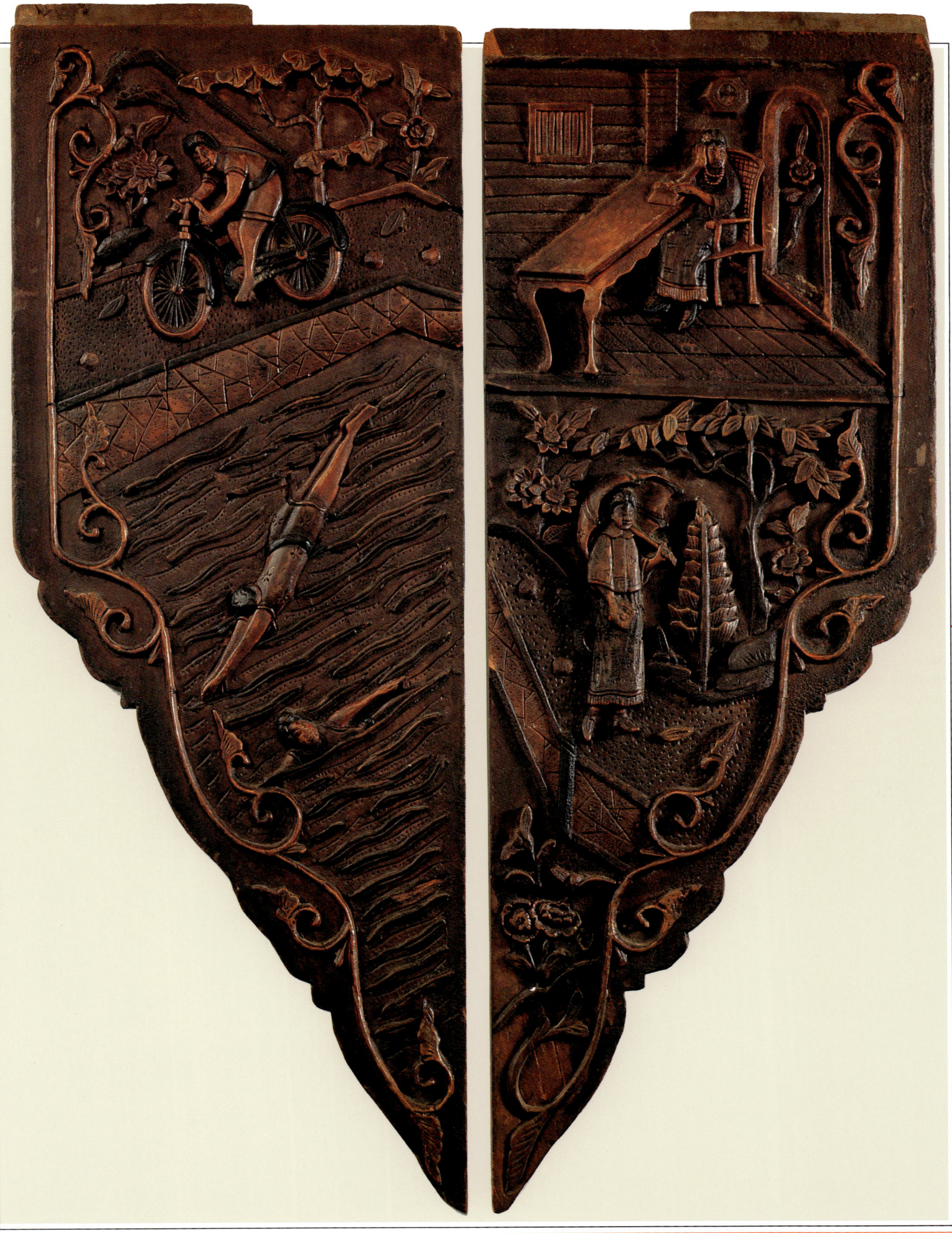

Wood relief carvings mostly depict immortals, emperors, generals and officials. Carved with female figures bicycling, diving and studying, these **wooden cupboard flanges** dating from 1912-19 are unusual in their depiction of female emancipation.

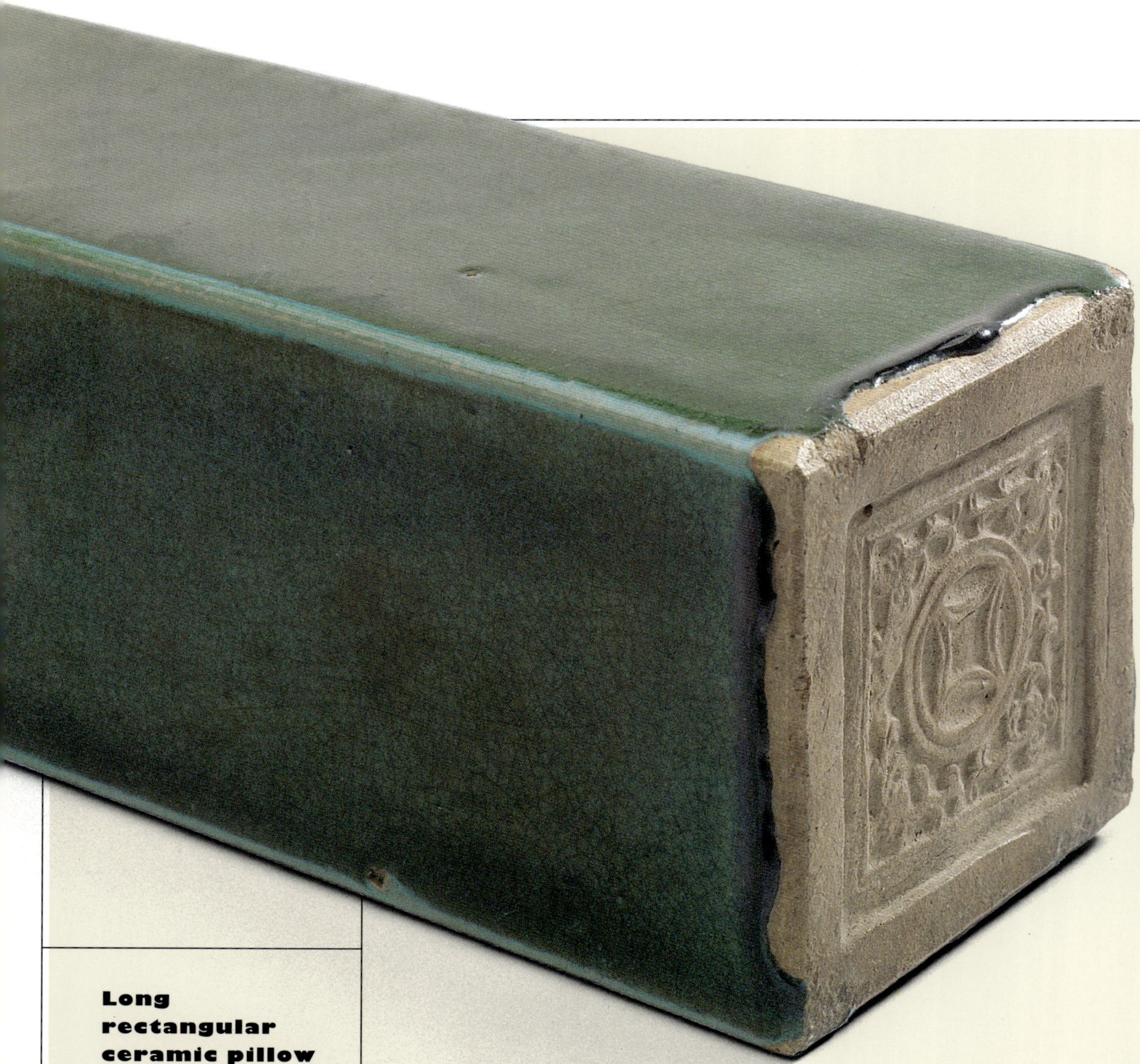

Long rectangular ceramic pillow with unglazed ends decorated in geometric and floral pattern, length 50 cm.

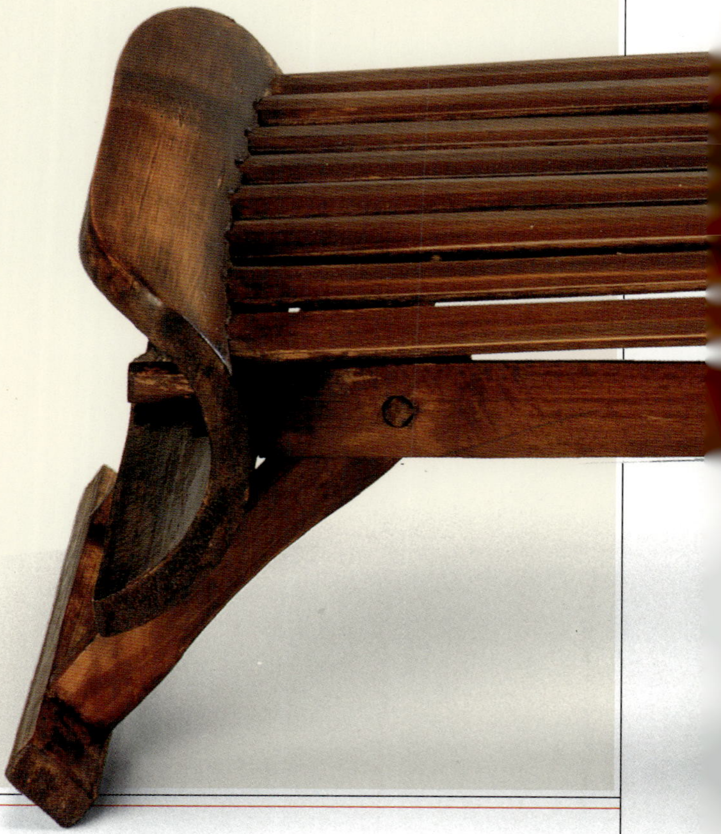

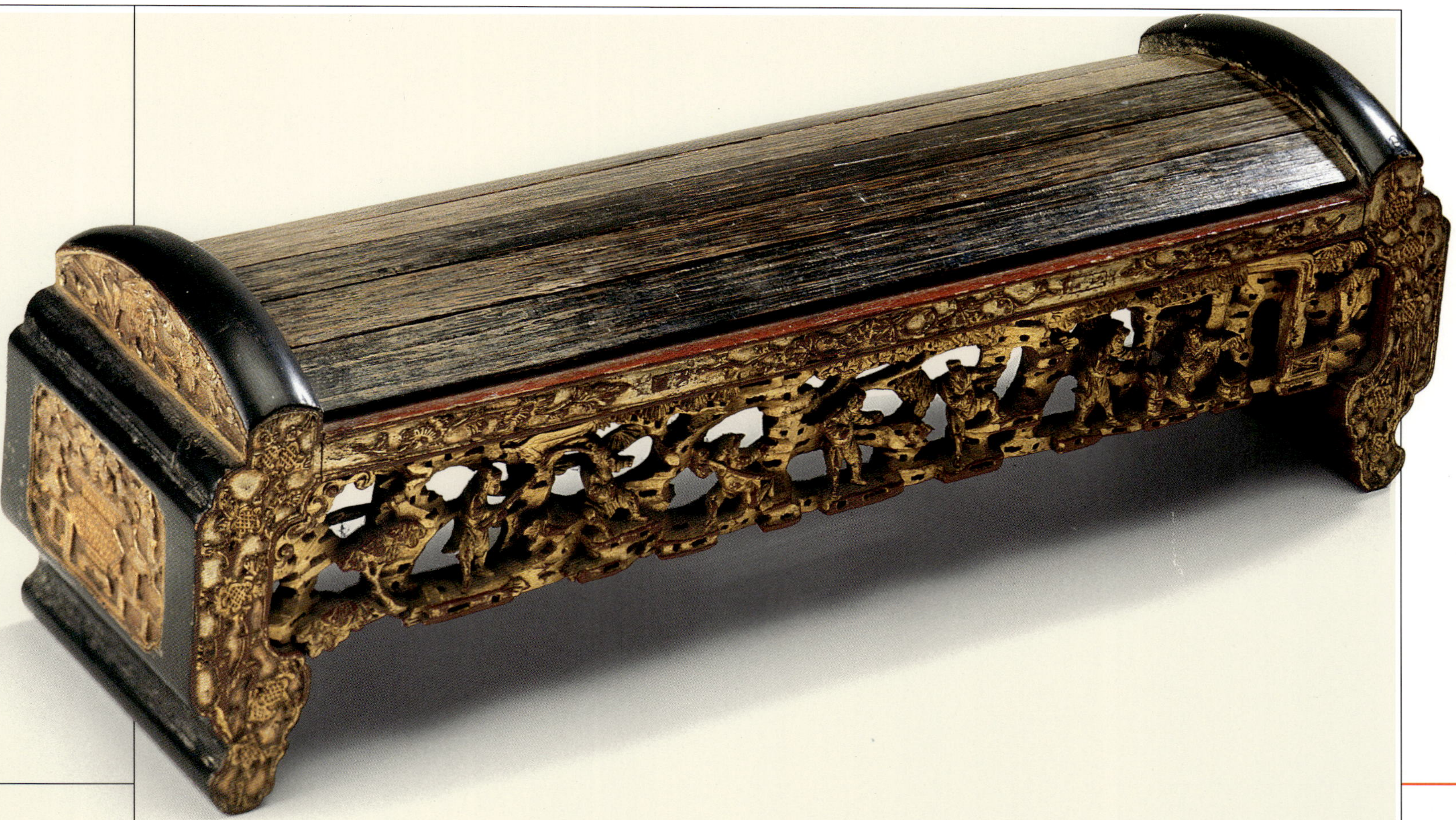

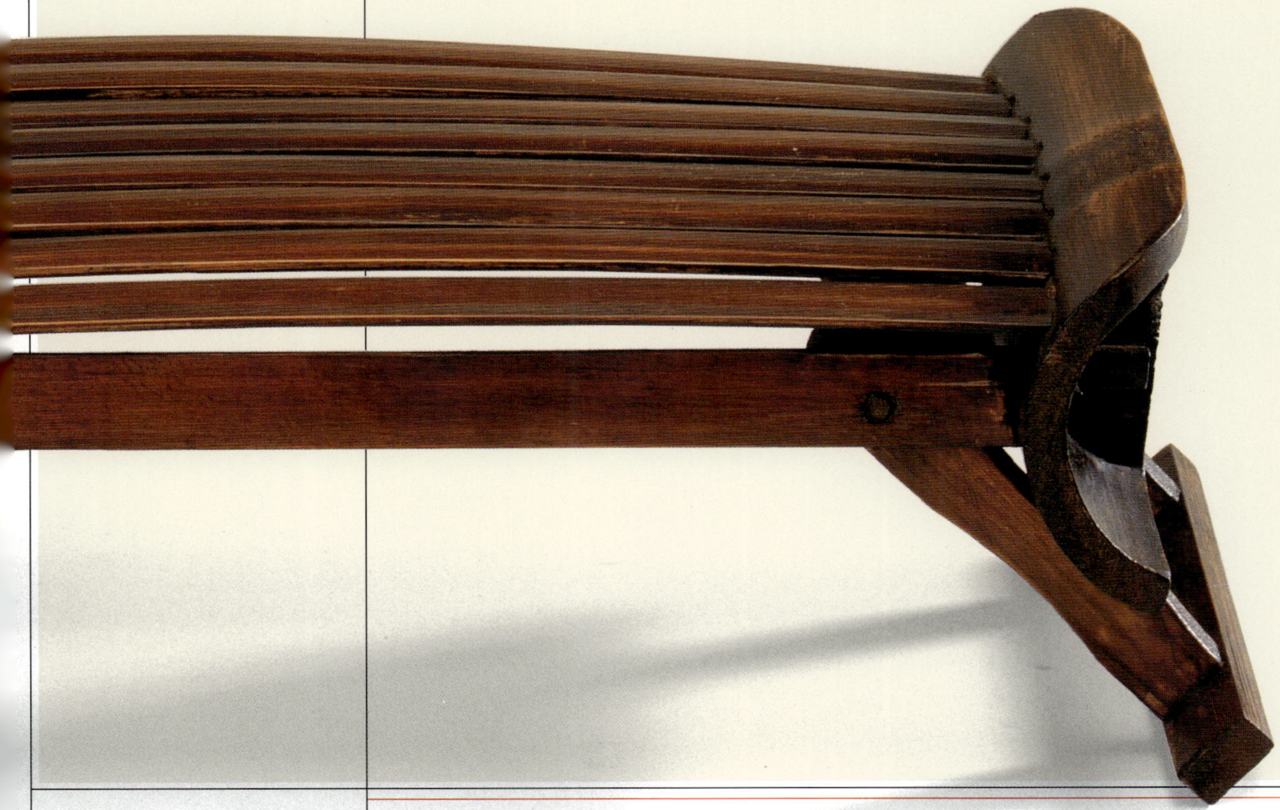

Centre **Portable pillow** in slatted bamboo for travelling, with legs that fold inward, length 26 cm. *Right* **Pillow with a head rest** of bamboo slats and sides of softwood in gilt openwork carving, length 60 cm.

LIVING

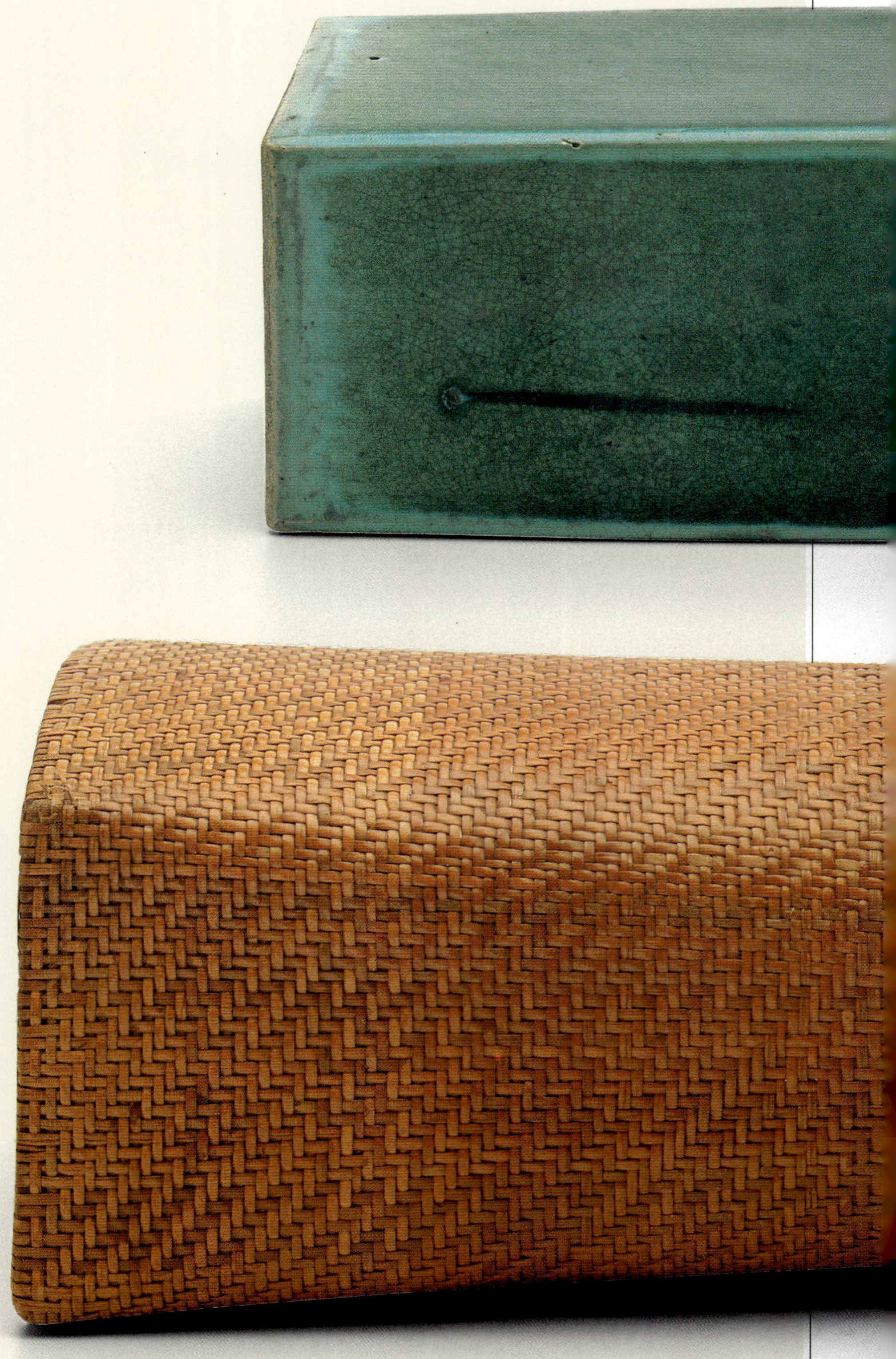

Top **Ceramic pillow** with a green glaze, length 50 cm. *Bottom* **Pillow in woven rattan** with slight concave indentation for head, length 45 cm.

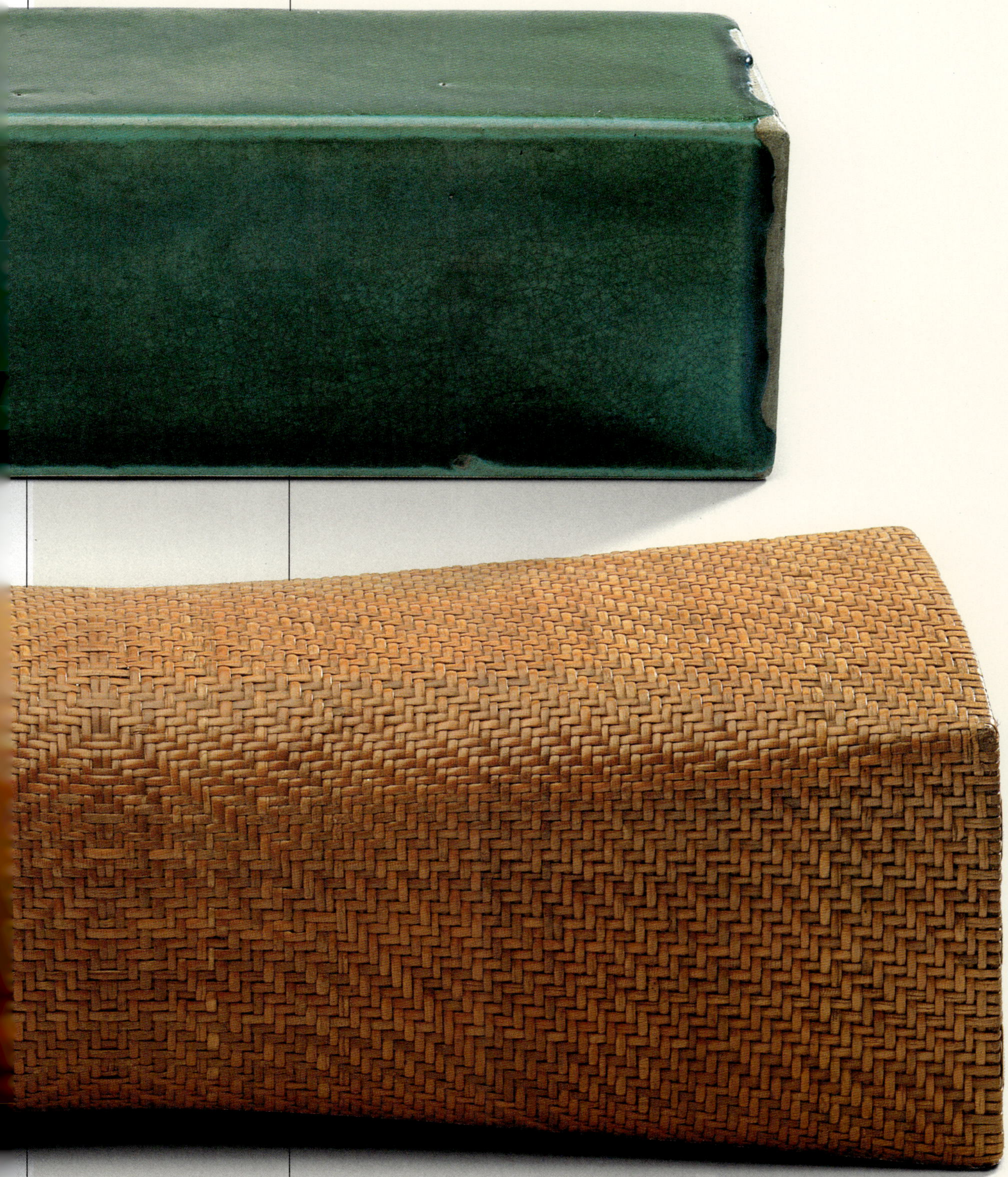

二

INSTRUMENTS OF OFFICE

INSTRUMENTS OF OFFICE

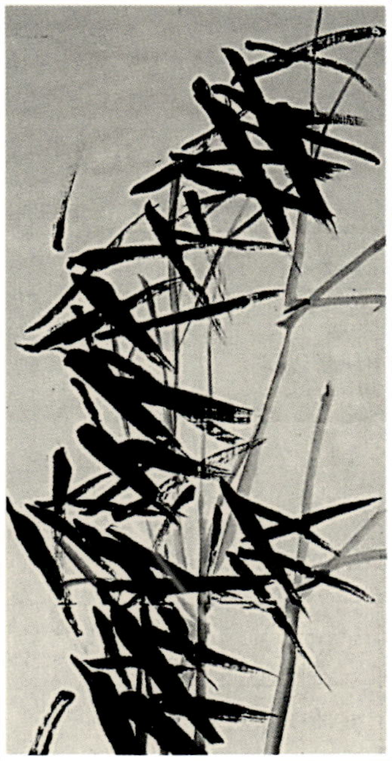

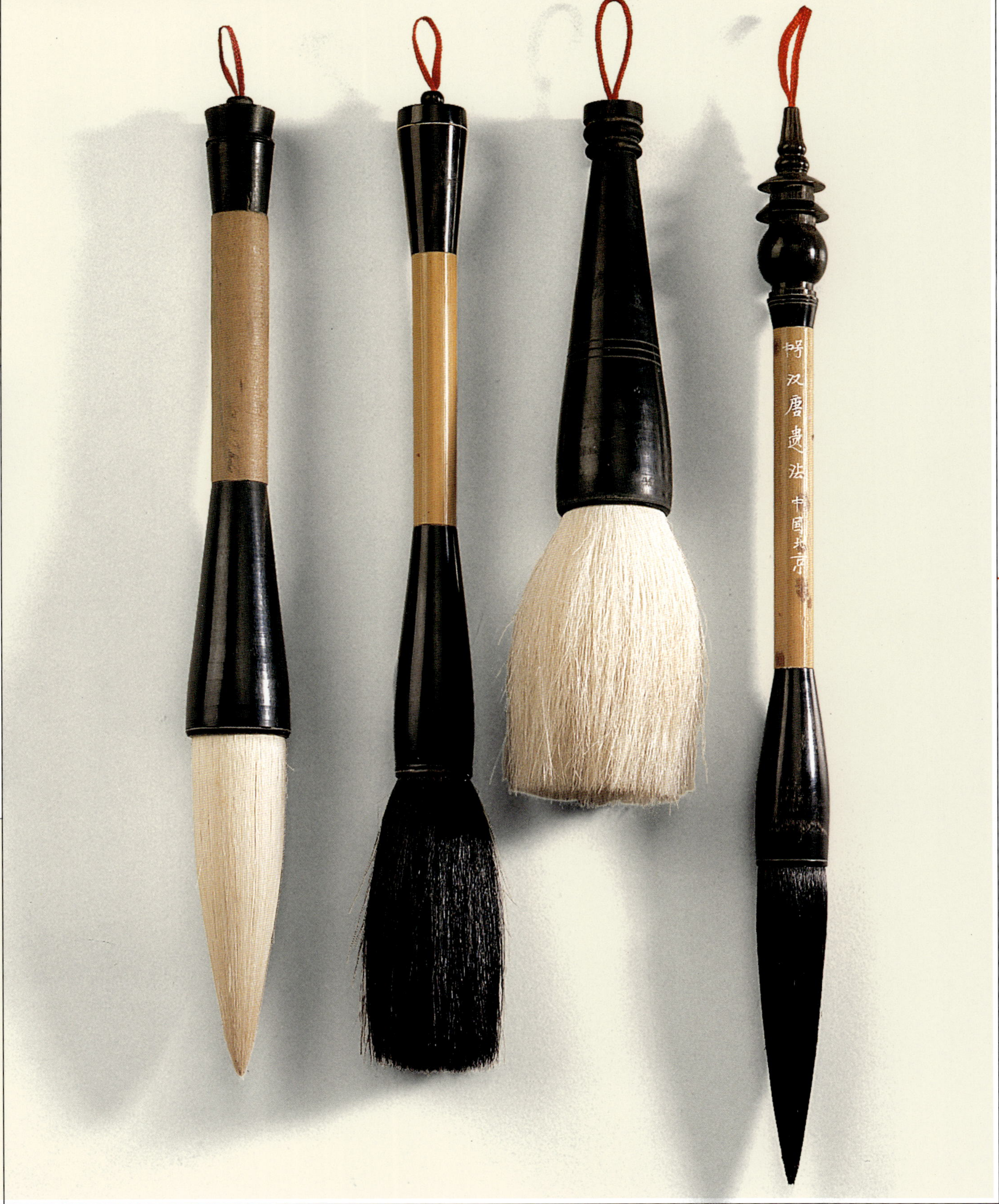

Writing brushes, the first of the Four Treasures of the Scholar's Studio (the others being ink stick, ink slab and paper). Set in oxhorn and bamboo, the ones of white goat hair are for writing calligraphy and those of black horse hair mixed with pig bristles are for painting.

INSTRUMENTS OF OFFICE

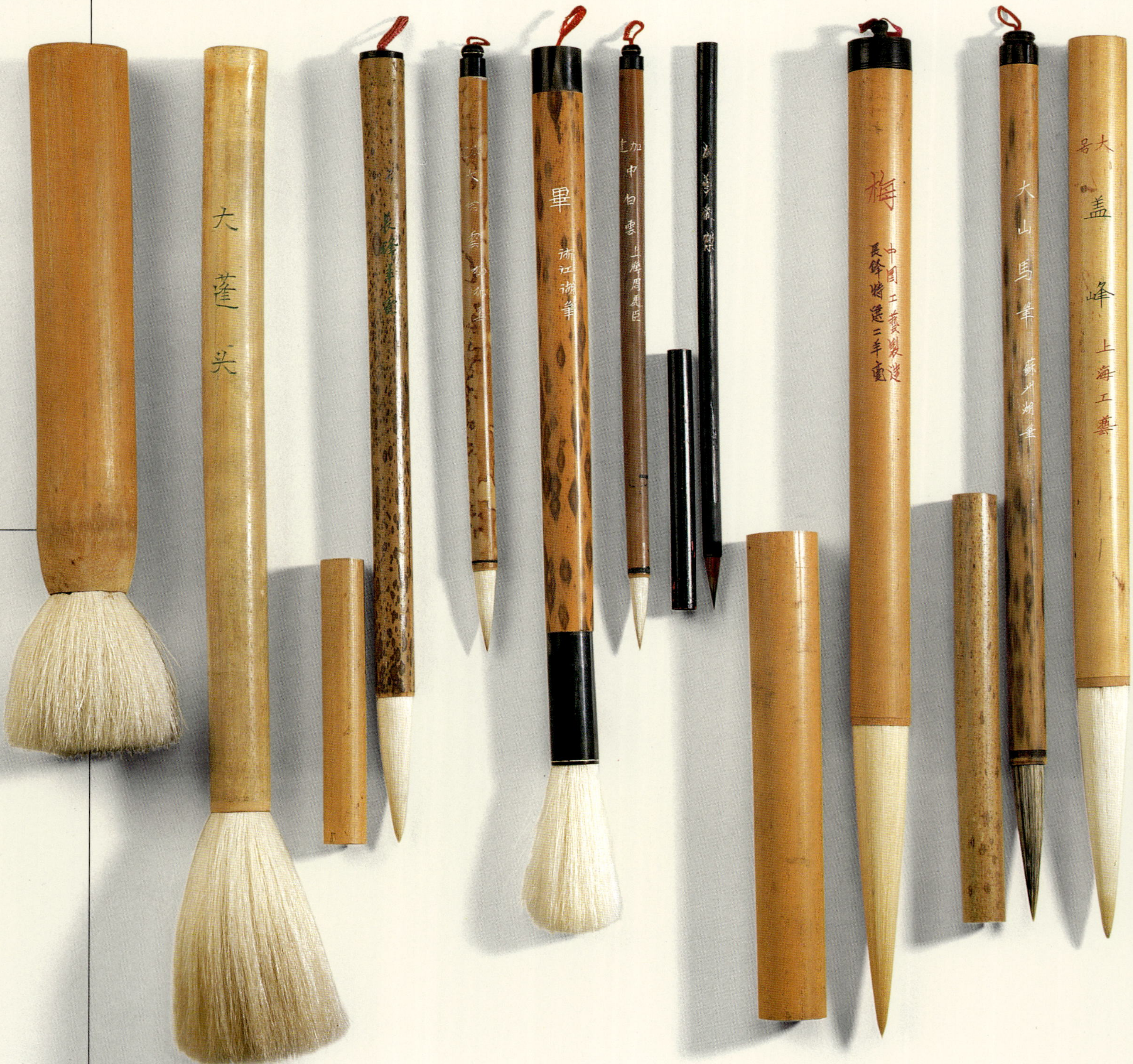

Brushes of goat and rabbit hair for painting and calligraphy set in bamboo and *(fifth from left)* section of black oxhorn, four with caps. In imperial times access to lucrative public office and social prestige was gained through success based on refined literary skills in the state examinations.

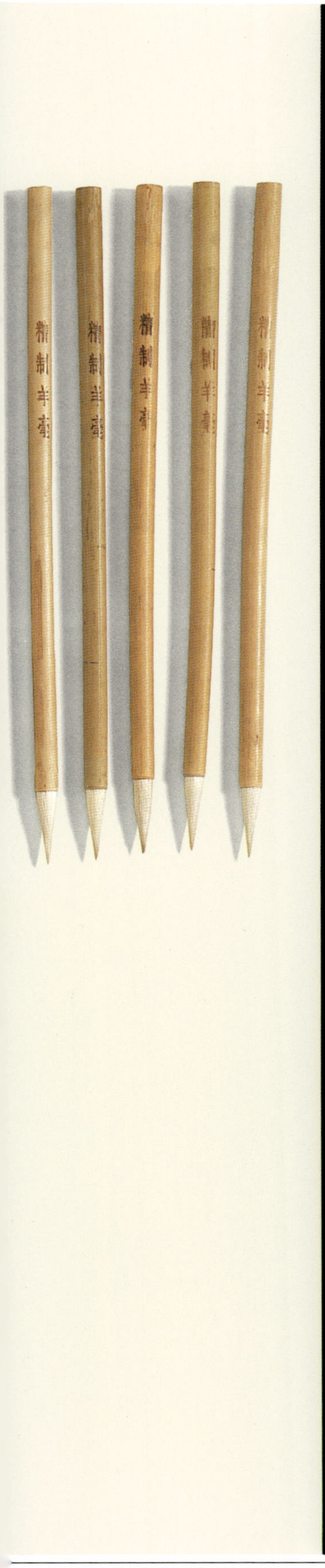

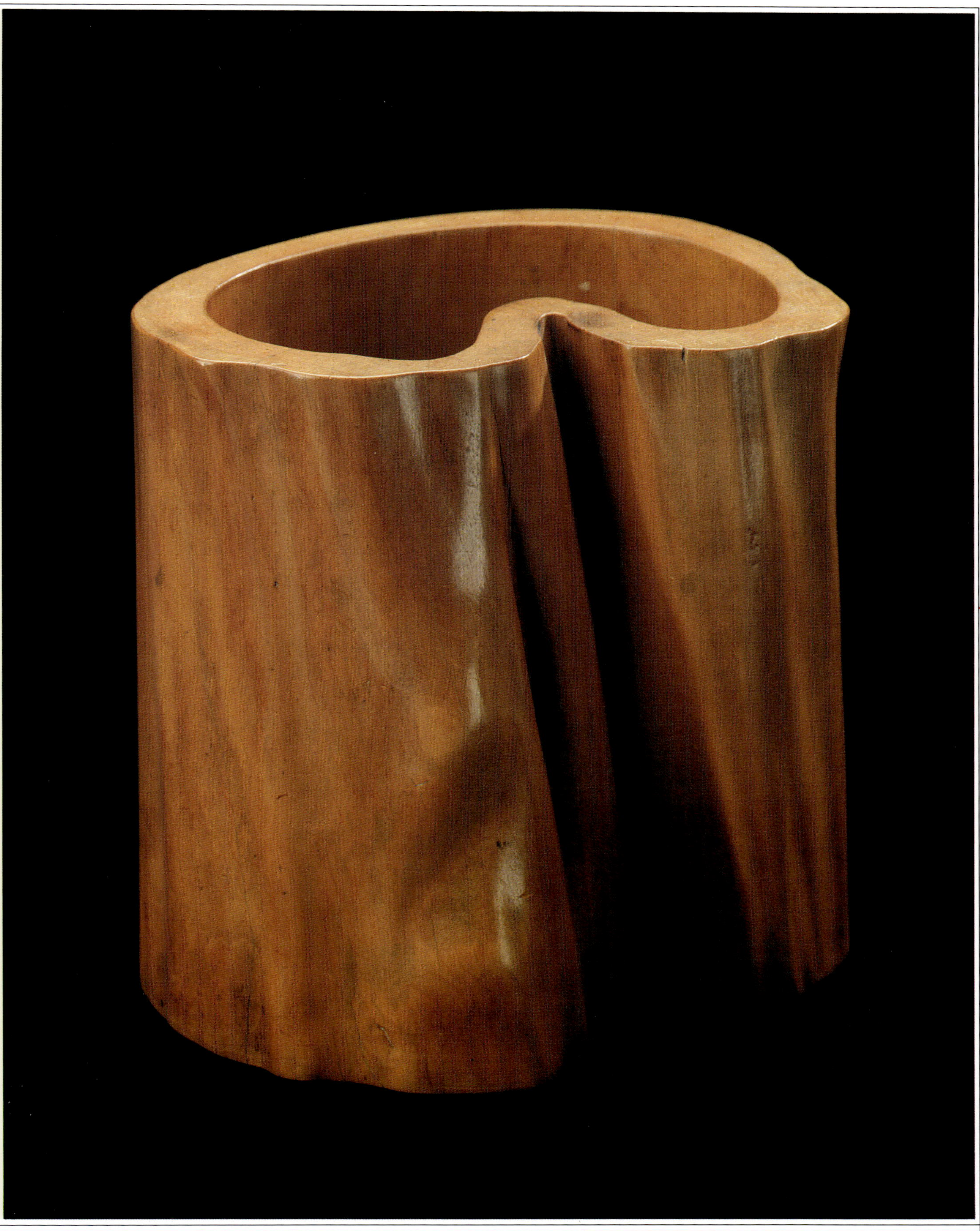

Brush pot made of boxwood, height 19 cm.

INSTRUMENTS OF OFFICE

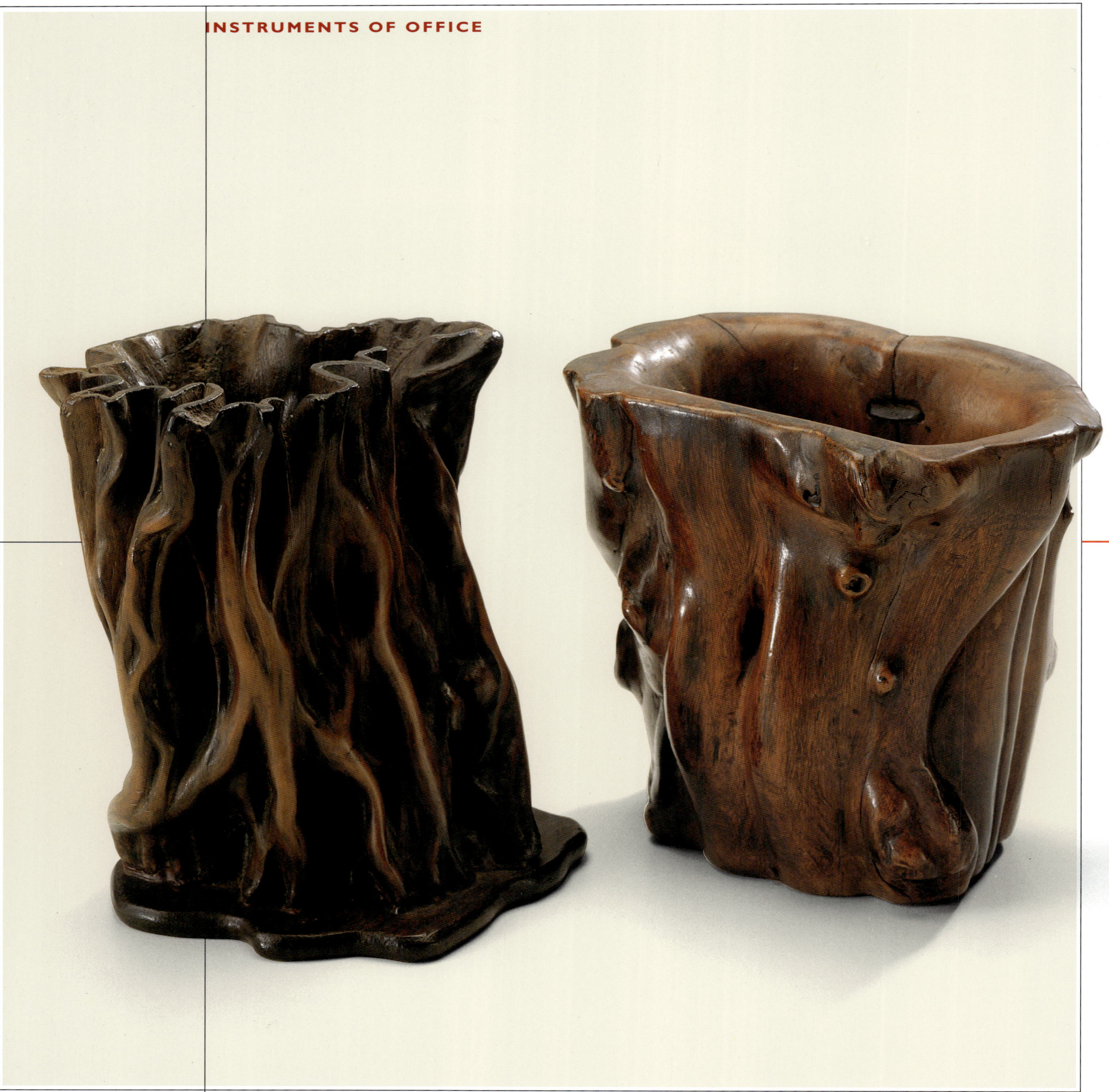

Pair of brush pots in blackwood *(left)* and old rosewood *(right)*, height 16 cm. Brush holders of expensive wood or stone, the fine paper, the embossed ink sticks and the smooth stone slabs on which they were rubbed and mixed with water to produce the shiniest and blackest ink – all combined to invest the scholar's desk with an aura of ritual and art.

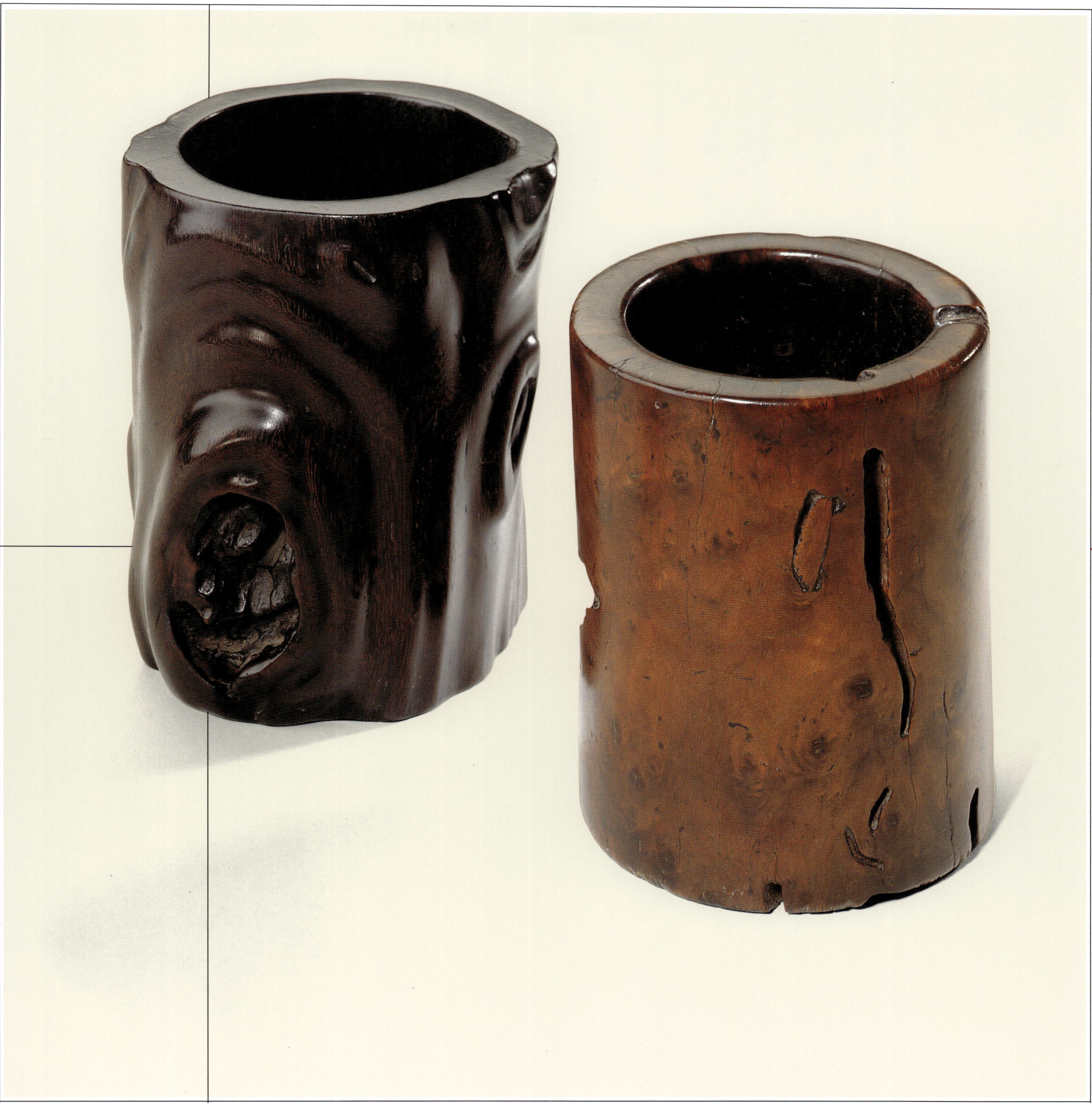

Pair of brush pots in blackwood *(left)* and peach wood *(right)*, height 16 cm.

Brush pot
made of lacquered
bamboo,
height 19 cm.

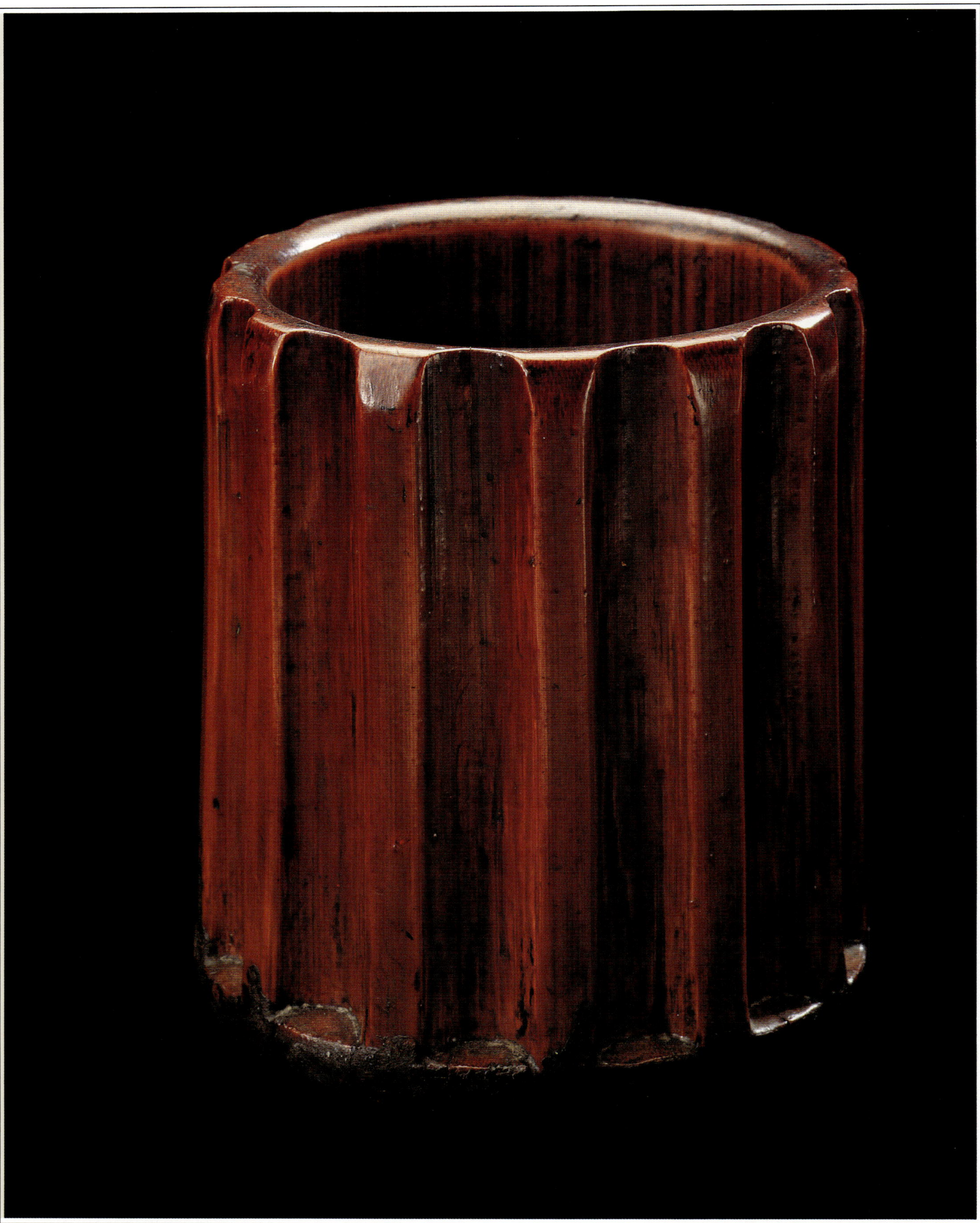

三

PLEASURES OF LEISURE

PLEASURES OF LEISURE

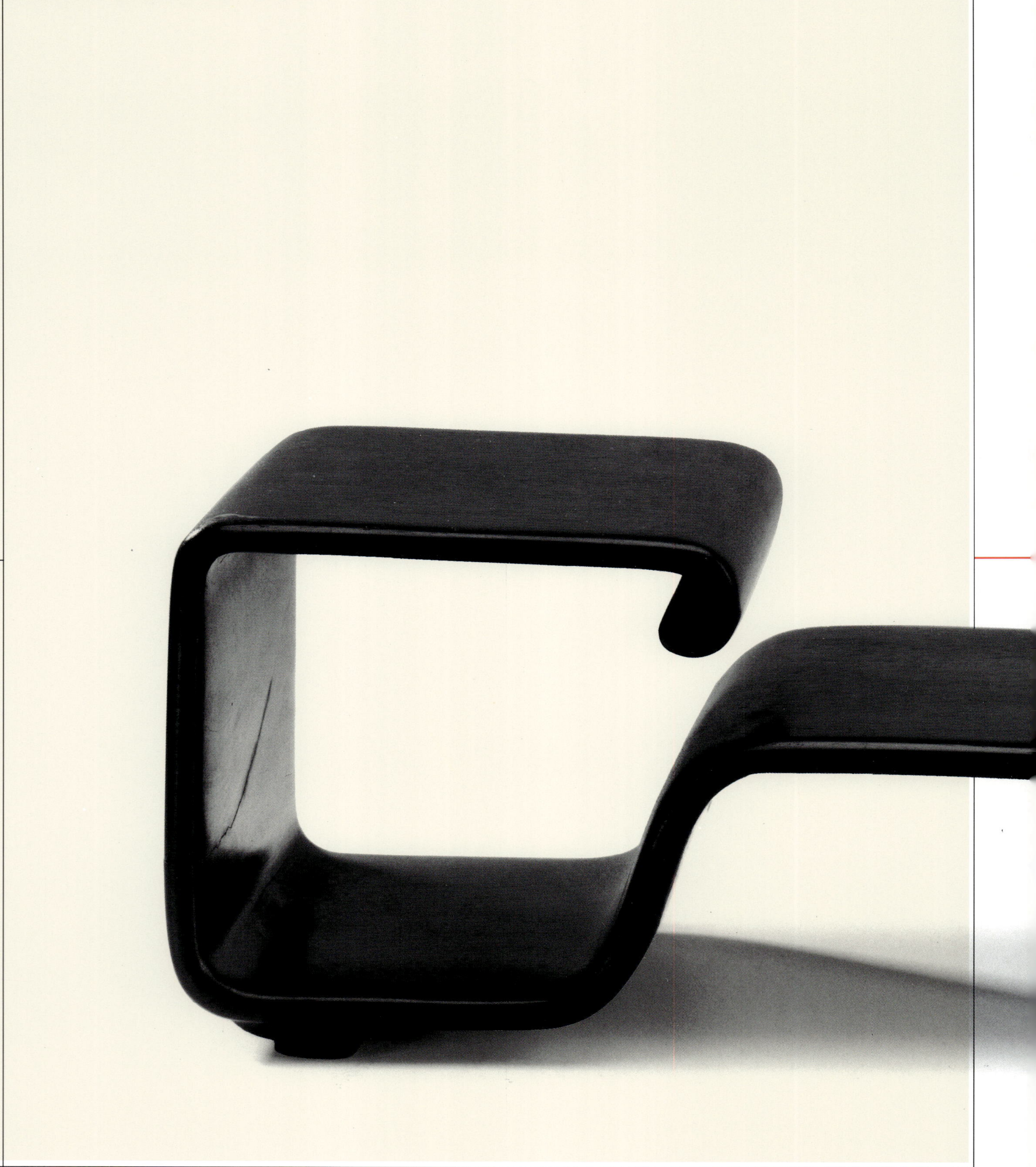

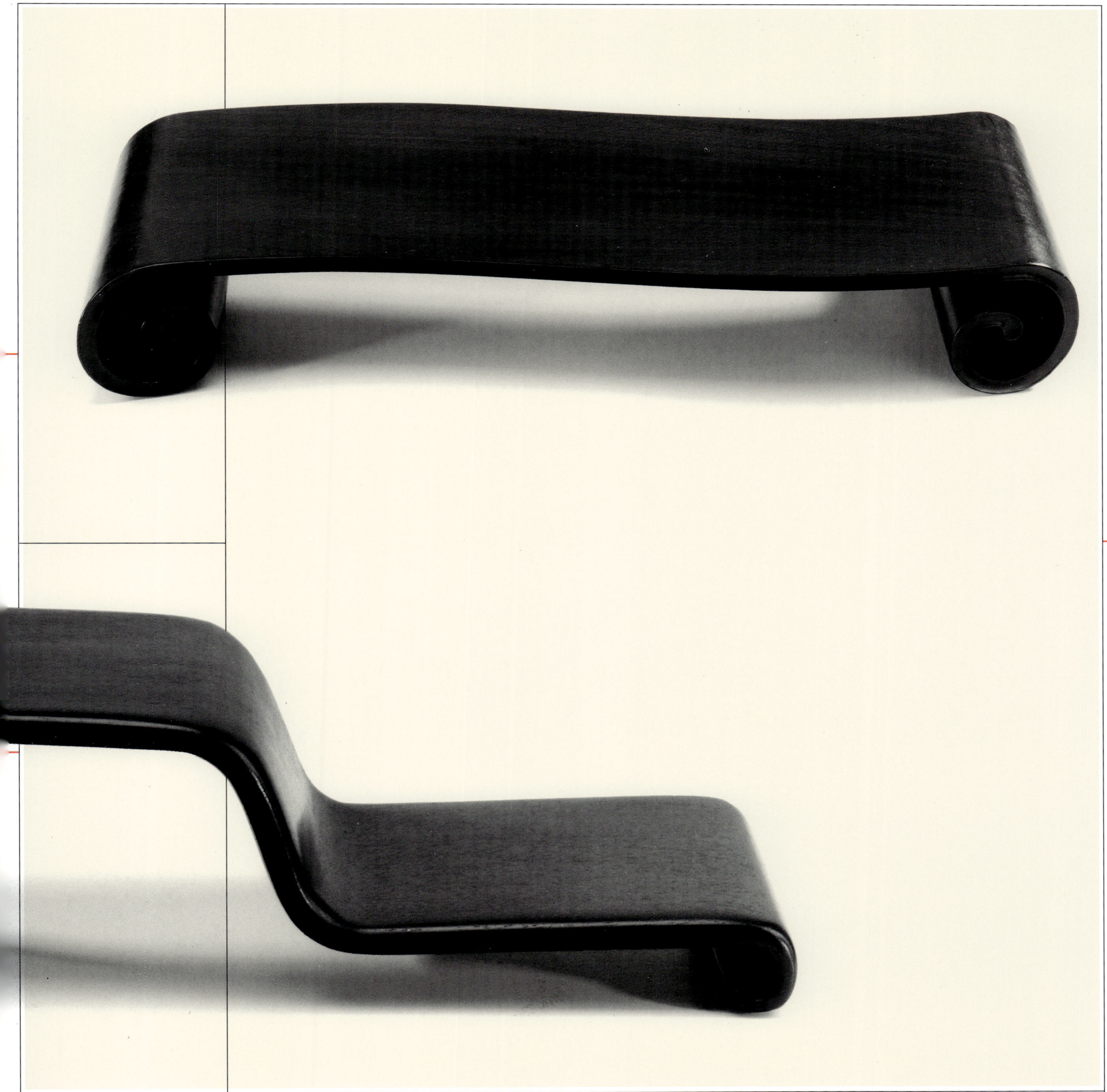

Hardwood display stands for ornaments, antiques or collectors' items, part of the paraphernalia of the gentlemanly pursuit of collecting and connoisseurship.

PLEASURES OF LEISURE

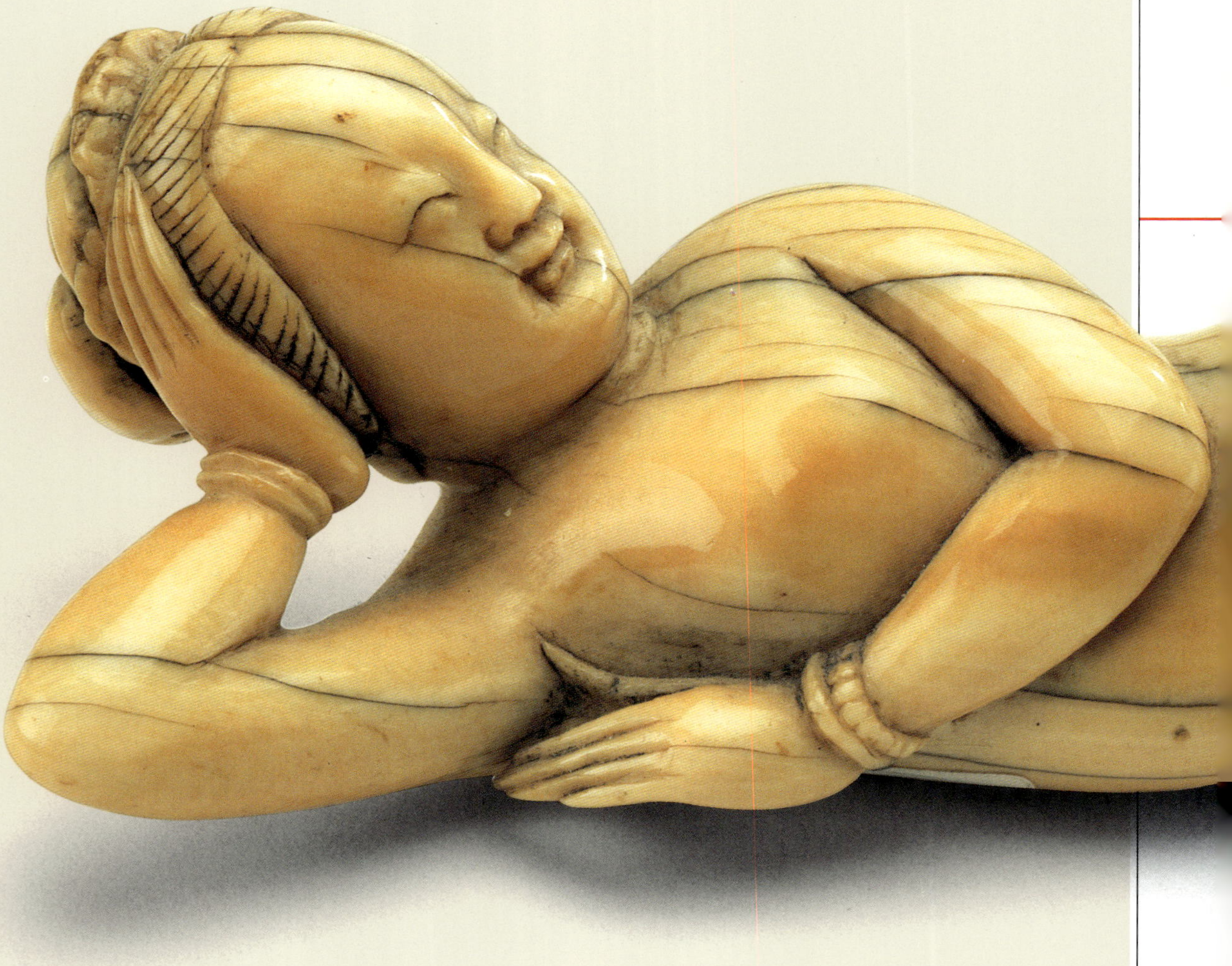

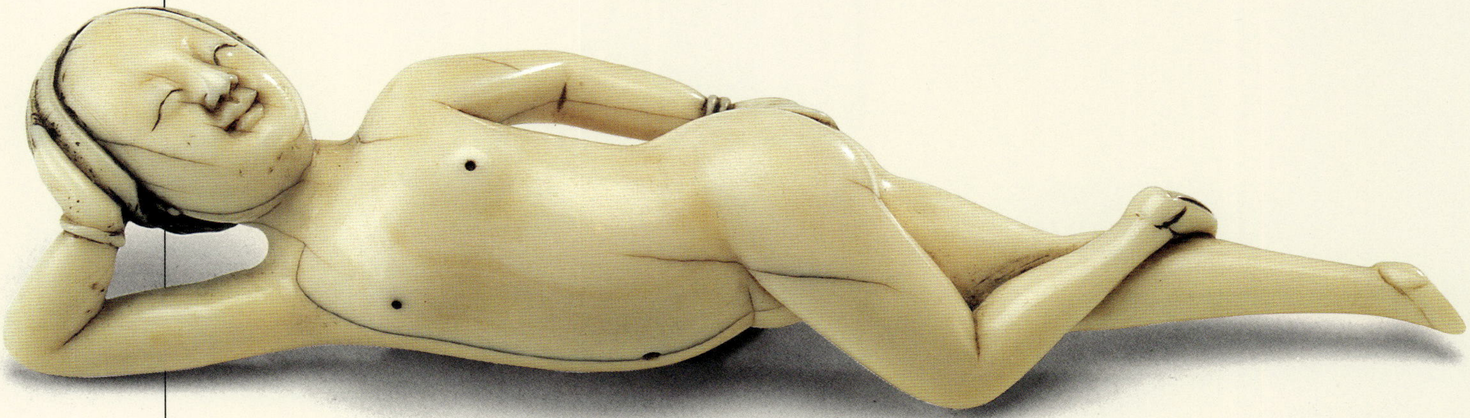

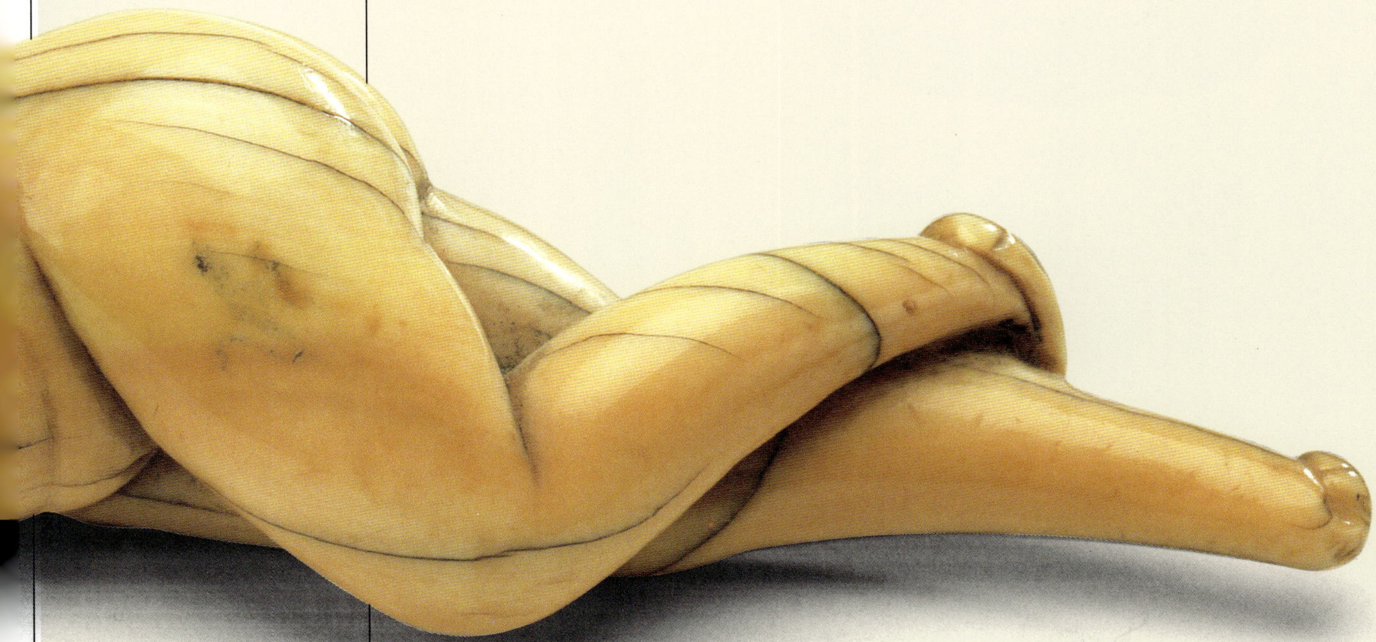

Reclining nude ladies in ivory that go by the misnomer "doctors' dolls", length 13 cm.

PLEASURES OF LEISURE

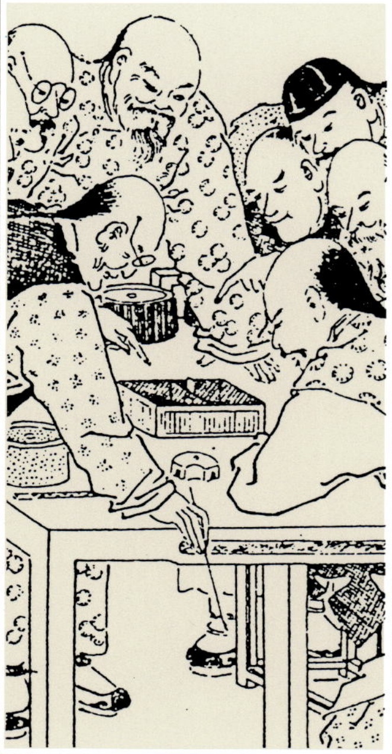

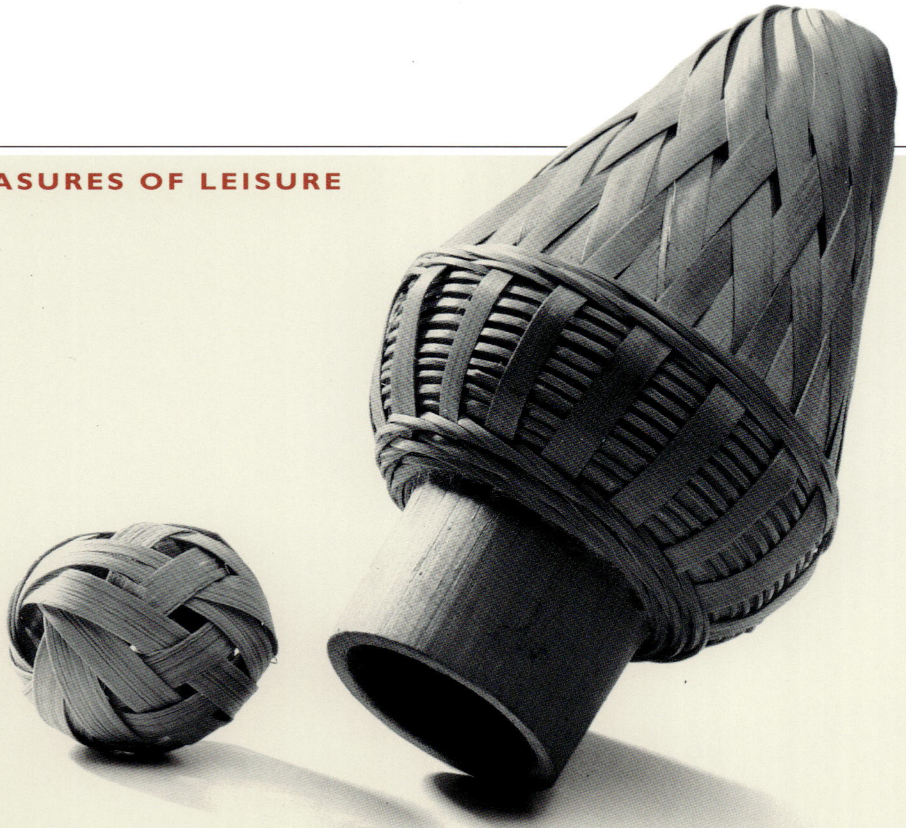

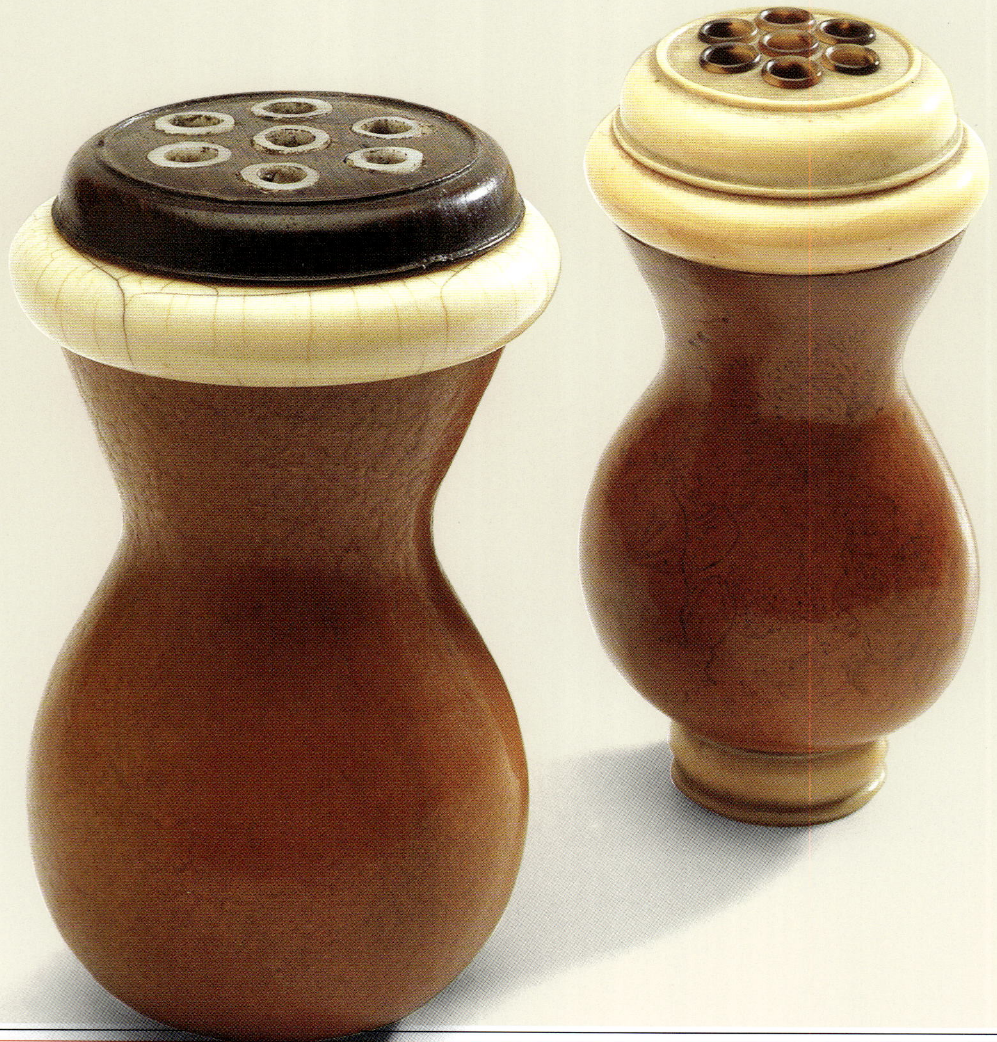

Top **Rattan cage** with stopper for keeping chirping crickets, height 14 cm. *Bottom* Pair of **cricket containers** made from hollowed-out bottle gourds fitted with lids perforated with air holes.

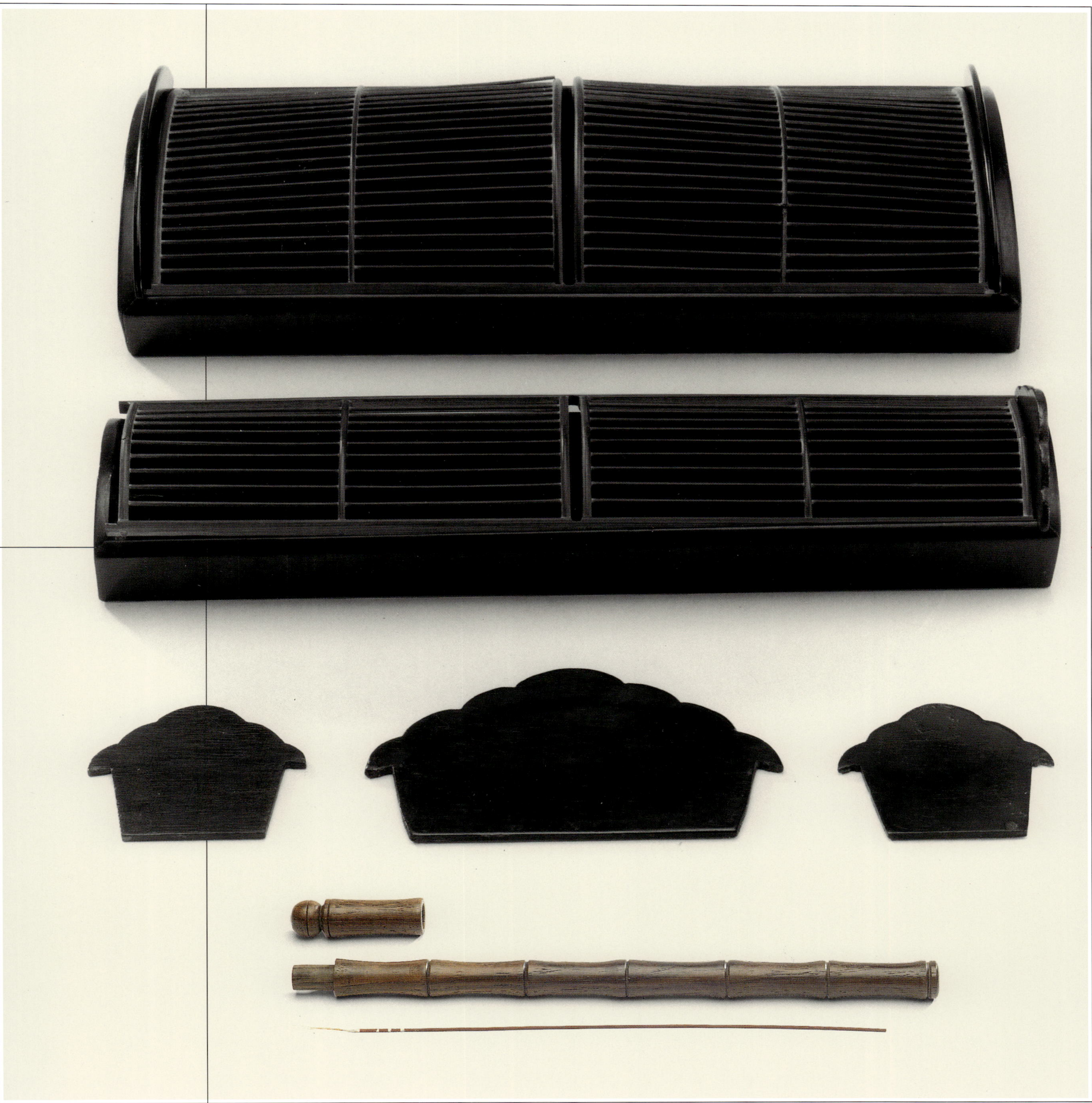

Top **Cage** in blackwood and bamboo for fighting crickets, a "duplex" kind with a middle partition that lifts off so that the two creatures can confront each other, length 24 cm. **"Tickler"** of camel hair *(bottom)* used for irritating the crickets and taunting them to fight is kept in blackwood container with lid carved to imitate bamboo, length 20 cm.

PLEASURES OF LEISURE

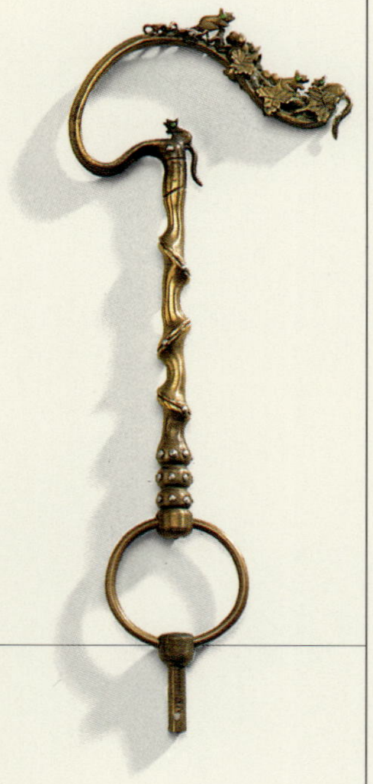

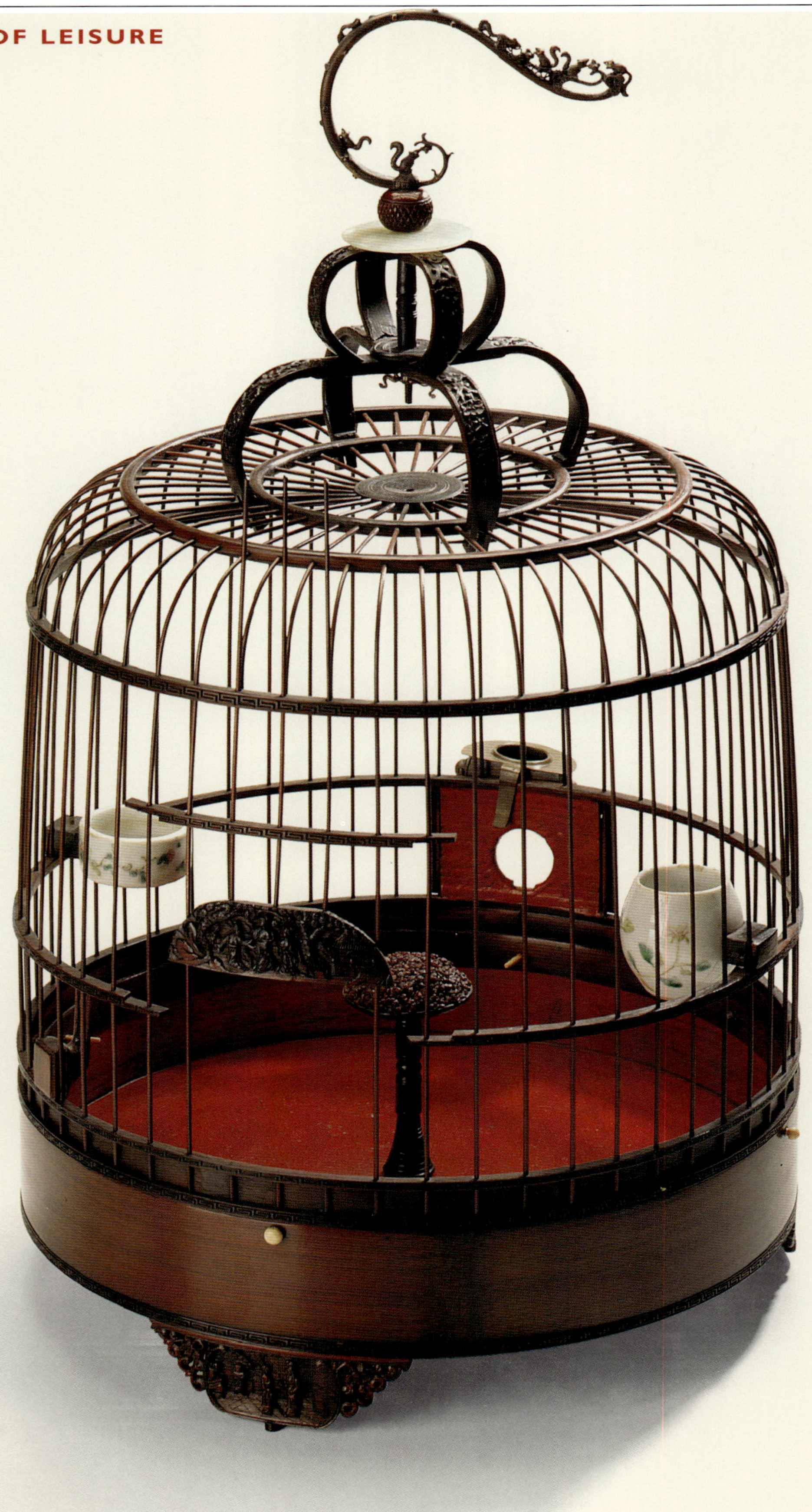

Keeping pet and singing birds is a traditional pastime popularly indulged in by fortunate idlers. The style of cage varies with region and type of bird: this one usually comes with a brass cup outside the latch and houses the lark favoured by bird-lovers in Peking, height 45 cm.

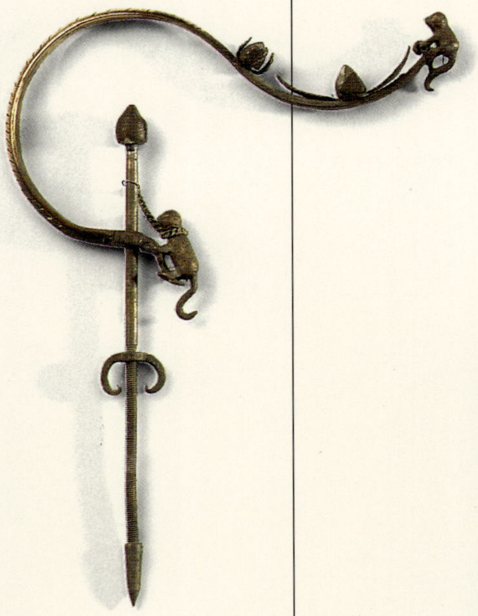

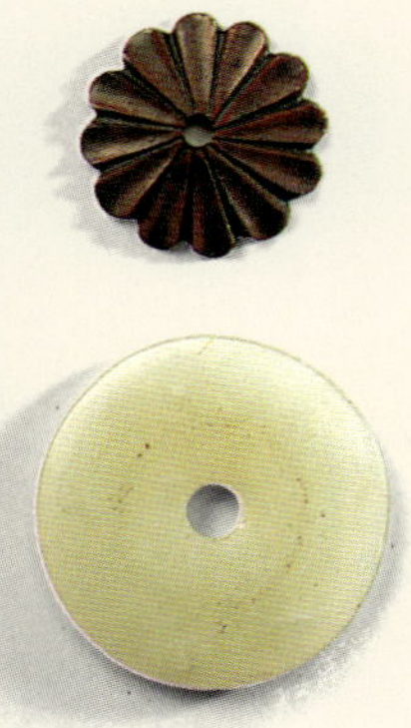

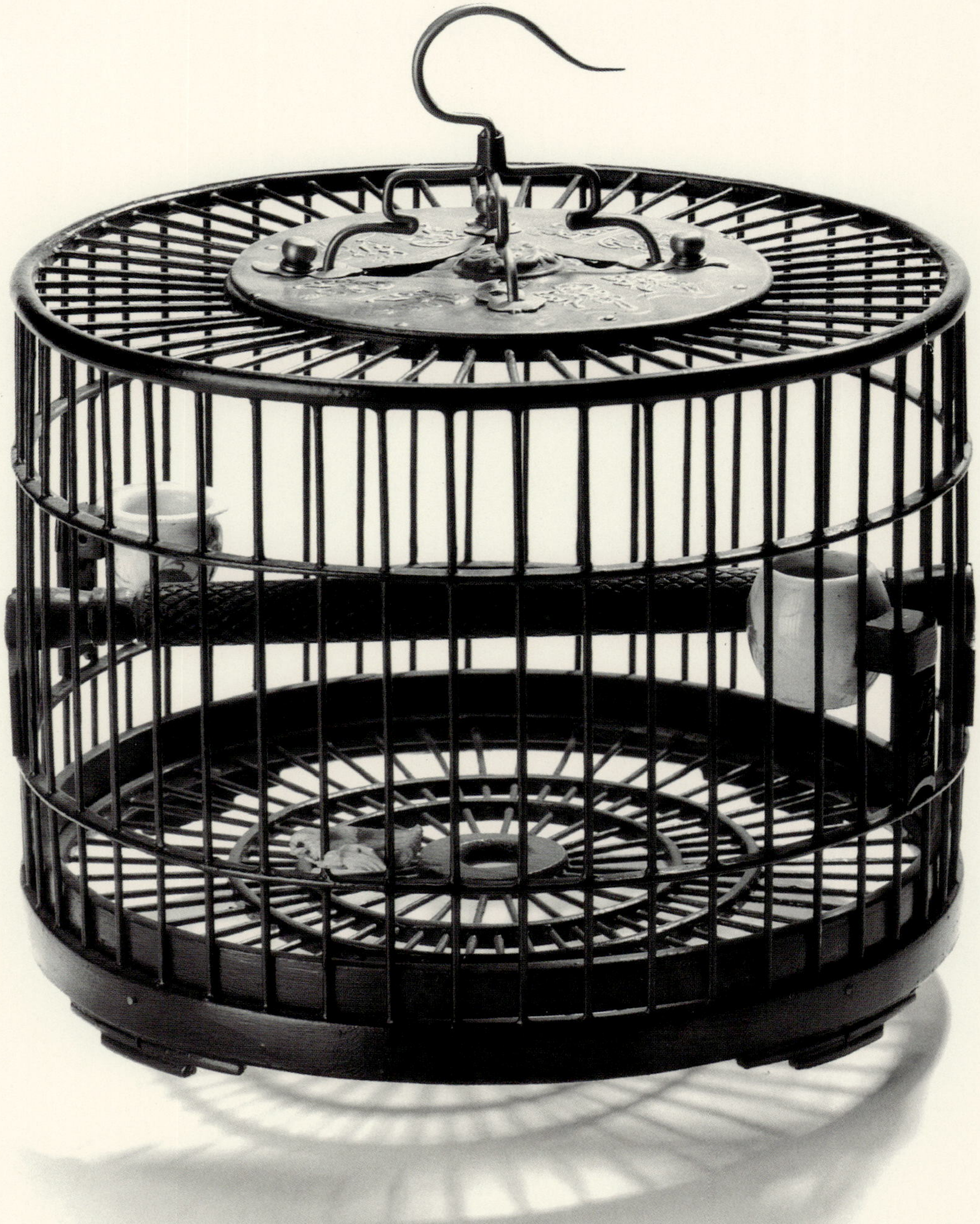

Birdcage for the ruby-throat and blue-throat from the Shanghai area, covered in the thick lacquer of Suzhou. Just as tender care is lavished by bird-keepers on their pets, so devoted attention is given to the decoration of birdcage hooks. The two ring fastenings are of bamboo and bone.

PLEASURES OF LEISURE

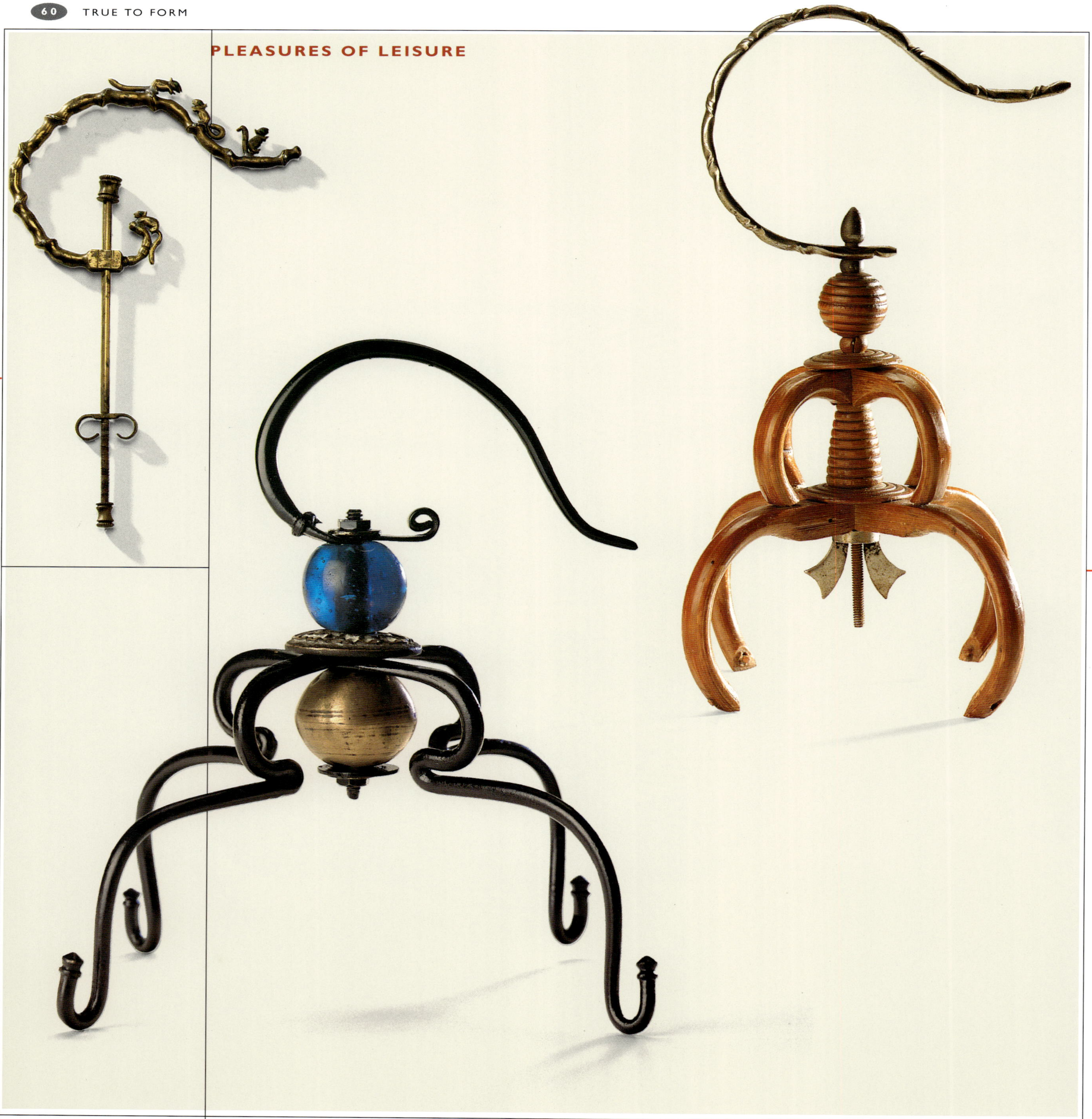

Hooks of metal *(left)* and bamboo *(right)* for suspending birdcages from eaves of home or teashop frequented by bird-lovers. To make their birds sing, the owners would air and rock the cage from its hook. The blue glass knob *(left)* may be an allusion to the sapphire button on the hat worn by Qing officials of the third rank. Hanger on the right goes with a cage for keeping thrush.

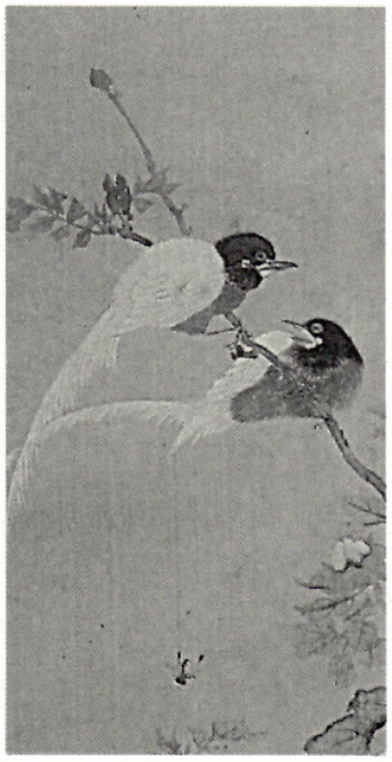

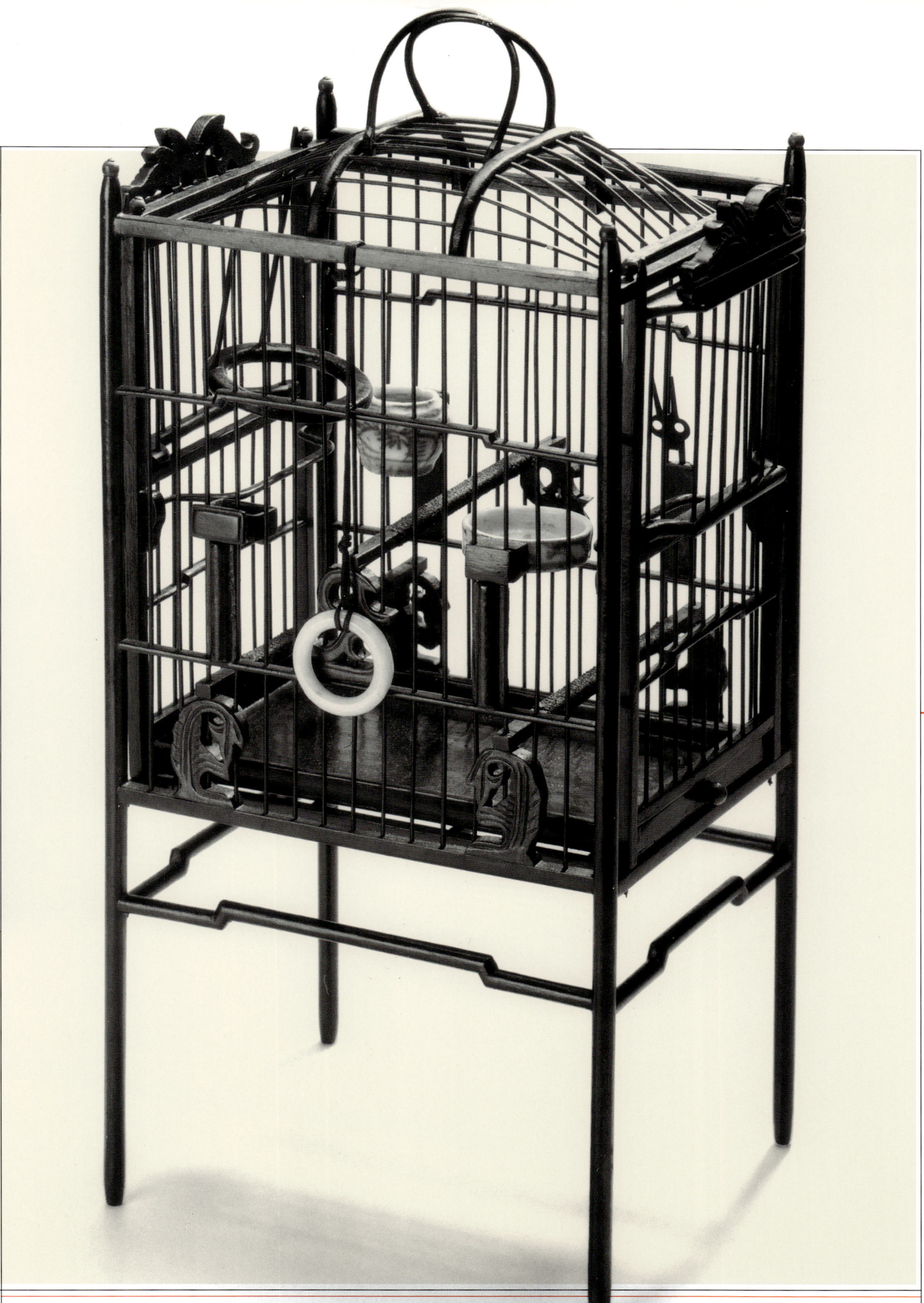

Of expensive blackwood, and with a jade lock, this **standing birdcage** would typically grace a room in a Shanghai home and house a canary or brambling, height 42 cm.

PLEASURES OF LEISURE

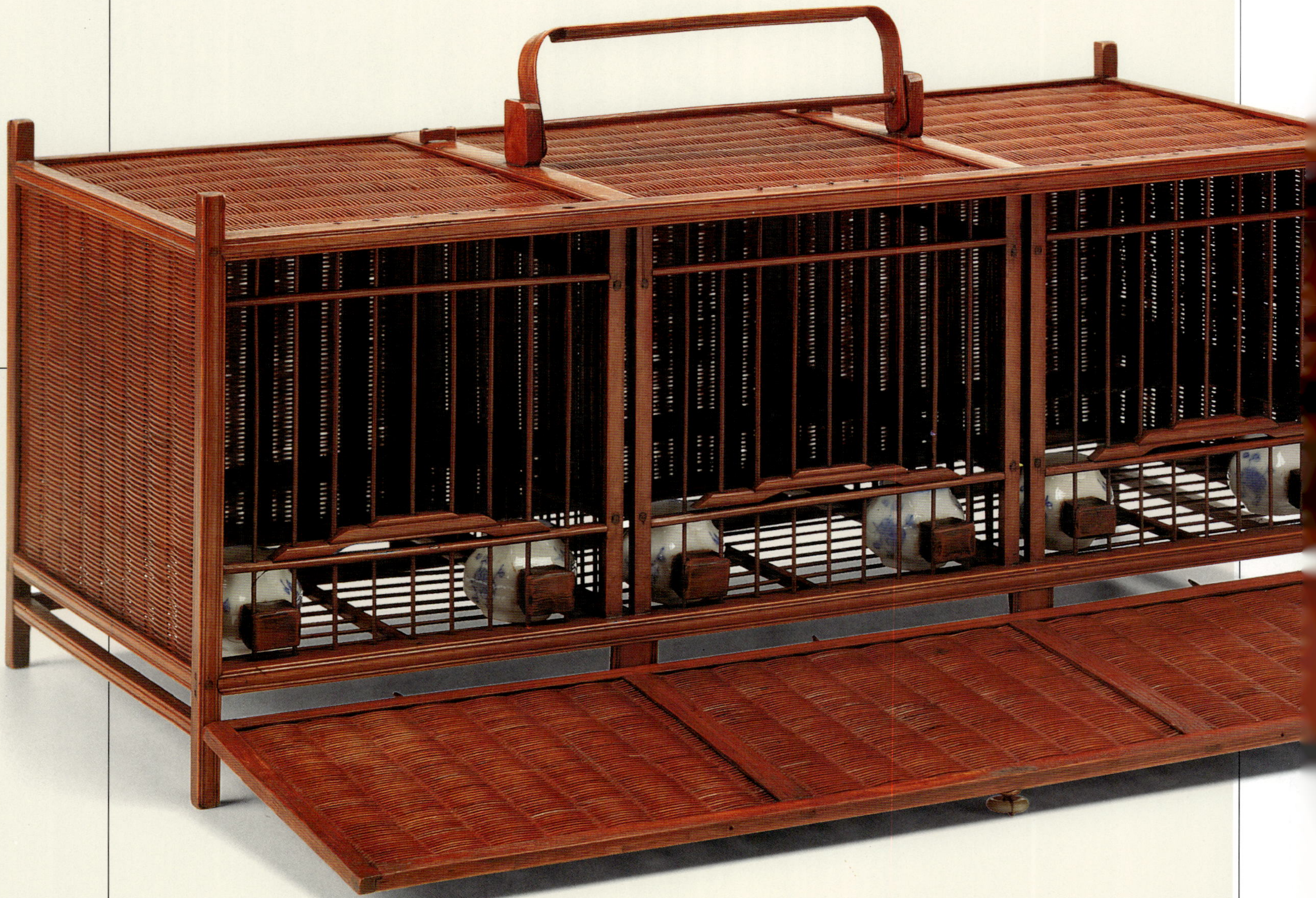

Fortune-teller's birdcage, housing a trick bird which has been trained to pick up cards from a spread-out pack and convey them to his master who then divines his customer's luck, length 45 cm.

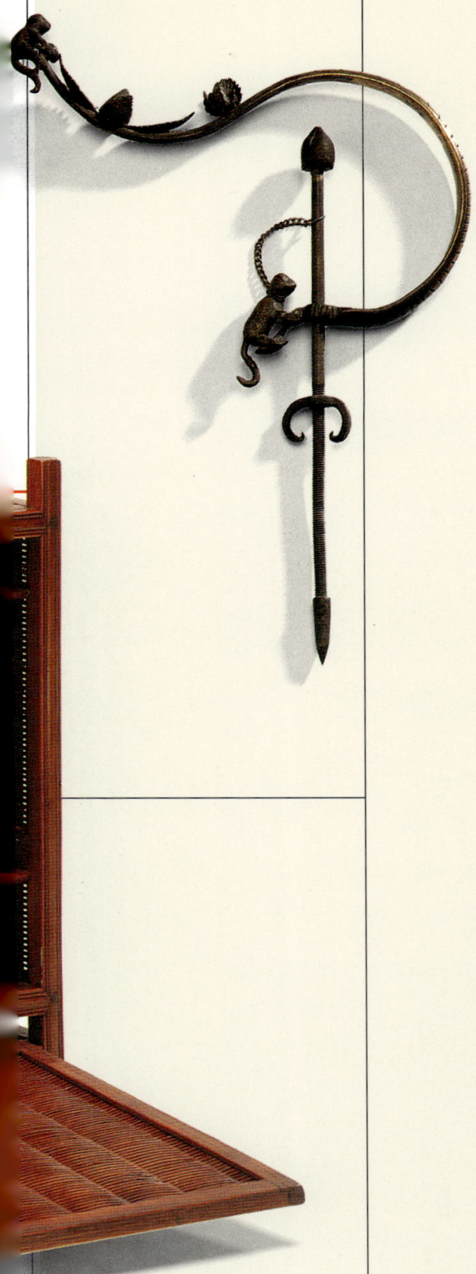

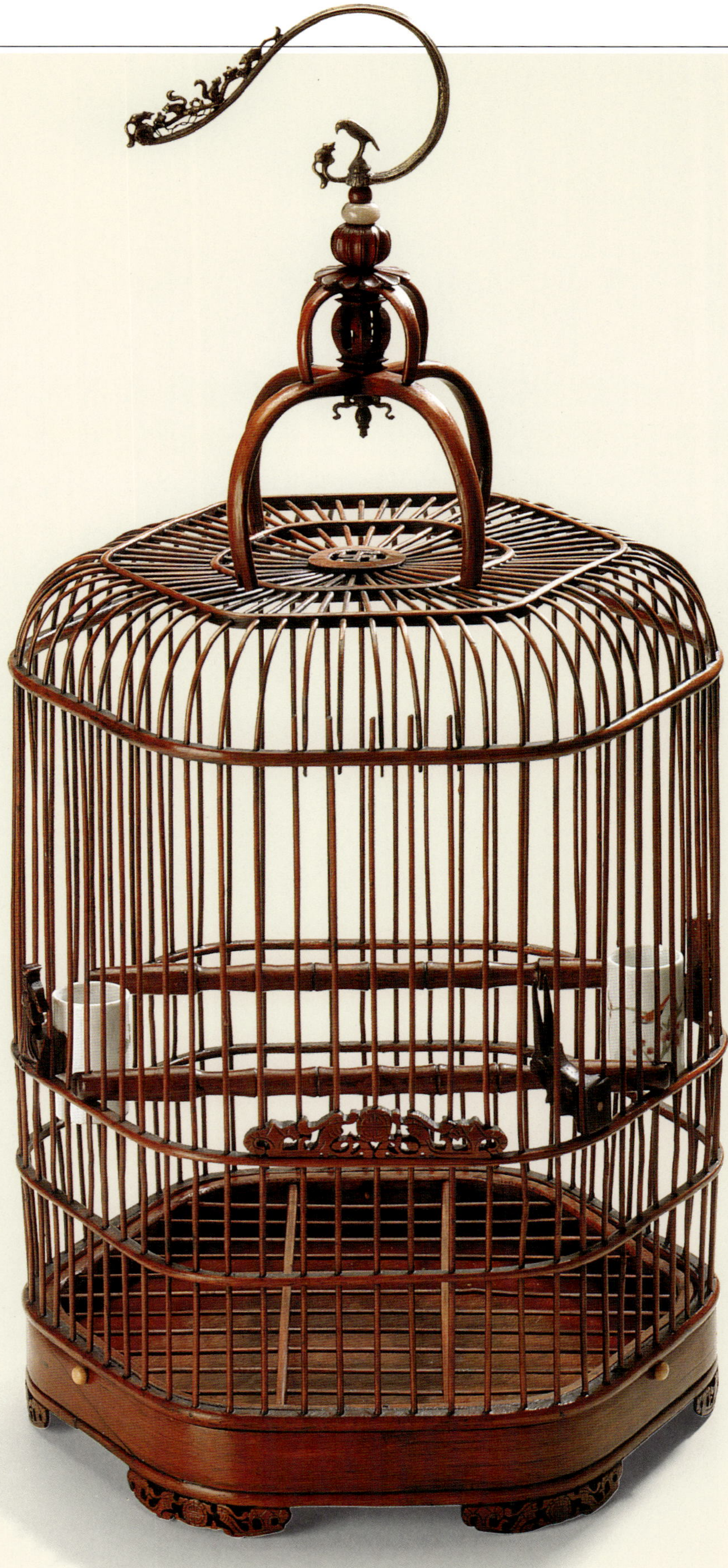

Hexagonal birdcage, typical of Peking, for keeping the red-billed leiothrix, height 40 cm.

PLEASURES OF LEISURE

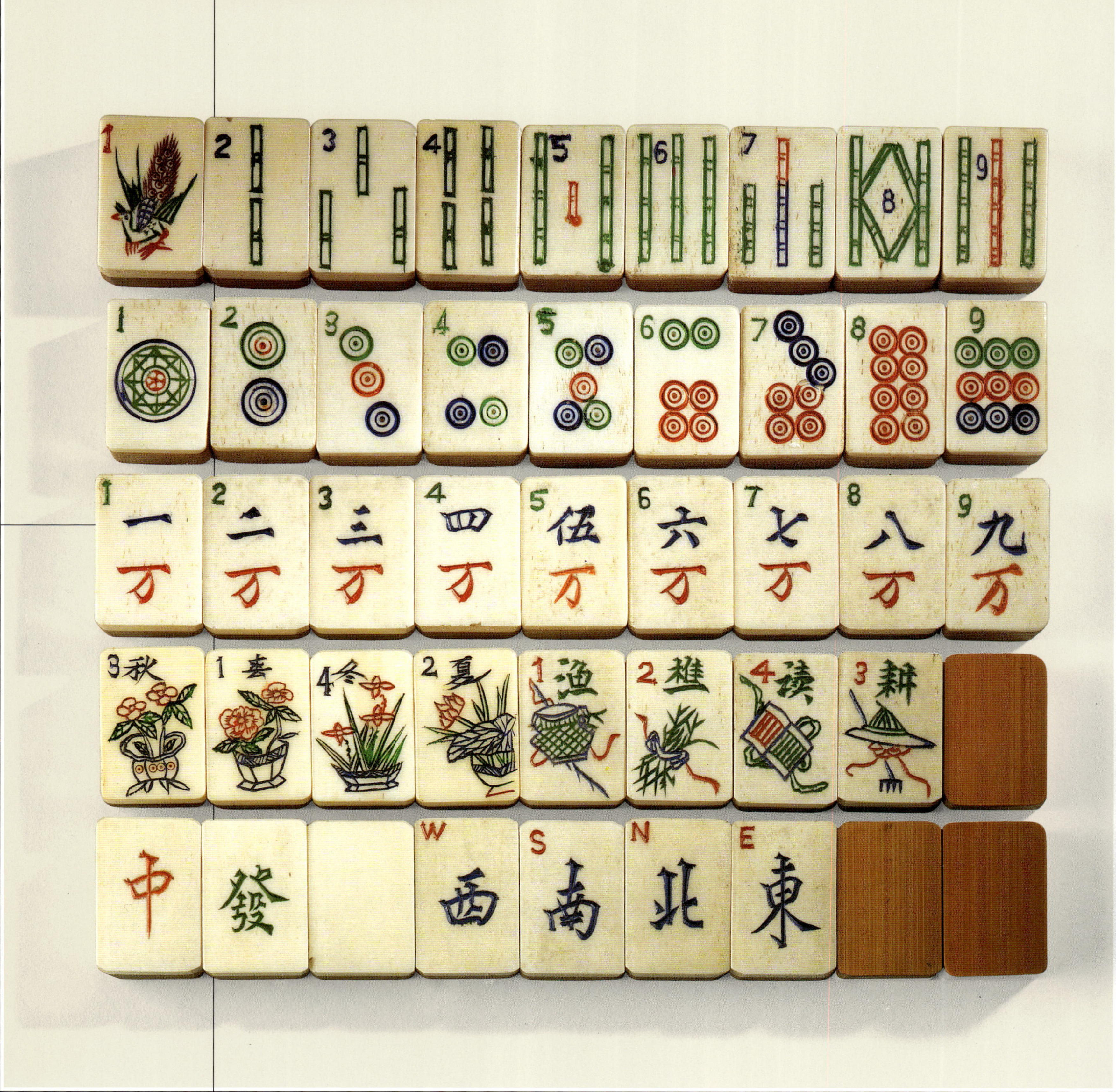

Mahjong tiles in ivory set in bamboo.

A Celebration of the Art of the Chinese Craftsman

WILLOW FLOSS IN the swift wind
races against the Spring Festival.
Hoisted by children,
Running everywhere,
A sheet of paper, wind-driven,
it desires to ascend to the heavens;
And the wandering thread,
ten thousand feet long,
cannot hold its course.
But when it hits the ground,
Suddenly it grows still.

On a Kite
Wu Weiye,
17th century

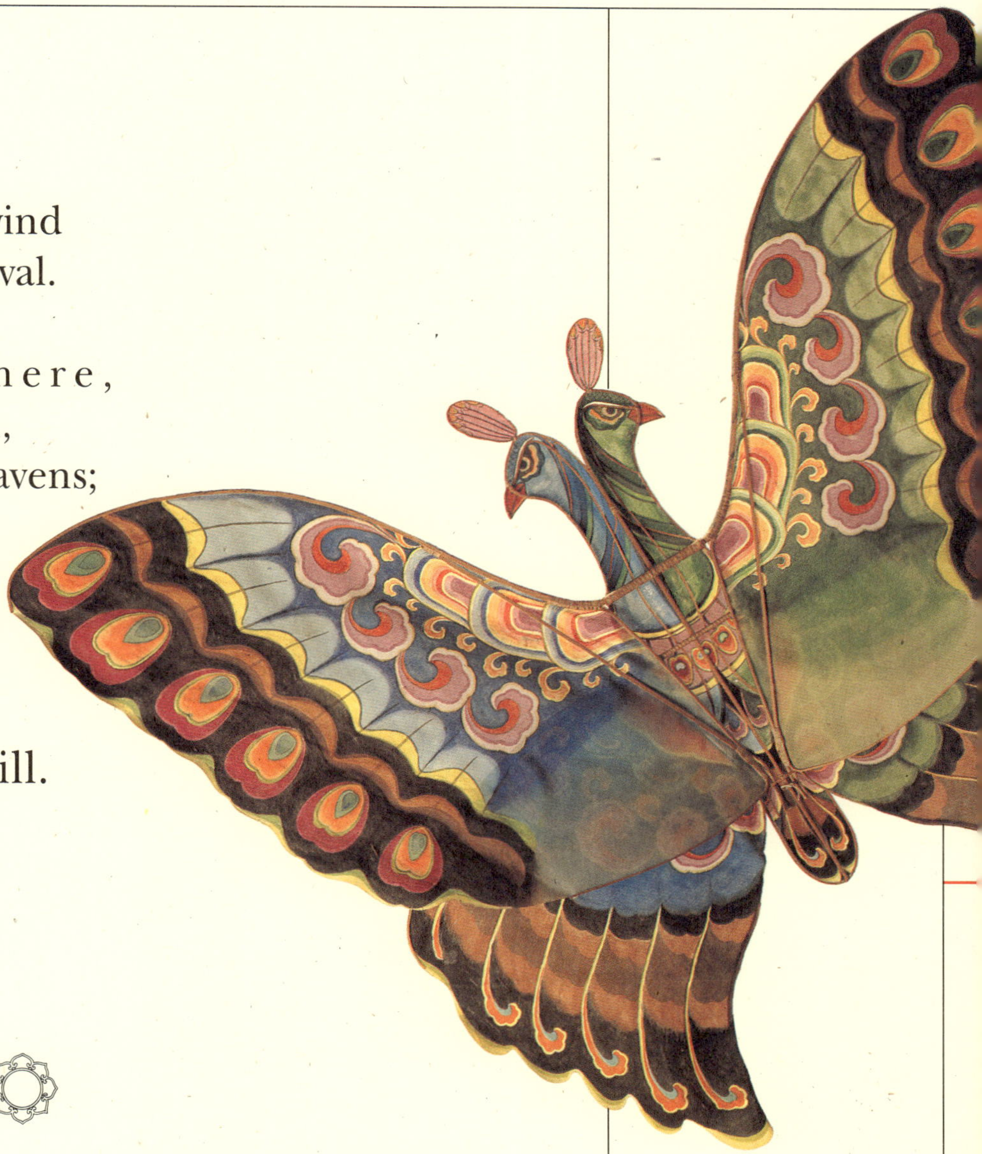

THE CHINESE WERE THE FIRST PEOPLE IN THE WORLD TO MAKE AND FLY PAPER KITES. They called them "paper birds" at first, then "aeolian harps" – "harps" because small bamboo flutes were tied to them to make them thrum as they lifted into the air with the wind blowing through them. Today kites come in all sizes and designs, gorgeously hand-painted in rainbow colours, fantastically shaped as swallows, centipedes, tadpoles, flamingoes, peacocks, butterflies, wild geese and gold fish with goggly eyes that spin and roll when the kite is in full flight.

It is the art that goes into producing paper kites and other Chinese crafts – the feel for form, the grasp of function, the mastery of the medium whether it be paper, clay, bamboo, wood, straw, fabric, brass, leather or even gourd – that this book sets out to celebrate.

Paper kite *flown by children and adults in north China in Spring, and especially on the fifteenth day of the first lunar month, to send off the God of Wealth on his way to heaven.*

The examples reproduced in it are for the most part simple articles made for daily use, a far cry it would seem from the sumptuous silks, jades and porcelains by which the world first came to know China. Yet in even the least object the Chinese touch is unmistakable. The classic shapes whose effect rests on their proportions and their deeply satisfying forms are found in plain bamboo baskets no less than in fine Ming dynasty porcelains. Such beauty is not created in a day. It must have long and rich roots and, far from having sprung out of a vacuum, even the humblest object is linked in some way to the finer traditions. It is a Chinese habit to make the same object over and over again to styles and conventions evolved in the earliest dynasties, and people craft what had pleased their parents and *their* parents and *their* parents for a thousand years and more.

Something else links the ages of the crafts pictured in this book, as recognizable in the items which go back a couple of centuries as in those produced only yesterday. There is nothing hit or miss about the way they have been made, and that is because their creators stand in a long line of craftsmen whose skills have been immemorially tempered in a hard school. The practice of Chinese craft has been the nimbler and the more accomplished for having been conditioned by a history of trying to meet the exacting requirements of cultivated patrons.

Let us play about with time a little and call on one such patron, a gentleman living near the famous West Lake in Hangzhou. We enter his mansion by a gateway, passing but hardly noticing – for they are far too common to remark – the painted images of door gods mounted on each side of the entrance to guard against demons and evil spirits. The roof comes into view above the trees, its tiles glazed jade-green, its timbers carved and painted, its eaves decorated with terracotta dragons and phoenixes. Then down along a covered arcade, where lattice windows reveal now a drift of bamboo, now a slant of sun, and now a thrust of ornamental rock. As we step into the reception room our host appears, robed as befits an official of lofty rank in 13th-century China in fine silk from Suzhou. A girdle buckled in rhinoceros horn clasps his waist. One hand flicks open a folding fan to reveal a celebrated painter's mastery of the brush.

A choice of teas, Hangzhou's own Forest of Fragrance and White Cloud blends, awaits us, served in cups of fine porcelain placed on trays of glimmering lacquered wood. The room is simply and elegantly furnished, with tall-backed

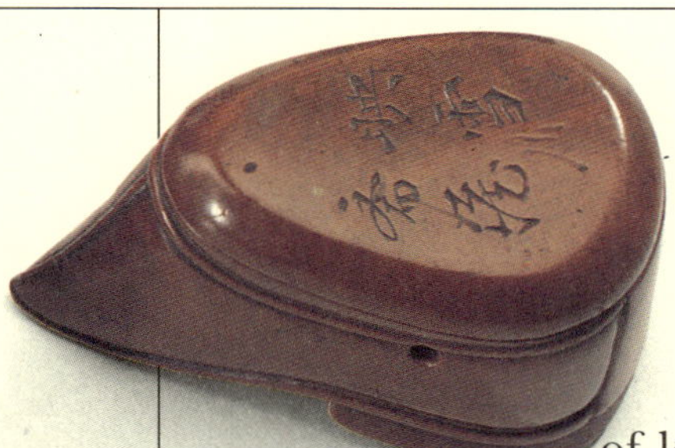

wooden chairs placed around a small rectangular table, and scroll paintings adorning the walls. Slender glazed celadon vases hold clusters of daphne and magnolia in full bloom.

As well as being a high official, our host is a cultivated man of letters, the sort to fall under the spell of the written word, whether embodied in poetry, or in those brush strokes that are the very essence of Chinese style in the arts. The study in which he spends many a pleasurable hour is replete with the familiar accoutrements of scholarship: brush pot and wrist rest, ink stick and stone, seals and seal box, brush and cap. There he now leads us, to share with us his pleasure in his art collection. He is no follower of fashion – he leaves that to the vulgar merchants – but still he has a passion for collecting that is so much the rage these days: paintings and calligraphy, antique jades and bronzes, curiously shaped rocks and other esoteric *objets d'art.*

As he unfurls hand scroll after hand scroll, landscapes bathed in cloud and mist with poems and colophons written on them in various styles of calligraphy, his delight and refinement are plain to see. Like his fellow literati, our host reveres calligraphy above all other arts. To him it goes without saying that the highest forms of art are those of the brush.

His love of beauty no less than his wealth ensures that his home is filled with the products of the country's finest craftsmen. Indeed his house is one glorious announcement of the craftsman's art. But though he treasures these things, it would never occur to him to "collect" them. Luxurious as they are, they are practical objects, there to be used in everyday life, and he would be astonished indeed to know that one day people would so prize his robust stoneware jars from the kilns of Junzhou, the ones covered with a lavender-blue glaze splashed with purple, that they would set broken pieces as ornaments and jewels. To him such things are mere domestic utensils, beautifully crafted to be sure, but hardly art. Their quality shows him to be a rich gentleman of taste, but it is his collection of paintings

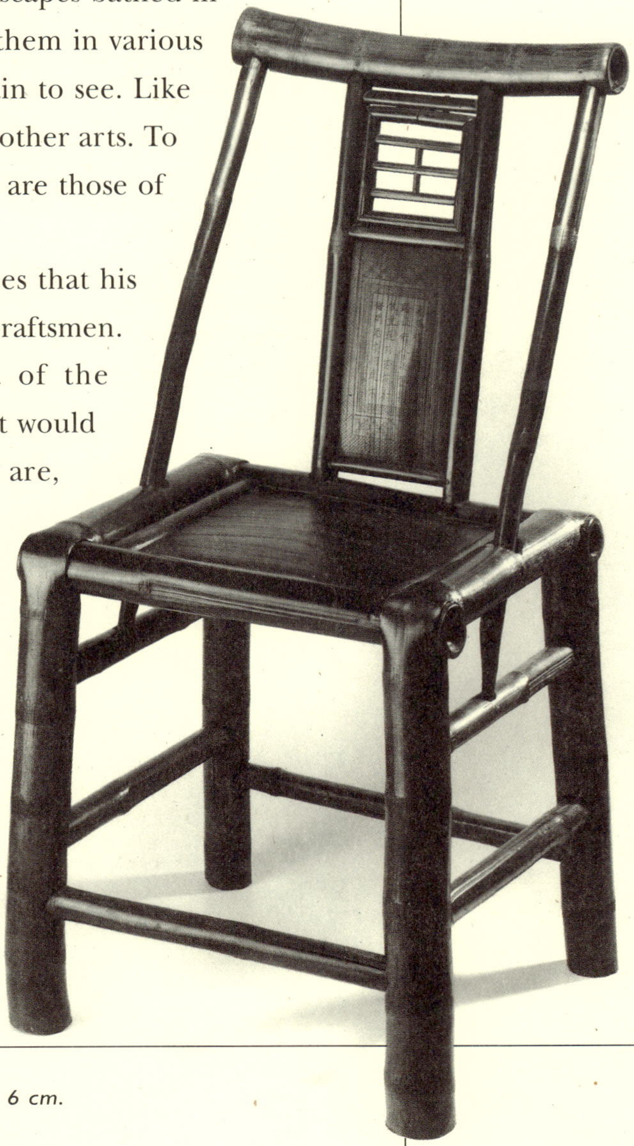

Top **Belt toggle** *carved from wood, width 6 cm.*
Bottom **Bamboo chair**.

and calligraphy that shows him to be a connoisseur.

In his mind there is a line dividing works of art from other objects. In China, the first works of art to be set apart by that line were pieces of calligraphy. As time passed, the line shifted to take in more and more different types of object, and many of our gentleman scholar's household utensils – ceramic vessels for wine and food, for example – are now cherished by collectors and museums as being art treasures in their own right. Hardly anything crafted, whether it be the terracotta animals above his roof tiles, or the rhinoceros horn buckle on his girdle, or even the pottery pillow which raised his wife's head from the bed so that her coiffure remained unruffled, would escape the attention of today's art dealer.

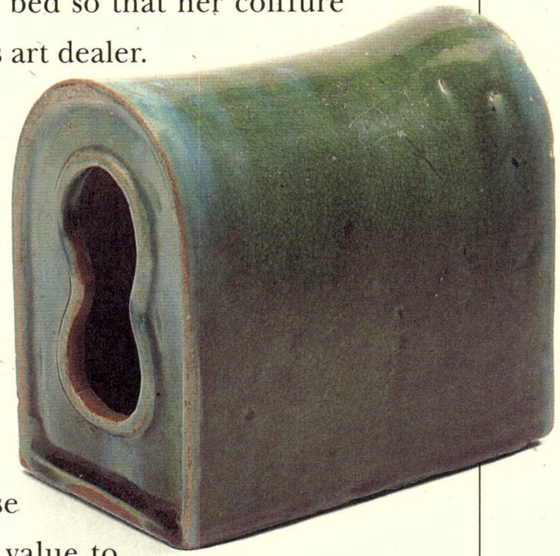

The majority of the objects pictured in this book are owned by collectors and dealers. Yet, save a few, they are things made for general consumption and not for any cultivated clientele – not, in other words, for the class of people to which our gentleman scholar belonged. If we were to emulate the Chinese connoisseurs of an earlier age we might dismiss half the objects as "vulgar", the work of the lowly and unlettered. But times have changed, and we think quite differently today. Of course age itself imparts an antiquarian quality and therefore value to them, but neither nostalgia nor rarity, nor even fashion or the attempts of art dealers to broaden the canon of marketable items, is enough to explain why things that had gone unnoticed before are now admired. What is also significant is that the very way we look at art has changed.

One of the changes is that, instead of regarding the arts as aesthetic wholes, we now distinguish between them, from the kind variously described as elite, sophisticated, serious or high (that is, the kind normally evoked when the word "art" is used without qualification), to the kind usually called folk. In this our views are affected by the late-19th century European recognition of folk art as a special category, a recognition that was bound up with the romanticization of the simple life, by the spread of local patriotism, and by aesthetic causes such as the English Arts and Crafts Movement. This last, under people like the poet and designer William Morris, deplored the ugliness and uniformity of the industrial age

Glazed ceramic hollowed pillow *with keyhole opening, height 15 cm.*

and set about the re-creation of traditional handicrafts, pioneering a new appreciation of "art made by the people and for the people" throughout Europe.

Away in the Far East the seeds it blew about were to prove especially fertile in Japan. The same could not be said of China, where such interest in folk traditions as existed has been of a different character: less widespread, more intermittent and far more politically inspired. We can perhaps best understand the Chinese experience by contrasting it with Japan's.

A Japanese William Morris arose in the 1920s to celebrate the "forgotten beauty" of folk crafts and the art of the "unknown craftsman" (or "country bumpkin", as Morris has called him). The art critic Yanagi Soetsu responded deeply to the aesthetic qualities of functional everyday objects – the bold striped pattern on an indigo-dyed cotton kimono, the green glaze dabbed over a saké bottle – and made it his lifelong purpose to open people's eyes to this neglected realm of beauty, neglected because Japan's intense modernization and its intellectuals' infatuation with the West were leaving many traditional craft forms out in the cold.

To Soetsu, there are broadly speaking two main forms of craft: artist craft, luxury items made by the few for the few; and folk craft, objects made for everyday use by the many for the many. He championed the latter, seeing in it the purest form of craft. "Naturally the English movement under William Morris was the subject of much discussion", we are told by his friend Bernard Leach, the British potter, "and I clearly recollect how he questioned me about an equivalent term for peasant or folk art, in Japanese", Since none existed, Soetsu had to invent one. The word he came up with was ***mingei***, written with the Chinese characters *min* (for "popular" or "of the people") and *yi* , for "art". Soon the word was on everyone's lips; it entered the Japanese dictionary, and was further spread by the influential Mingei Movement.

民藝

In China there was no movement to compare to the Mingei, and such interest as folk crafts aroused among the educated on the whole lacked conviction, as if the seal set upon culture by the taste of the gentleman scholar was too secure to be broken. Besides, the Mingei Movement's wish to preserve art forms rapidly retreating before industrialization was altogether missing in China, where the belated arrival of modernity allowed country traditions to survive longer.

What did occur in China was a nationwide cultural upheaval (the May

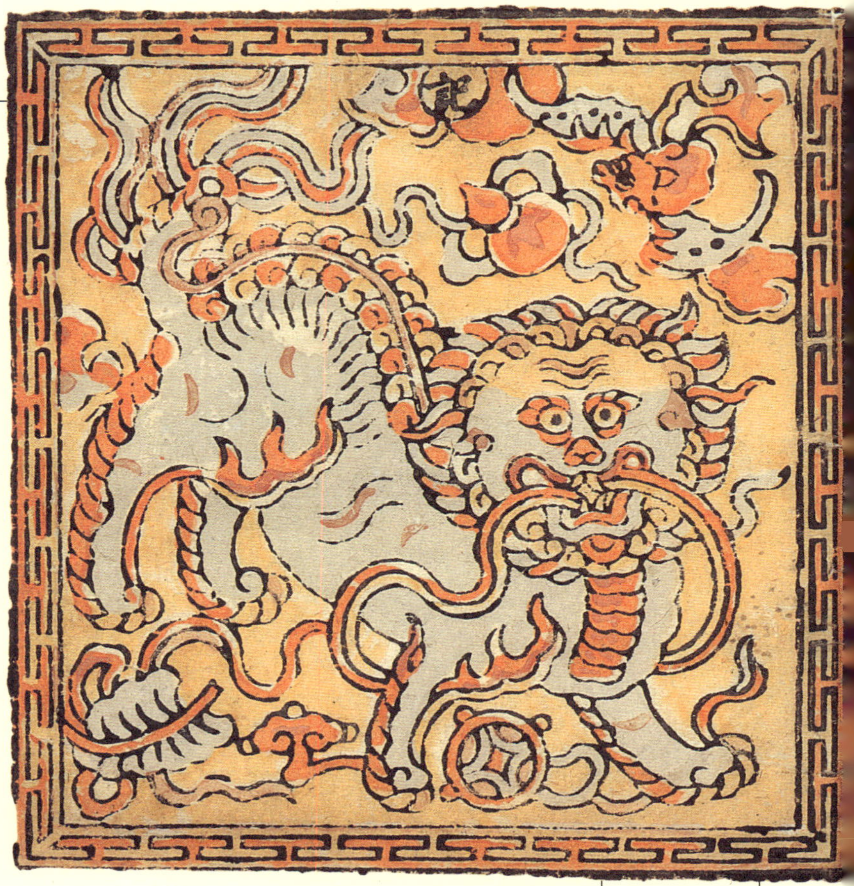

纸馬

Fourth Movement of 1919, as it came to be known), when young hearts were set on fire by ideas like democracy and socialism; when all-out attacks were mounted on "old ways" such as Confucianism, arranged marriages and classical education; and when writing in the vernacular was pitted against the intensely difficult classical Chinese that for so long had dominated letters in China.

As part of the interest in developing a literature based on the vernacular style of ordinary speech, scholars at Peking University began to study folklore and to collect folk ballads and proverbs. The compass of their research forays presently widened to include examples of folk art – the so-called *zhima*, images of folk deities printed on paper by peasants for burning, being one such genre. Later the seeds sown in Peking flowered in the south, in Canton's Zhongshan University, where calls were made in 1928 to give folk art, folk beliefs and folk customs, so long submerged under the heedless sway of literati values, the attention they deserved.

Such calls did not exactly fall on deaf ears, but still they hardly amounted to a change in the standards of beauty or a widening of art appreciation. "Folk art" entered the Chinese vocabulary, but it was as a type of folk product, rather than as art, that peasant craft first aroused interest. It was primarily ethnographers, not artists, who sought it out, and unlike Soetsu's theirs was not an aesthetic cause.

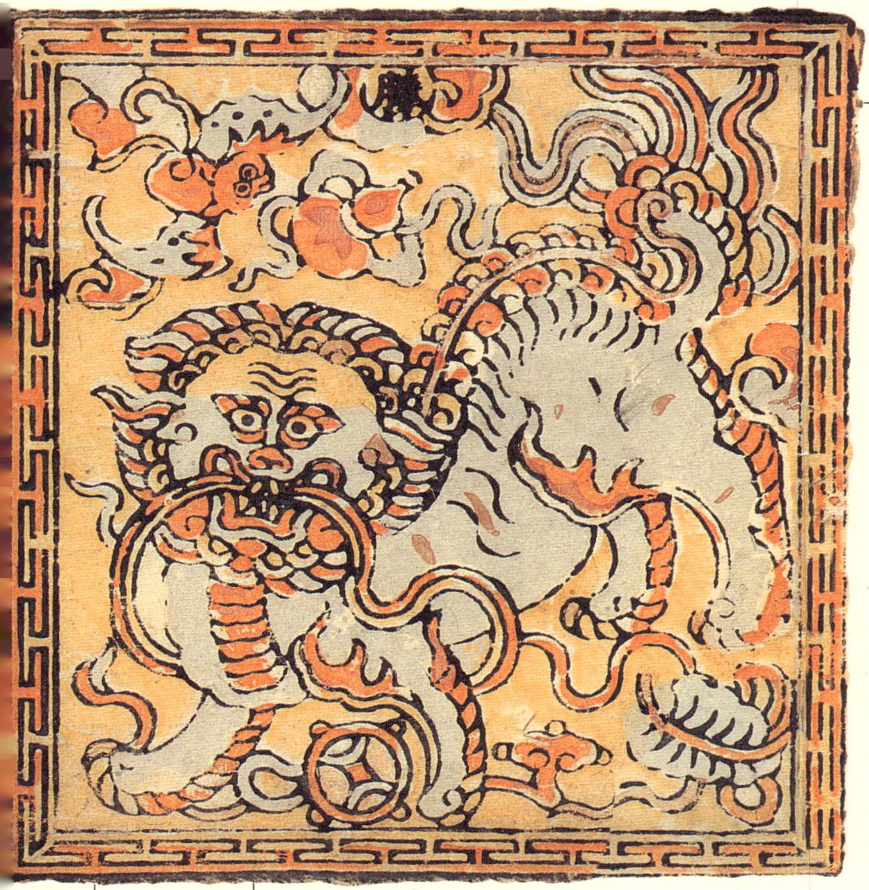

In the 1930s, it was sought out by the communist revolutionaries who had established themselves in the hills of Yan'an, the terminus of the Long March, as something which had lain beneath the notice of the upper classes and which they, for that very reason, should do their best to promote. But these new champions of peasant art did not see it in terms of aesthetics either, but as a vehicle for spreading their own political propaganda. The result was the appearance of paper cuts illustrating land reform and other favourite communist themes.

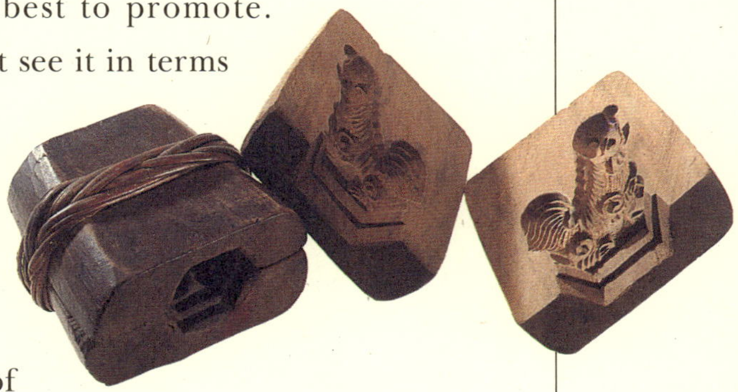

In any case, in China there is no cult of rusticity to equal Japan's, no particular attraction to those qualities – austerity, restraint, purity, asymmetry, imperfection – which permeate that cult's (and the Mingei Movement's) aesthetics. If there is a Chinese counterpart to the Japanese scholar retiring to the country to take pleasure in using the roughest utensils, he is more likely to be seen fondling an ancient piece of sculpted jade, the most immaculate example of its kind, with no hint of the rustic about it.

We very often think of the rustic when we think of folk art, and just as no

Above centre **Paired wood block prints** *of lions playing with silk balls produced before the 17th century by an old family printing house in Macau, 15 cm square. Above* **Wooden mould** *for biscuits in three-dimensional rooster design with rattan bands to bind mould during baking.*

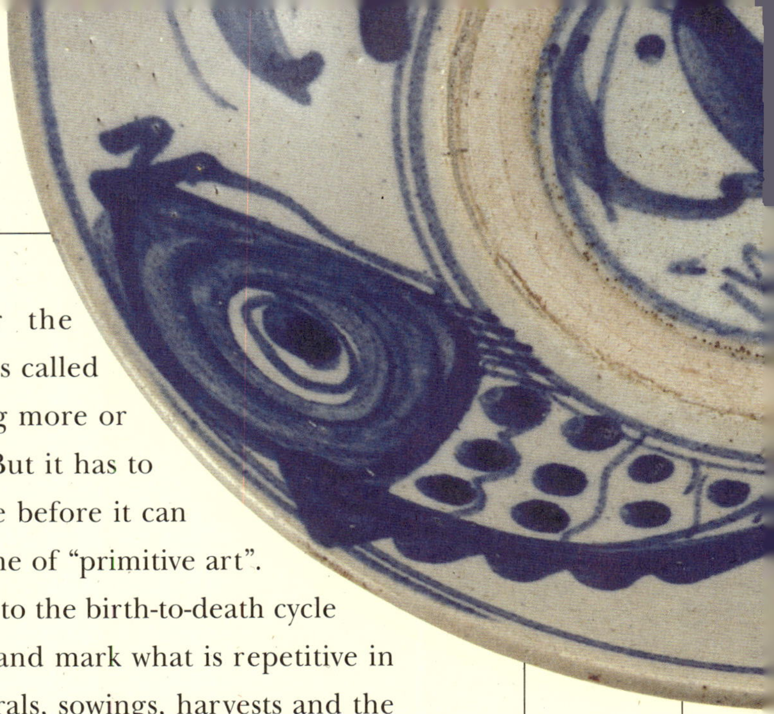

one would consider the Osaka secretary or the Birmingham factory worker as belonging to the class called folk, so it is the works of peasants and artisans living more or less apart from city dwellers that we term folk art. But it has to exist as an unsophisticated art within a great culture before it can be called "folk art"; otherwise it would go by the name of "primitive art". Produced in rural environments, close to nature and to the birth-to-death cycle of human existence, such works usually accompany and mark what is repetitive in country life: anniversaries, festivals, marriages, funerals, sowings, harvests and the daily round. Folk art, in other words, is the art of the "country bumpkin", to borrow William Morris's phrase.

By that reckoning then, none of the crafts in the home of our host in Hangzhou could be described as "folk". They were made in the towns, in workshops or factories, to satisfy the refined taste of the upper classes in furnishings, clothing and diversions, part of the luxury trade that put ceramics, lacquers, textiles, combs, fans, necklaces, hairpins, pendants, toggles, bamboo wares, wicker cages, children's toys, printed books and all sorts of other articles on sale in the shops.

Many of the artisans blurred the line Soetsu draws between artist craft and folk craft, since their products catered simultaneously to the few (the aristocracy) and the many (the ordinary people). Take the marionettes and shadow puppets, a form of theatre enjoyed by all classes, whose members were to be found jostling together in Hangzhou's "pleasure grounds": covered bazaars where jugglers, storytellers, acrobats, men exhibiting performing insects or bears, snake charmers and other street entertainers put on shows for high and low society alike. Shadow puppet plays were sometimes staged before high officials, courtiers and even the Emperor himself. "Folk" seems hardly the right word for them there. And what are we to make of paper kites, which most people assume to be a folk creation, when they were in fact invented by a palace courtier? In earlier times flying kites was not a popular pastime but a sport of the aristocracy.

Clearly there are many borderline cases. The folk distinction is at its most unmistakable, though, in the paper cuts Chinese peasants call "window flowers," the wood block prints or "New Year pictures", festival lanterns, batik, baskets, wooden cake moulds, clay toys and figures, and such examples of the country needlewoman's craft as embroidered pillow ends and children's aprons.

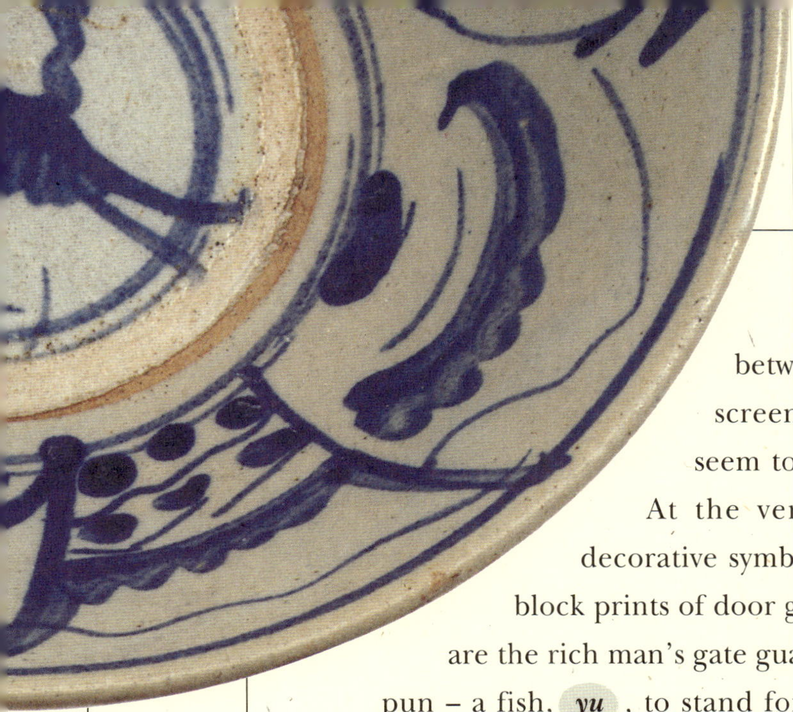

Between popular and upper-class taste, between a simple "window flower" and a carved lacquer screen inset with jade and lapis lazuli, a great gulf may seem to lie; and yet there is no denying that a link exists. At the very least, they share a common vocabulary of decorative symbols and motifs inherited from the past. The wood block prints of door gods pasted in front of peasant homes, for example, are the rich man's gate guardians popularized. Symbolism based on rebus and pun – a fish, *yu*, to stand for plenty or abundance, the Chinese character for which, *yu*, is written differently but pronounced the same – is ubiquitous in Chinese society, high or low. The image of peaches, which is emblematic of immortality, longevity and felicity, appears everywhere in Chinese art – as for instance in the cake moulds portrayed in this book. Such allusions, and the stock of legendary and literary figures in which they are entangled, are a heritage conditioning Chinese in all walks of life.

魚

Among the objects pictured in this book, the ones lying furthest from the folk end of the spectrum include the brush pots, the standing birdcage, the wooden display stands and the reclining nude female figure carved from ivory. Brush pots, part of the paraphernalia on the gentleman scholar's desk, were symbols of classical literacy, refinement and high social standing. The birdcage is of the sort to be found in a well-to-do home in Shanghai and would not have belonged to anyone lowly. Nor the hardwood display stands, which were used for showing off art objects and so were an item of cultivated conspicuous consumption. As for the nude figures, dealers will tell you that they are "doctors' dolls", handed through bed curtains to aristocratic female patients so that they could point to the place where their pain or ailment was located, decorum having obliged them to hide from male gaze and touch. In fact they were commercial erotica, very titillating to the men who bought them in the big cities.

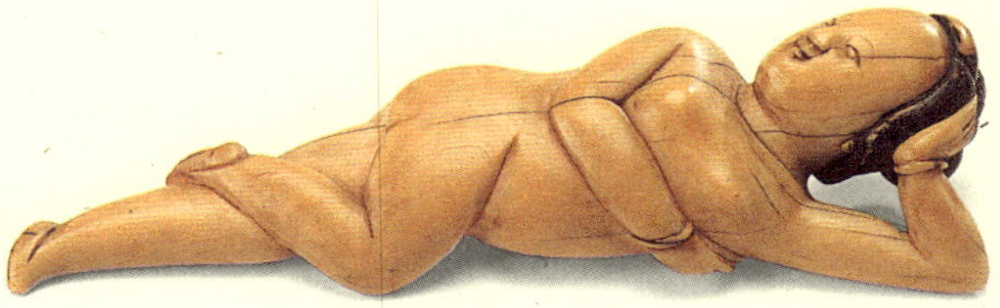

Above centre **Ceramic plate** *decorated with fish, a symbol of abundance.*
Above **Reclining female figure,** *an object of erotica, length 15 cm.*

A BURNING TOWN, or seeming so,
Three thousand furnaces that glow
Incessantly, and fill the air
With smoke uprising,
gyre on gyre,
And painted by the lurid glare,
Of jets and flashes of red fire.

Keramos
Henry Wadsworth Longfellow
1877

AT THE HEART OF AN ESSAY ON TRADITIONAL CHINESE CRAFTS MUST STAND A PASSAGE ABOUT THE MEN AND WOMEN WHO MADE THEM. Out of so many, let us meet just one. Yun Yiping is a potter at Yixing, a town whose name is synonymous with unglazed purplish brown clay teapots (four examples of which appear in this book). A native of Yixing, she was born in 1954 and started work at the kilns aged eighteen, studying potting techniques with the master craftsman He Daohong, himself a Yixing native. Later, under the tutelage of another master instructor, she began designing teapots herself, specializing in wares in streamlined forms with pine, bamboo and prunus motifs. She works surrounded by men, because the practice of craft, with the exception of paper cuts, embroidery and basketry, has been a male preserve until modern times. The scale on which things have always been made in China means that the potter with clay in his nails was less the single self-conscious artist creating alone than the production line worker. If we were to visit him at work, we might well find ourselves at a place like the one evoked by Longfellow. The "three thousand furnaces", the fire from which was said to light up the night sky, were the kilns of the famous potteries of Jingdezhen in south China, an industrial centre unparalleled in the world until the Industrial Revolution in England and the source of almost all the ceramics in the early export trade with Europe. In 1712, we are told by a French Jesuit who visited the place to steal the secret of porcelain making methods for France, no fewer than three thousand kilns were in operation, three hundred of them in the imperial factory which supplied all the Emperor's porcelain.

Production was organized on a division of labour, and a porcelain jar could pass through dozens of pairs of hands as it was being shaped, glazed, painted and fired, with even the painting divided up, one man doing the outlines and another filling in the washes. If we were to visit Jingdezhen today, we would find many of the stages of production little changed.

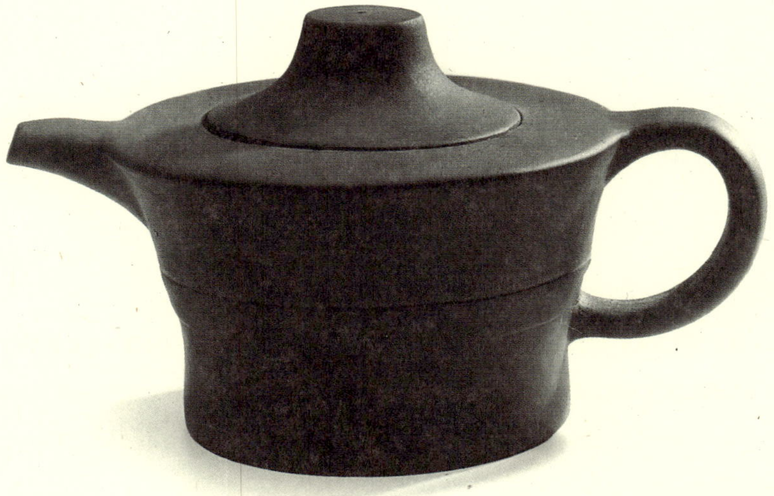

The practitioner of craft today is heir to skills and traditions evolved, broadly speaking, in three types of setting. From the earliest times there were imperial workshops throughout the empire to turn out wares for the palace, and also bureaus to inspect and oversee operations. An eye was kept open for gifted artisans, and the most accomplished were creamed off by the imperial factories. Then there were the private workshops in the cities, where the artisan worked either in the guild appropriate to his calling, or under the patronage of rich officials or merchants. A third class of artisans travelled from place to place, father, son and grandson together, wherever their skills were needed, sculpting bas reliefs in tombs or carving Buddhist statues in grottoes as they went. Goldsmiths and cabinet-makers might come with their tools and materials to the home of their rich

Clay teapot *from the kilns of Yixing, Jiangsu province.*

工多藝熟

customer and make jewellery or furniture, as the case may be, on the premises, under the supervision of the major-domo. I remember that every autumn a veritable workshop of tailors, seamstresses and furriers would move into my maternal grandfather's house in Shanghai to produce a winter wardrobe for all the family, to line their silk gowns with sable, and to unpick the coverlets and eiderdowns to fluff out the silk padding and to sew new bedding.

One practice united them all: the secrets of their craft were passed on from father to son, or from master to apprentice. If you looked up the Ha family in a Chinese craft handbook, for instance, you would find the names of four generations of paper kite makers: grandfather Ha Deshan, father Ha Changying,

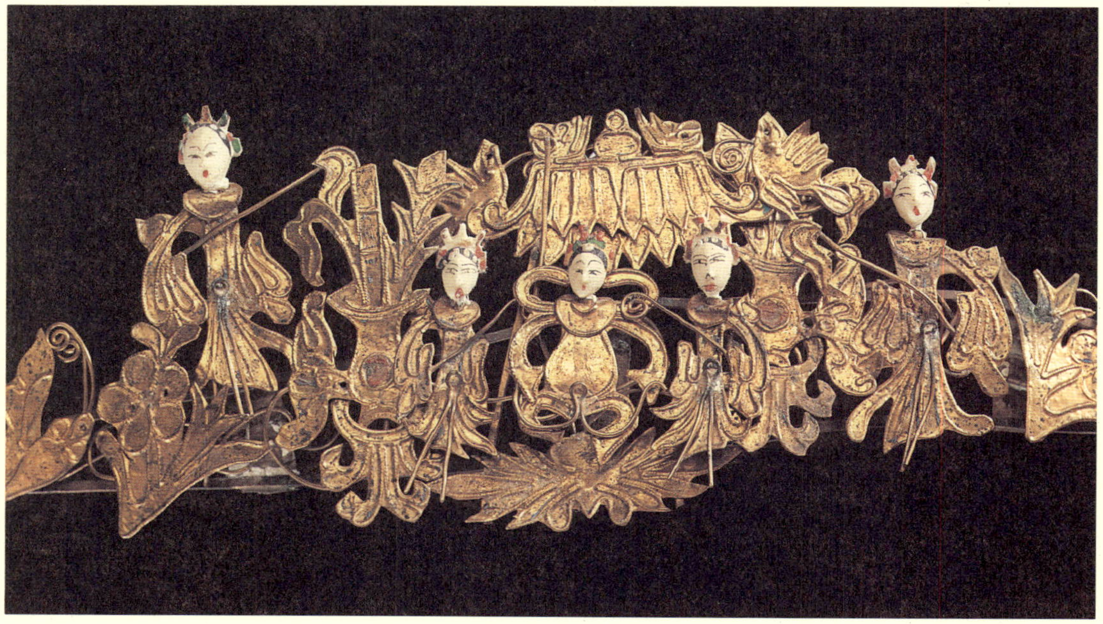

son Ha Kuiming (who happens to be the most famous kite maker in Beijing today) and grandson Ha Yiqi. Master-apprentice traditions have always been strong at a place like Yixing, and many generations have been guided into their vocation the way Yun Yiping has.

Few illustrated better than the Chinese craftsman the saying **"PRACTICE MAKES PERFECT"**. The workshops were forcing houses of talent, and having to meet the high standards of sophisticated patrons in palaces, in the rich and fashionable families which emulated courtly taste, and in the export trade whereby lacquerware, furnishings, carvings, watercolours and paintings, as well as a myriad of curiosities, were shipped from Canton to satisfy the European taste for exotica,

Tiara, *gilded, with heads of painted bone,*
from the mountains of Yunnan province, south-west China.
Such hair ornaments were worn by womenfolk at a wedding, the
birth of the first son, or at a clan elder's eightieth birthday.

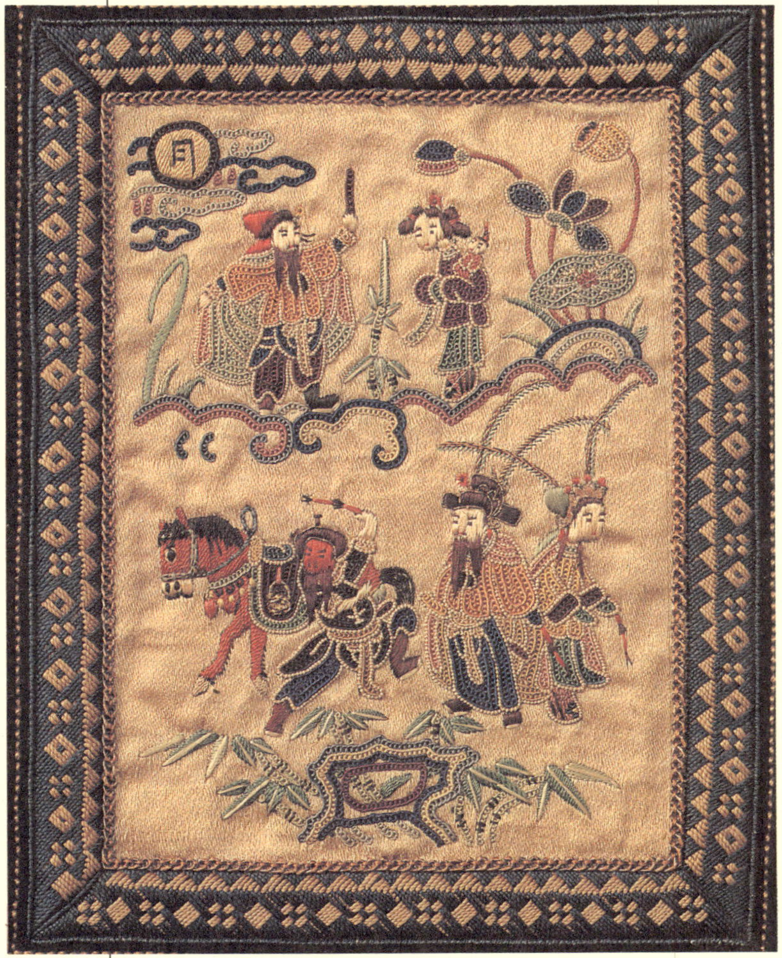

no doubt helped to hone skills and enhance workmanship. Indeed it is hard to see how, without such patronage, China could have become a place unrivalled for the excellence of its craftsmen. One has only to think of the hundreds of painstaking man-hours needed to carve a jade dragon writhing in pursuit of its fiery pearl – man-hours which could only have been paid for by commissions – to know that this is true.

On the whole their skills were not highly regarded, and craftsmen were seldom put on pedestals; but once a craftsman got taken up by the upper classes, his work would acquire a certain cachet. Signed works came to be treasured, and people like Zhu Bishan, the 14th-century silversmith, and Shi Dabin, one of the best known of the 16th-century potters at Yixing, became the Aspreys, the Wedgwoods, the Laliques and Fabergés of their day. Some crafts were deemed a cut above others: seal cutting and bamboo carving (of which more later), for example, basked in the reflected glow of calligraphy and had their gentlemen practitioners. Others, namely weaving, embroidery and paper cutting, have traditionally absorbed country women during the slack winter season.

It is not ruler or measuring tape, but eye and hand and even ear, the feel of the tool in the palm and fingers, that tell the carver of lacquer or bamboo whether a line is straight, how hard or gentle a pressure to apply, where the incision is to be made. Here is what a bamboo carver in Shanghai, in an essay that is one of my perennial delights, says of his tool: "As for the knife, there is no fixed type or form; whatever suits your hand is best; and it is no bad thing to make and sharpen it yourself, according to the needs that become apparent to you in the wielding thereof". And further on in the essay, he devotes a whole paragraph to just the coir

Silk embroidered pillow end *included in a girl's dowry, height 20 cm.*

匠心獨運

brush used for dusting off the shavings in the cuts.

Similarly, in fashioning his hoe, the traditional Chinese ironmonger considered not just the purpose of the implement but the texture of the local soil, how hard, how coarse or fine, how it would respond to the tool as its blade struck earth. One has only to watch a master craftsman work to realize that skill and tool are inseparable. It is for this reason, and because the tools are things of beauty in themselves, that we have thought fit to include them in this book.

It is an eclectic selection that the reader finds here, one which takes in things falling outside the conventional Chinese compilation – chopsticks, mahjong tiles, abacus and broom, for example. Though crafts are not usually called crafts unless they are handmade, or at least made with few tools, we have also thought to include machine-manufactured things, such as the red packets for the Lunar New Year gifts of money, that may seem to some readers to belong more properly to a book on modern design. They will not appear to be out of place though, if they are seen to illustrate the continuity of traditional forms and designs, of styles and decorative symbols that have been handed down from the past.

In any case, it is hard to say where handicrafts end and industry begins, where the manufacturing techniques of the factory system take over from the village workshop. Remember Jingdezhen, with its suggestions of "dark satanic mills". And yet, even if the work were shared out, it still demanded sureness of touch and dexterity. More than dexterity, it required ingenuity. In Chinese, "ingenuity" is a synonym for "craftsmanship"; it is written with two characters, *jiangxin* , which mean, if one were to translate them literally, "craftsman mind".

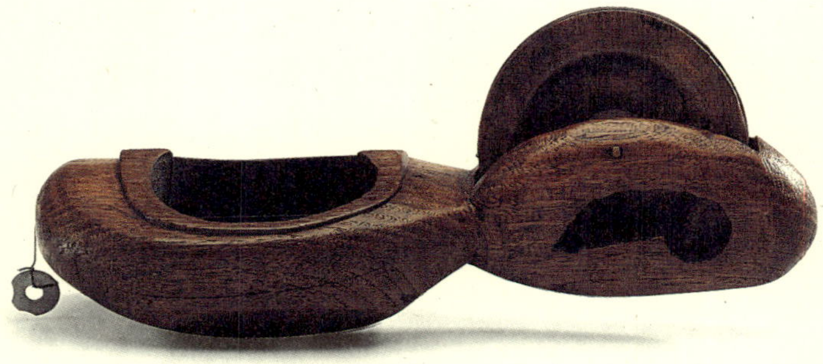

Carpenter's line marker with inkwell, *handle and string, length 22 cm.*

FLUSTERING WIND
Shakes the broad bamboo leaves;
Amid the rustling sound
Float down new bamboo skins.

Bundles of hay for a bed,
Dry rushes for roof,
Pottery for frying pan,
And gourd for a ladle.

Four-season Song on the Hardships and Joys of Farming Life
Zheng Xie,
17th-18th century

AND FINALLY, THERE IS THE MEDIUM. A true craftsman is he who masters his material. All is grist to the Chinese craftsman's mill, and there can be few people so ready to coax art out of any available material. It is true that he is often tempted, as the Chinese would put it, "to draw a snake and add feet to it", failing to leave well alone and ruining an effect by adding something superfluous, but it is also true that he is matchless in his ability to bring out the unique qualities, the intrinsic beauty of a natural material. Can there be anyone "truer to form", more respectful of his medium, than the creator of the pair of bamboo sections shown on an earlier page of this book? He has allowed nothing to detract from contemplation of their form. Consider also the wooden brush pots: their makers did not so much carve them; they honoured the wood's natural kinks and contours, let the material speak for itself, and in a manner of speaking "followed the way". One thinks also of those grotesqueries that Chinese carvers love to fashion from gnarled and knobbly tree roots.

But natural materials are not cherished for their loveliness alone; they are emblems, as bamboo supremely illustrates. Sturdy yet elegant, remaining green even in winter, this most "calligraphic" of plants (its leaves so reminiscent of the brush strokes used in writing characters) came to symbolize the gentleman scholar himself. In a more popular vein, the bottle gourd (which appears in this book in the guise of cages for crickets, a Chinese insect pet) has a symbolic tinge to it too. Indeed, it is almost a cult in China, connoting abundance and fertility, and

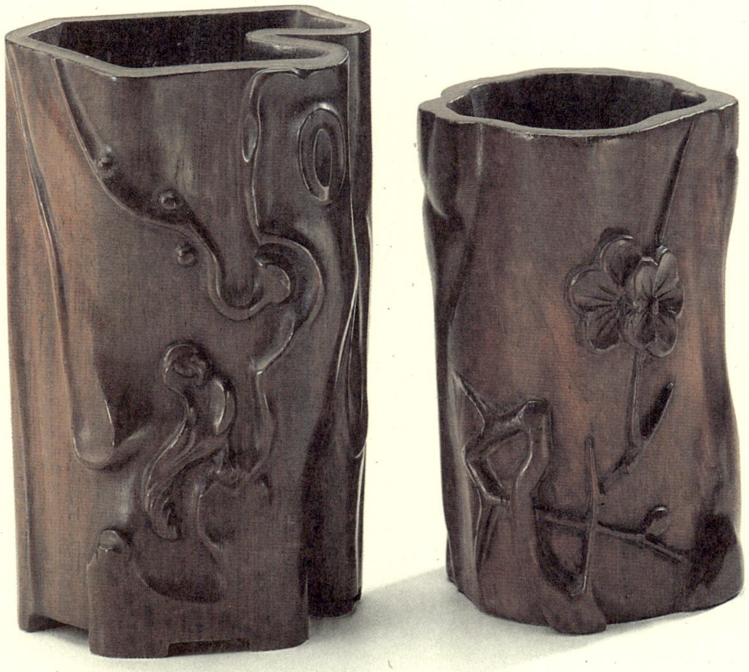

appearing as a receptacle for the elixir of life that hangs from the staff of the Star of Great Age, the popular deity always pictured as a dear old man with a long white beard and a big bald forehead out of all proportion to the face.

Two of the most distinctly Chinese materials, jade and cloisonné, make no appearance in this book, where the reader finds form given on the whole to humbler stuff. The abundance of bamboo, willow, rattan, wheat straw, rush and reed in the Chinese countryside means that the materials for cane products and wickerwork come readily to hand, and in countless villages nimble fingers plait and weave them into baskets, mats, hats, bags, trays, brooms and ornaments. Paper is

Brushpots *carved from blackwood.*

another plentiful material, cheap enough to be within the reach of most people, and paper crafts are highly developed in China. The pages of wood block prints and wooden relief plates in this book are a reminder that printing techniques were a Chinese invention. Originating in Buddhist and Daoist monasteries, the techniques were used for making holy images and religious tracts for distribution, and later extended by the laity for producing astrological works, almanacs and books.

Availability of material is part of the story of regional specialities: Fuzhou would hardly be "Lacquer City" if the lac tree did not grow there; and it was not just any wood but the local boxwood and longan that its carvers have fashioned into figures of Buddha and immortals, screens, architectural trims and panels with layers of birds and flowers.

The raw material will always be there, but will the art? I began as a celebrant and will try not to end as a mourner. But when plastic puts paid to the pains one must take with lacquer, and movies replace shadow puppets, something is lost even as something is gained. Preservation sponsored by government, through vehicles like the Shanghai Arts and Crafts Research Institute, the Suzhou Embroidery Research Institute, the Jingdezhen Ceramics Teaching Institute and so on, can ensure the survival of skills and products that grew from a way of life now passing out of existence; but it does so only up to a point. The Arts and Crafts Movement spawned a progeny of studio potters and engravers, the "arty crafty" with their aura of the homespun and rustic. Japanese art students still make *mingei* in studios. Figures of Chinese immortals resembling ancient votive statues are sculpted for sale as ornaments.

But they are no longer quite the same thing.

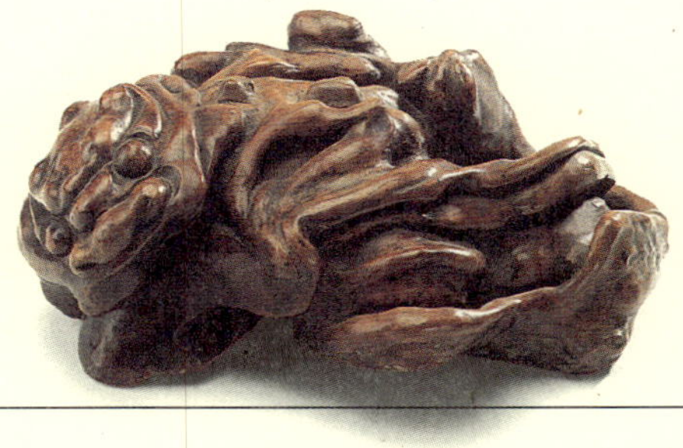

Boxwood carving *that exploits the natural knurls of tree roots, width 30 cm.*

四

DAILY ROUND

DAILY ROUND

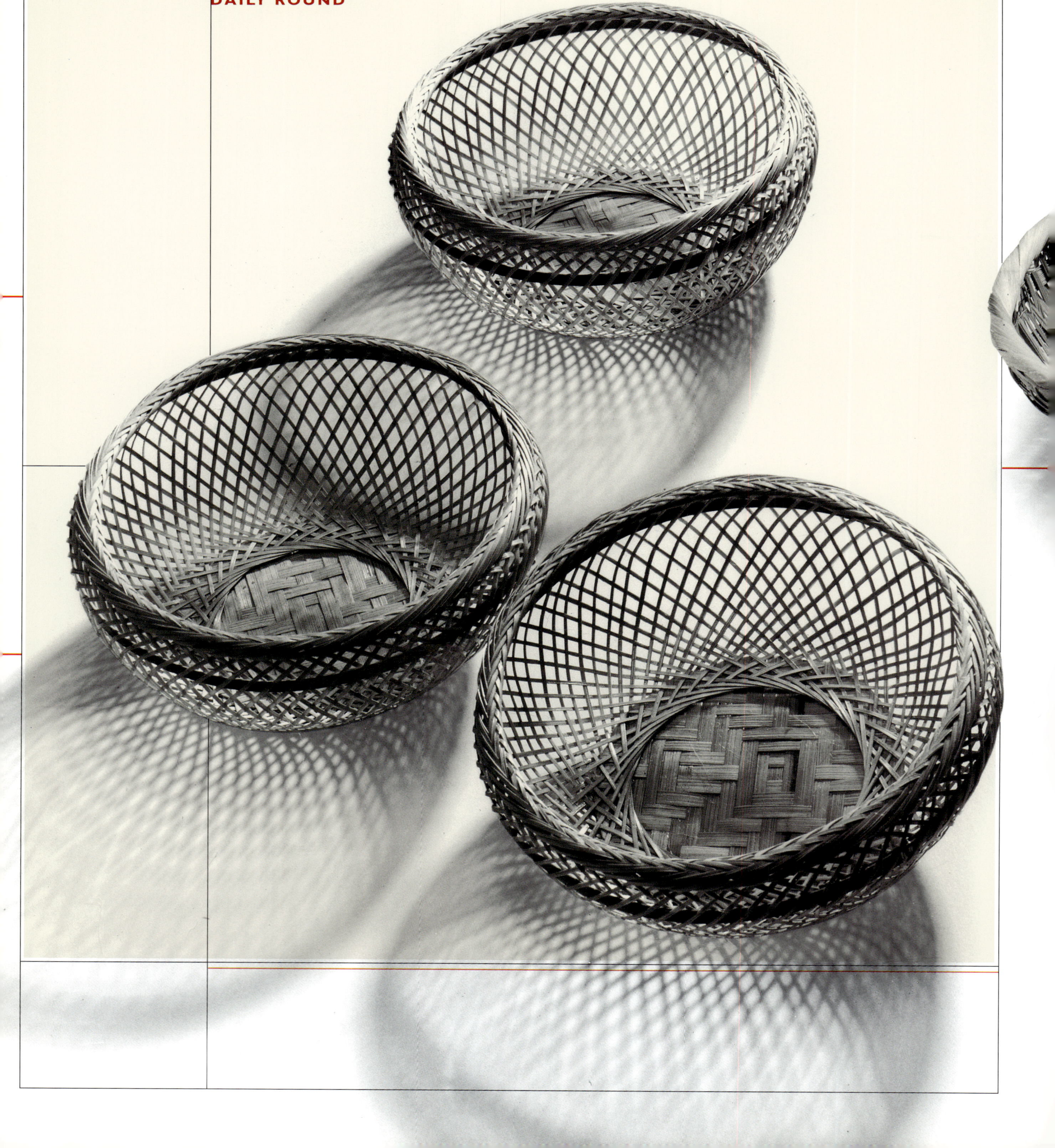

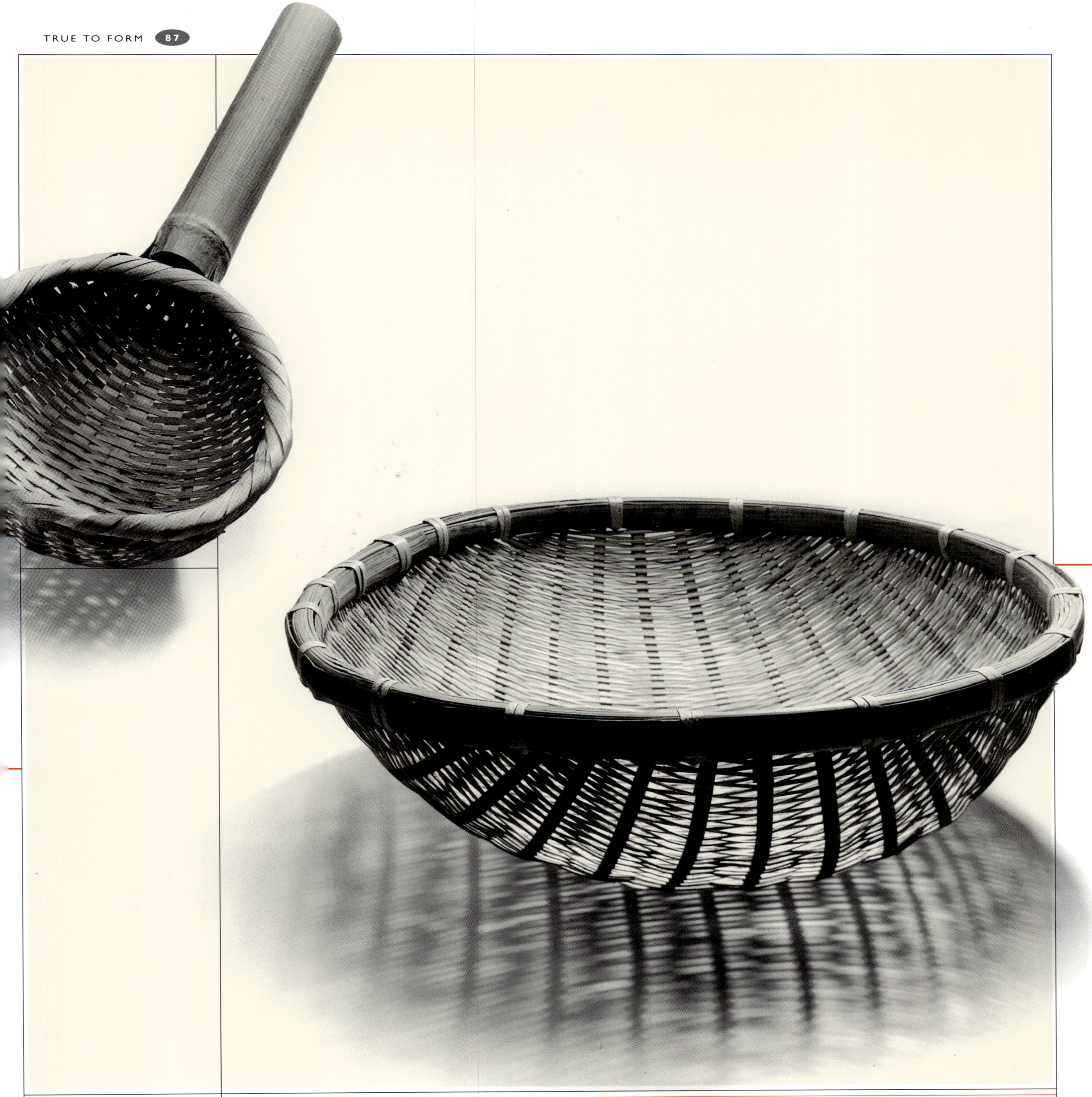

Bamboo kitchenware: dipper and colanders.

DAILY ROUND

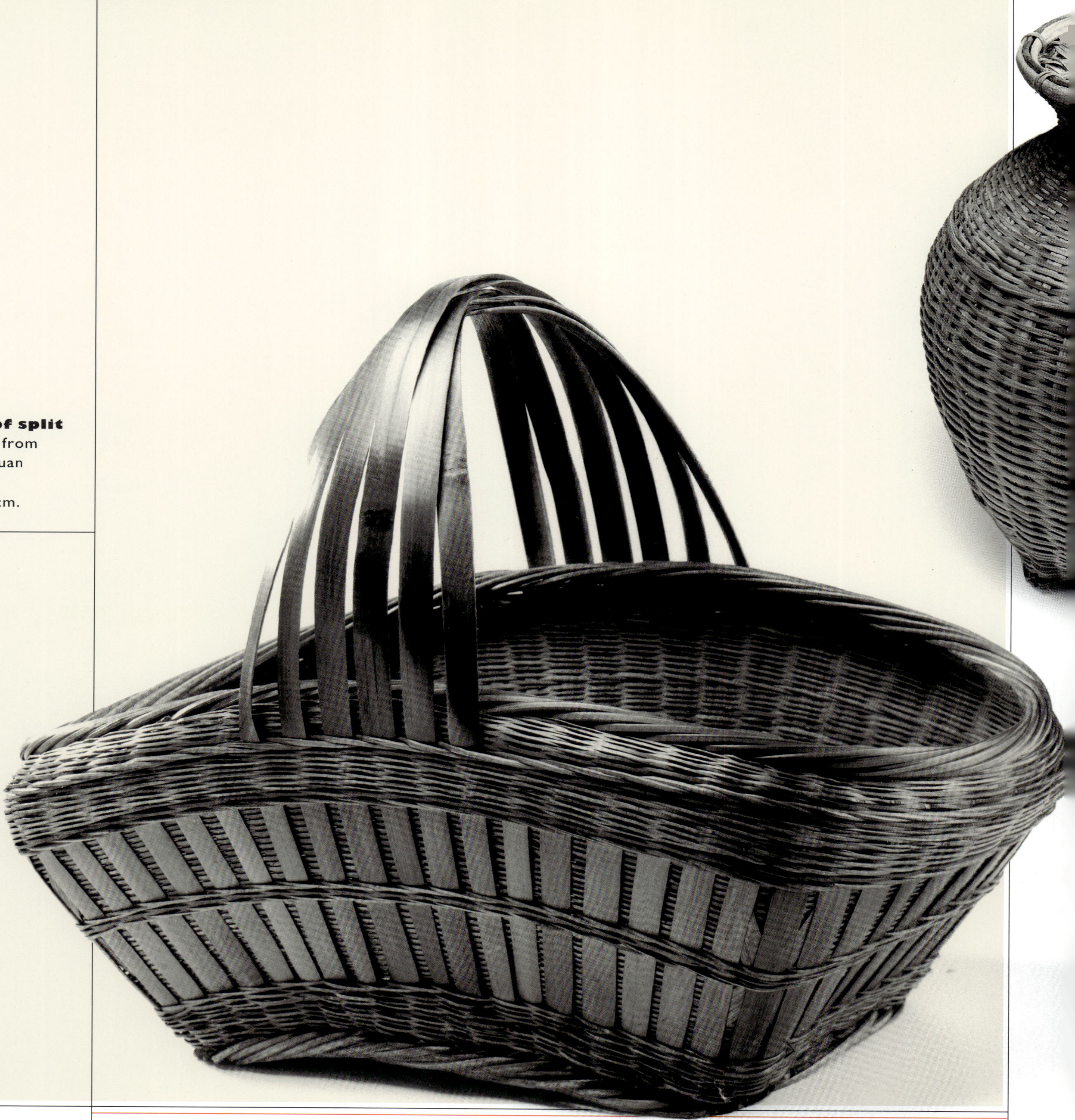

Basket of split bamboo from Dazu, Sichuan province, height 42 cm.

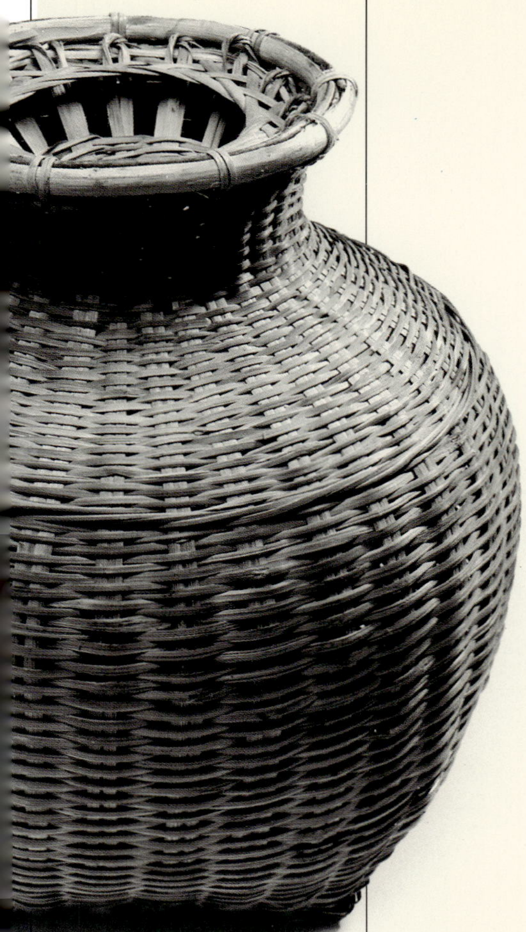

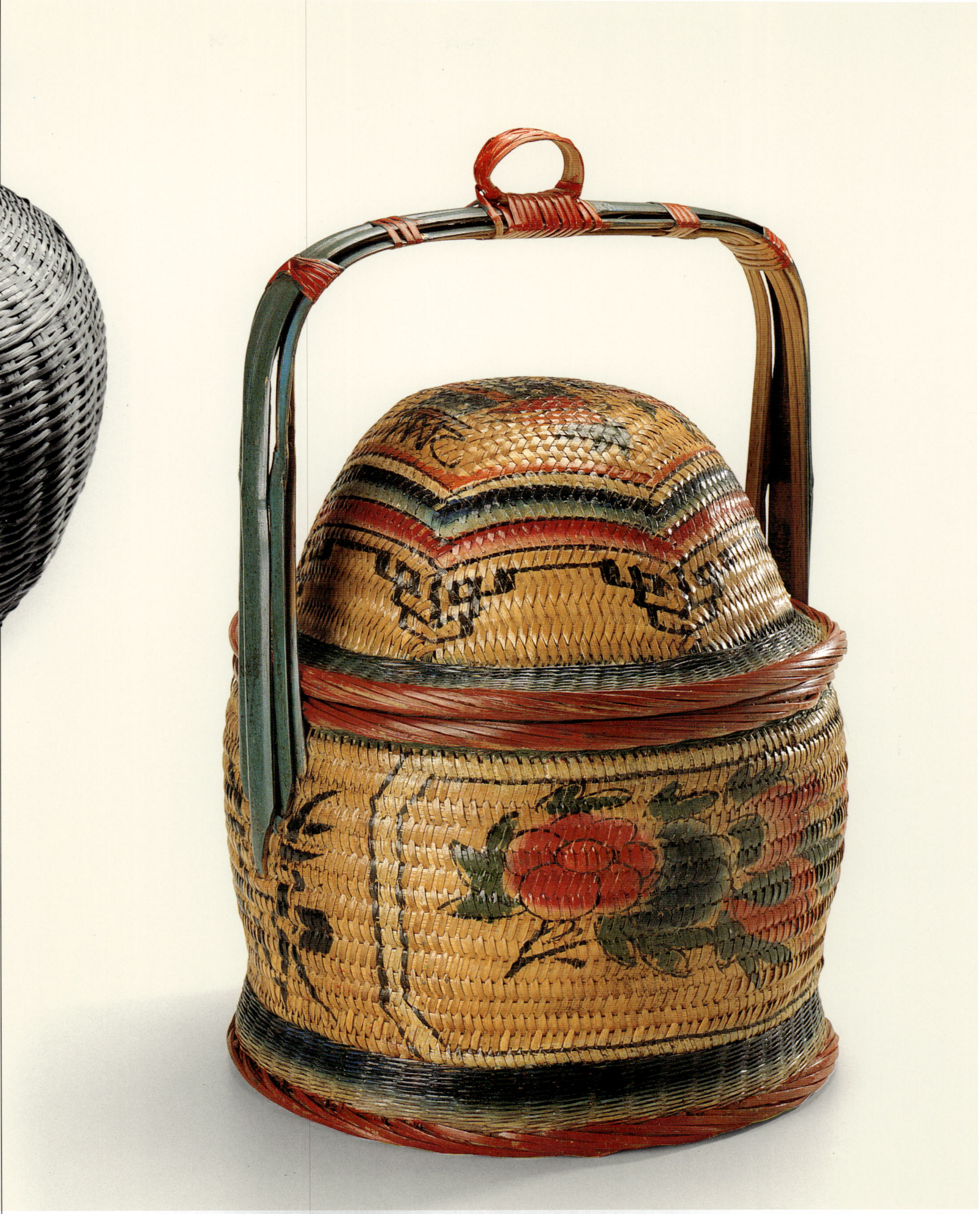

Left **Rattan fish trap** from Canton, height 40 cm. *Above* **Painted basket** from Swatow with loop to hang it from a shoulder pole, for carrying sweetmeats and cakes made of Chinese chives and radish to friends and relatives on feast days.

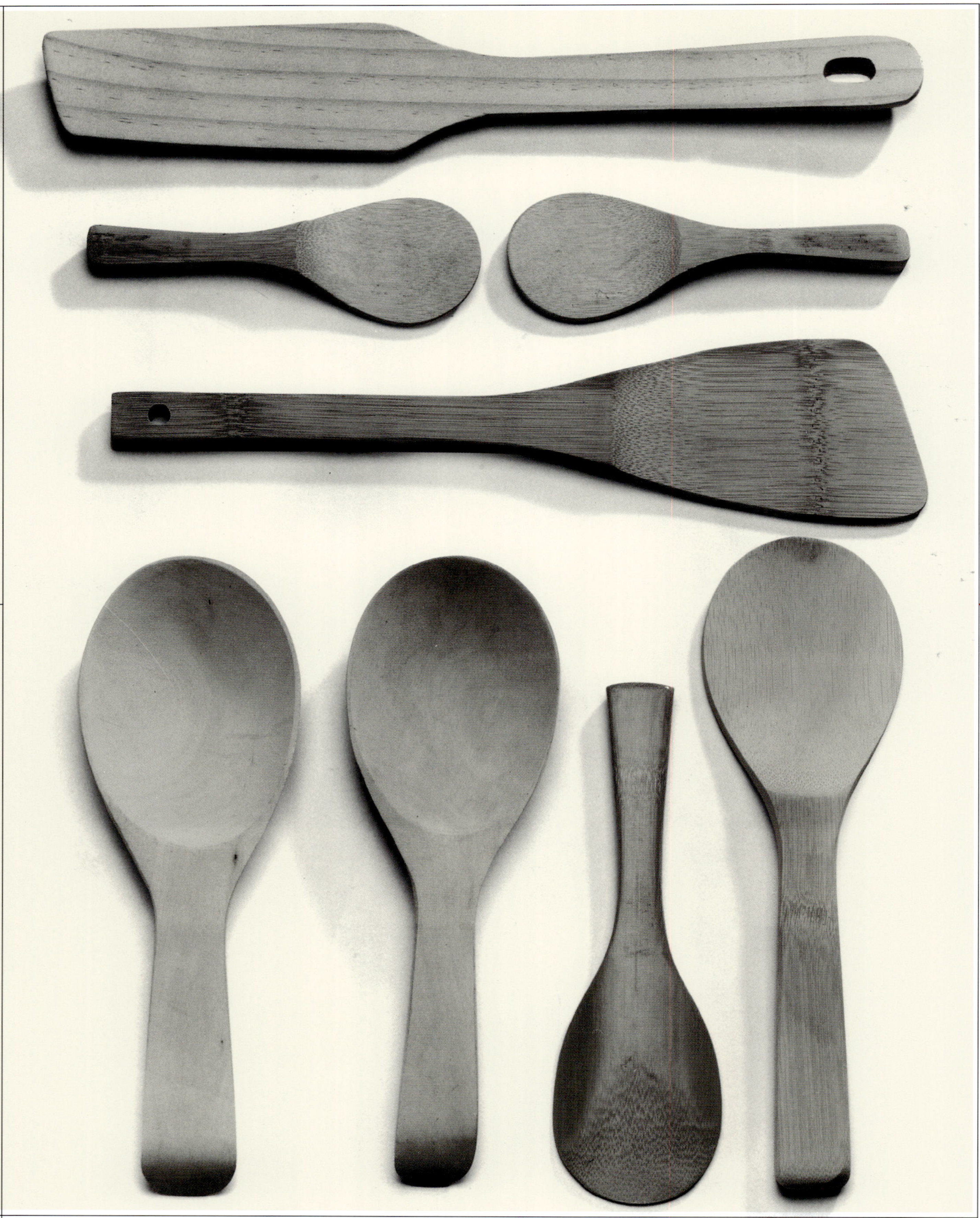

Wooden ladles, rice scoops and slices for stir-frying.

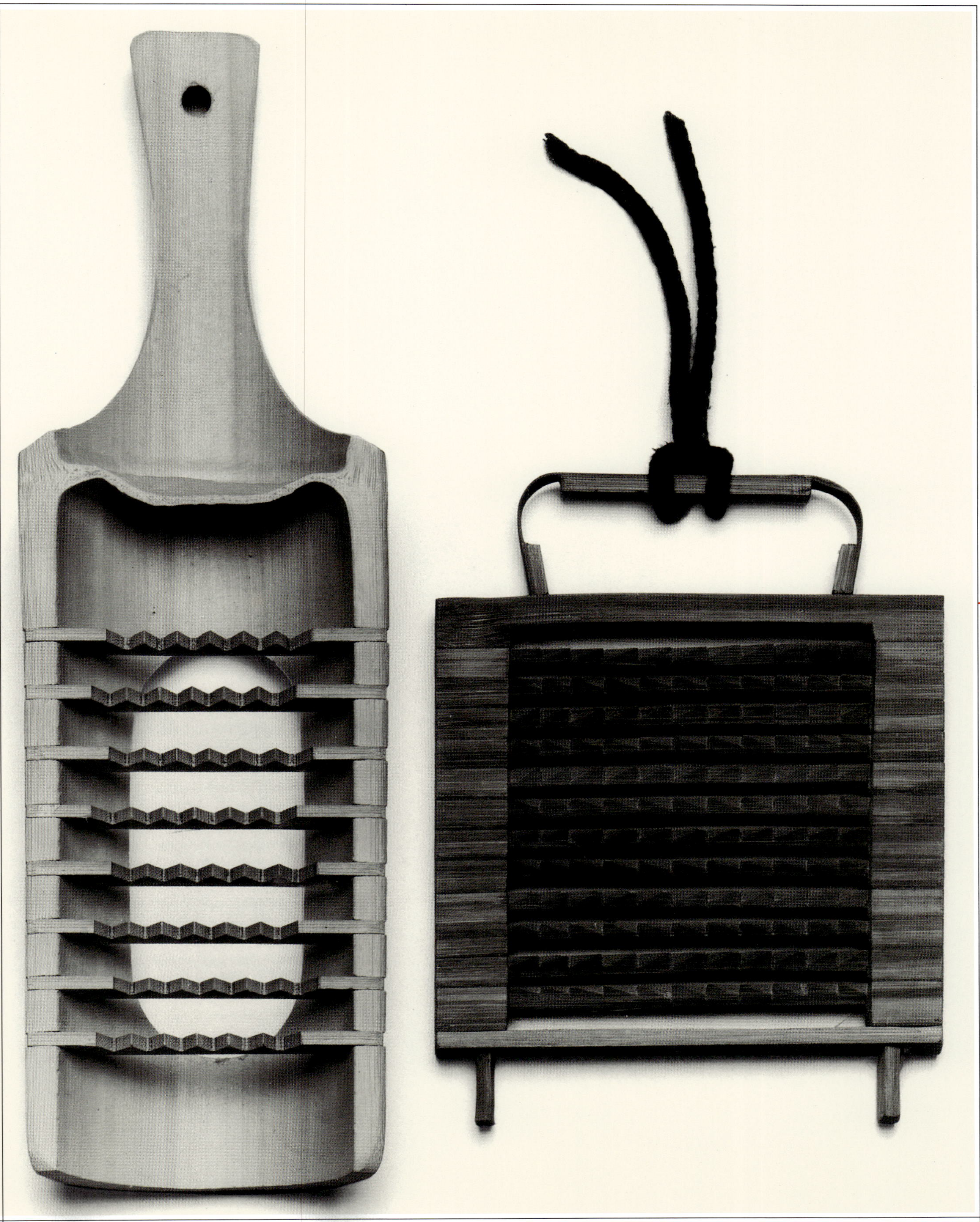

Ginger graters
in bamboo.

DAILY ROUND

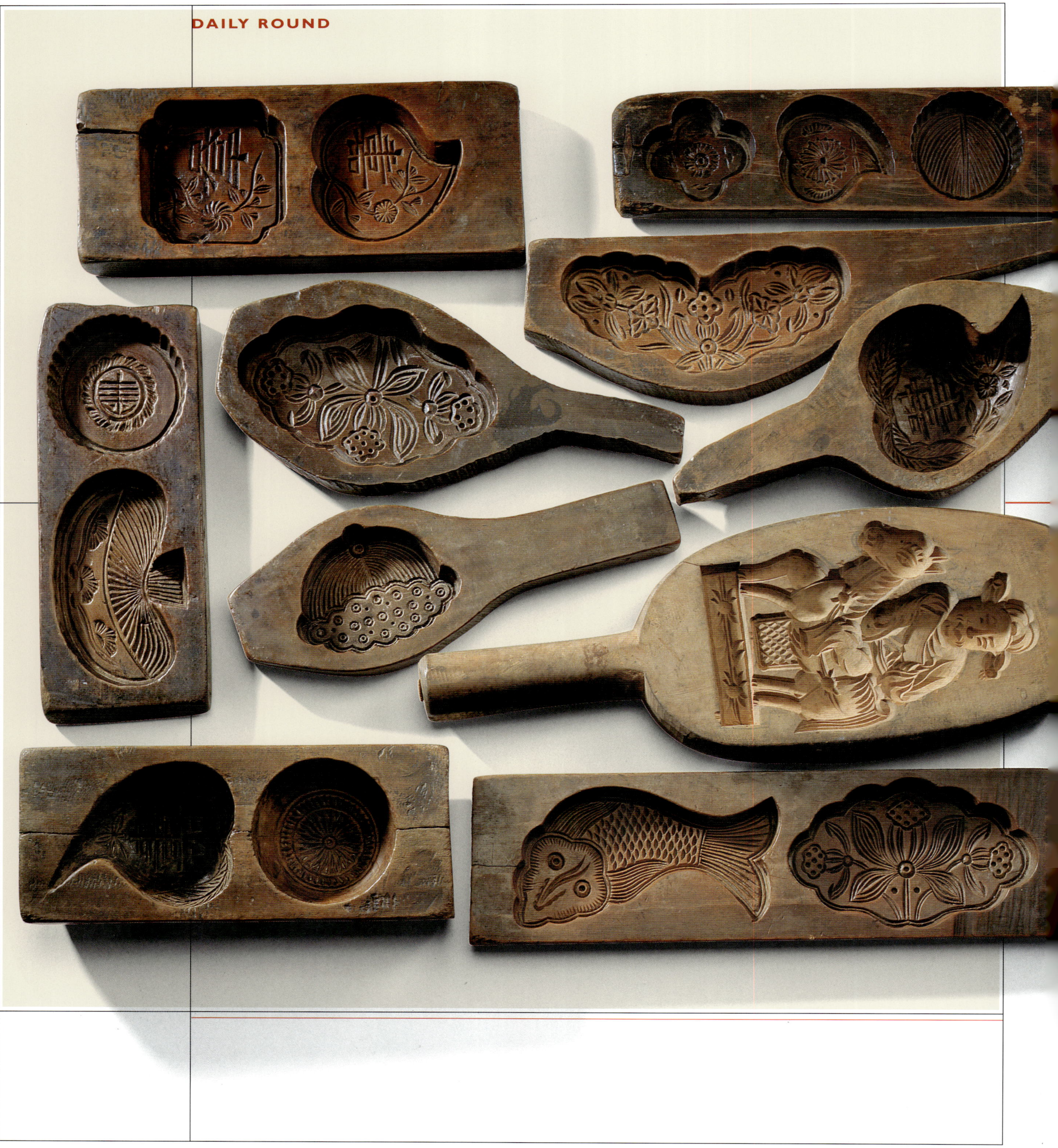

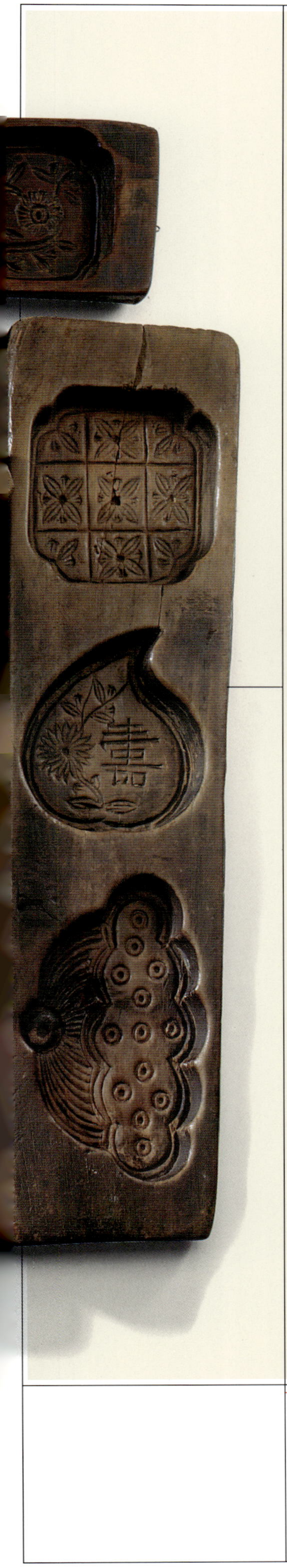

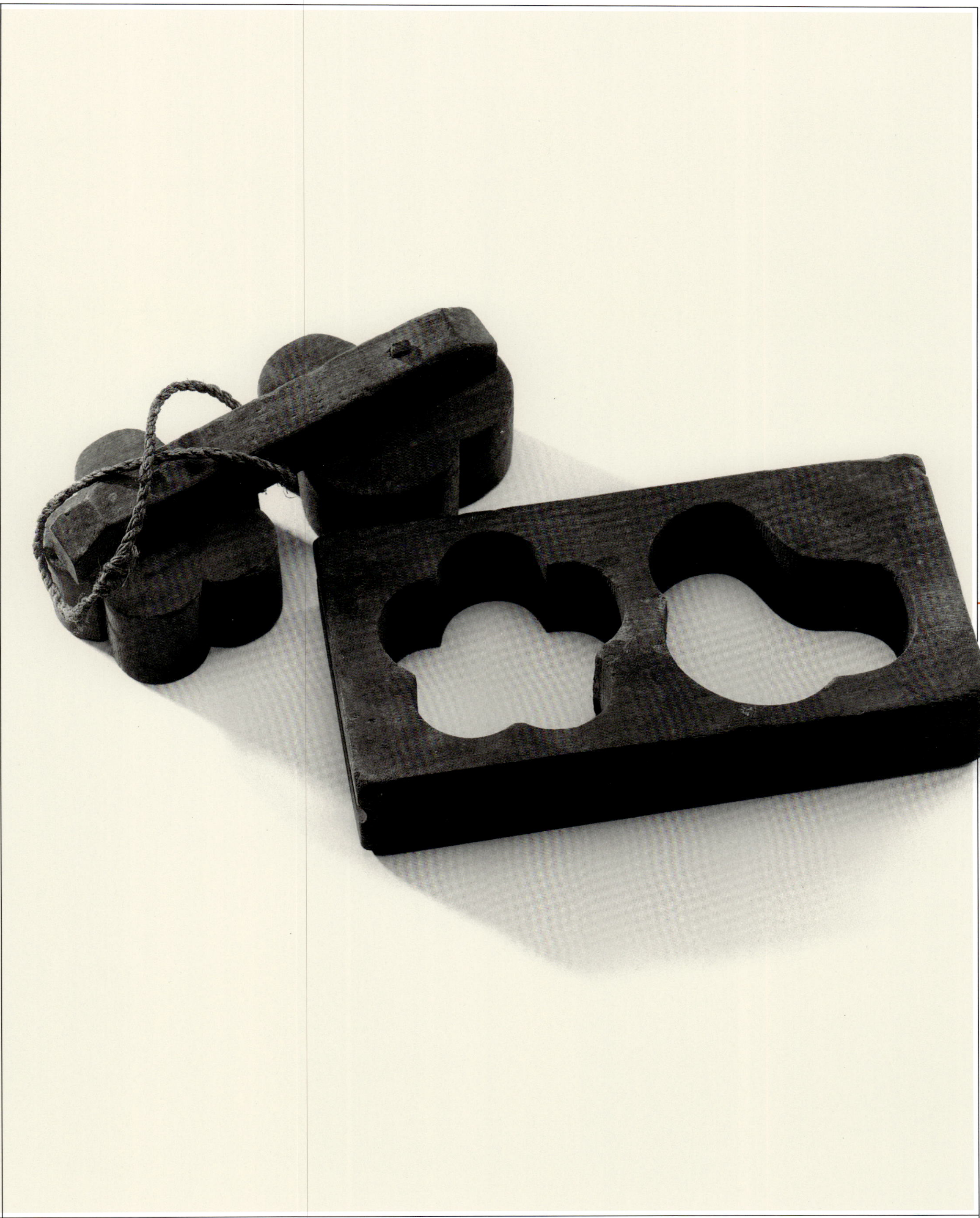

Left **Wooden moulds** for making cakes in the shape of auspicious symbols such as fish, symbolizing abundance, and pomegranate, auguring many sons. The character in the peach-shaped moulds is "longevity". *Right* Biscuits imprinted with a motif on one side are made by filling the scalloped holes with dough and then pushing it through with the other board.

DAILY ROUND

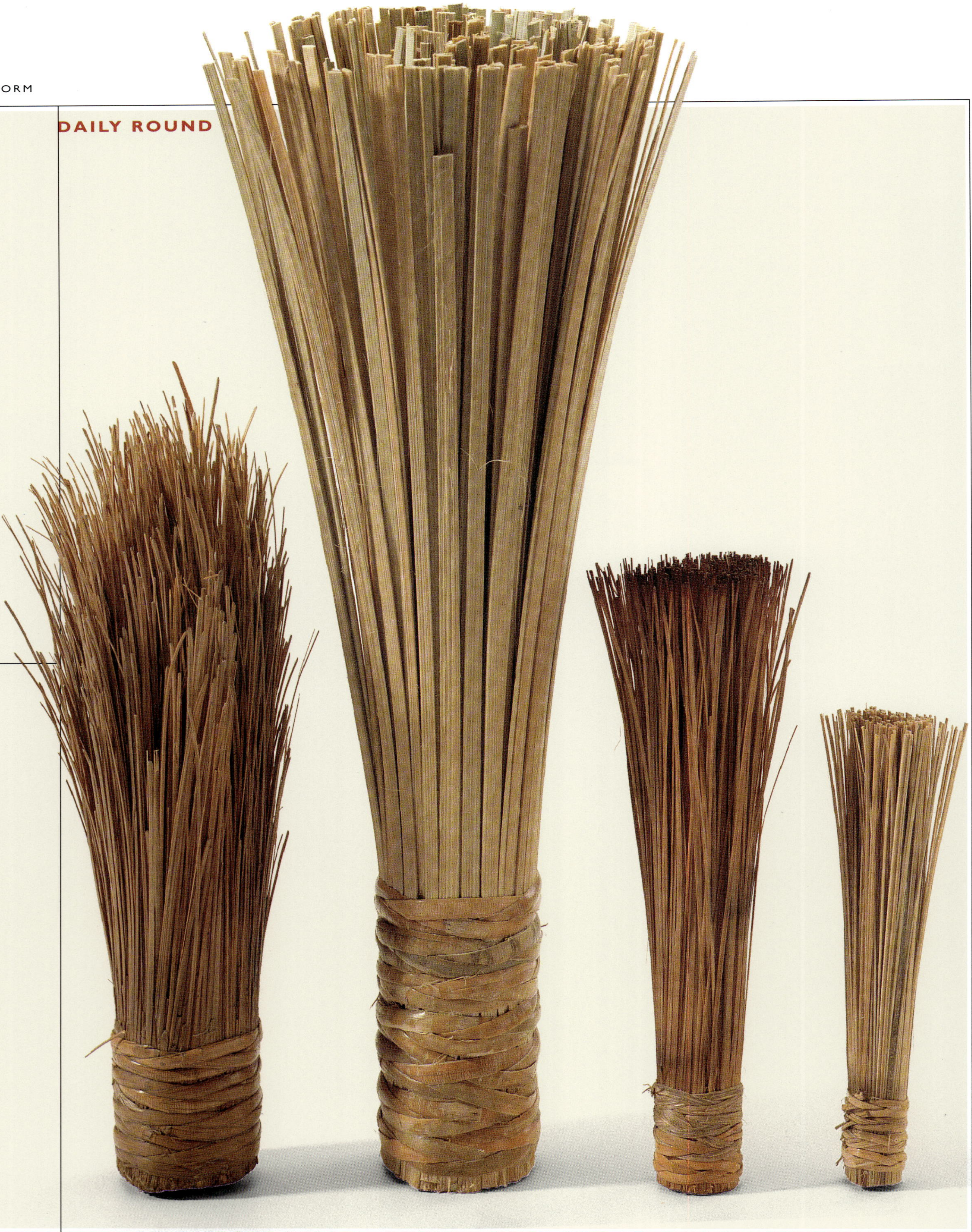

Wok cleaners with bristles made of bamboo splints bundled together. In a more primitive version found in southern China, the brush would have been made by fraying the end of a single piece of round bamboo, cutting it longitudinally into many parallel slits to form the bristles.

Straw and rattan broom

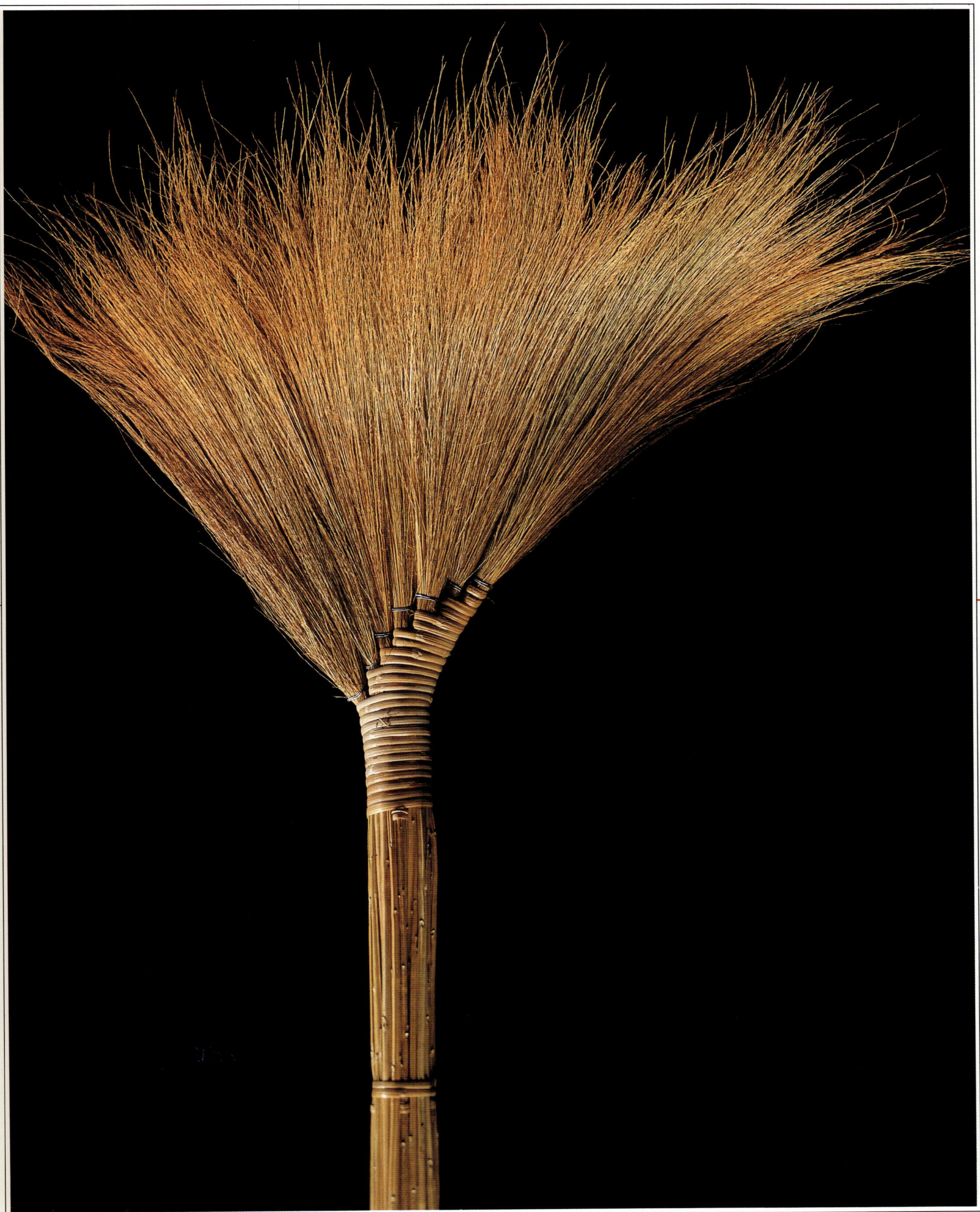

DAILY ROUND

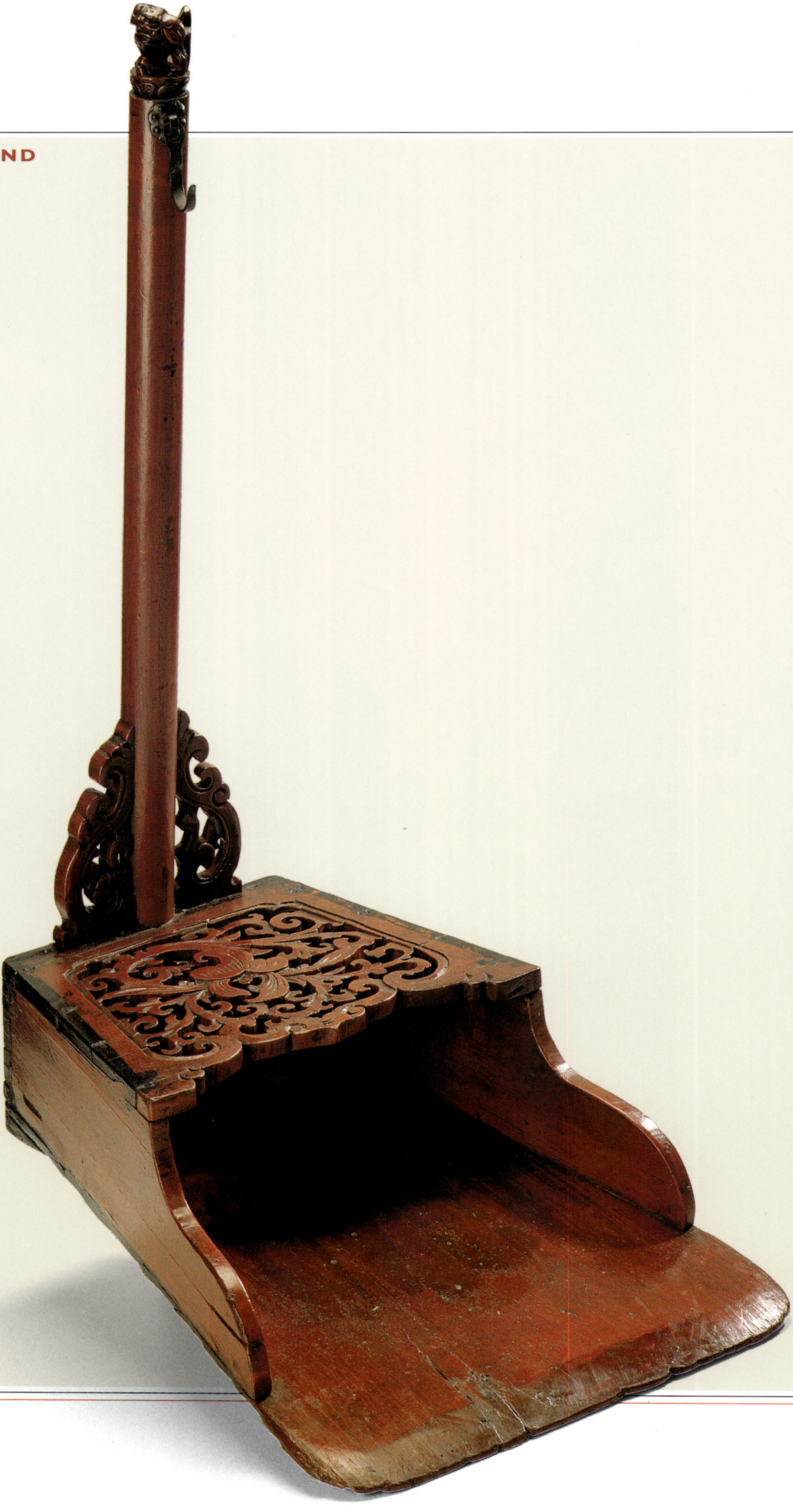

Dustpan in red lacquered wood with the handle surmounted by a carving of a *fo* dog, the conventional Chinese lion mounted in stone at the gates of Buddhist (*fo* in Chinese) temples.

Bamboo rake

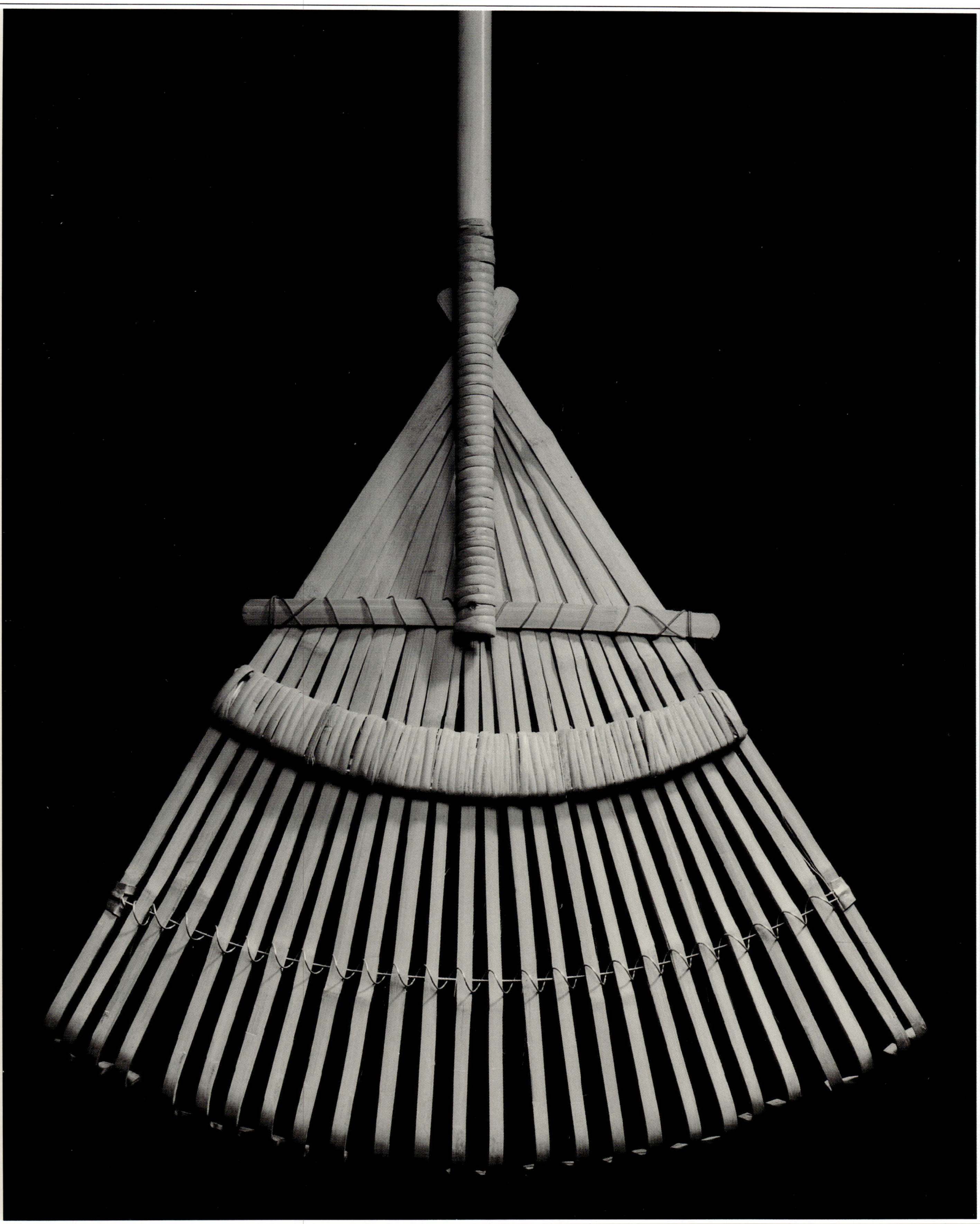

DAILY ROUND

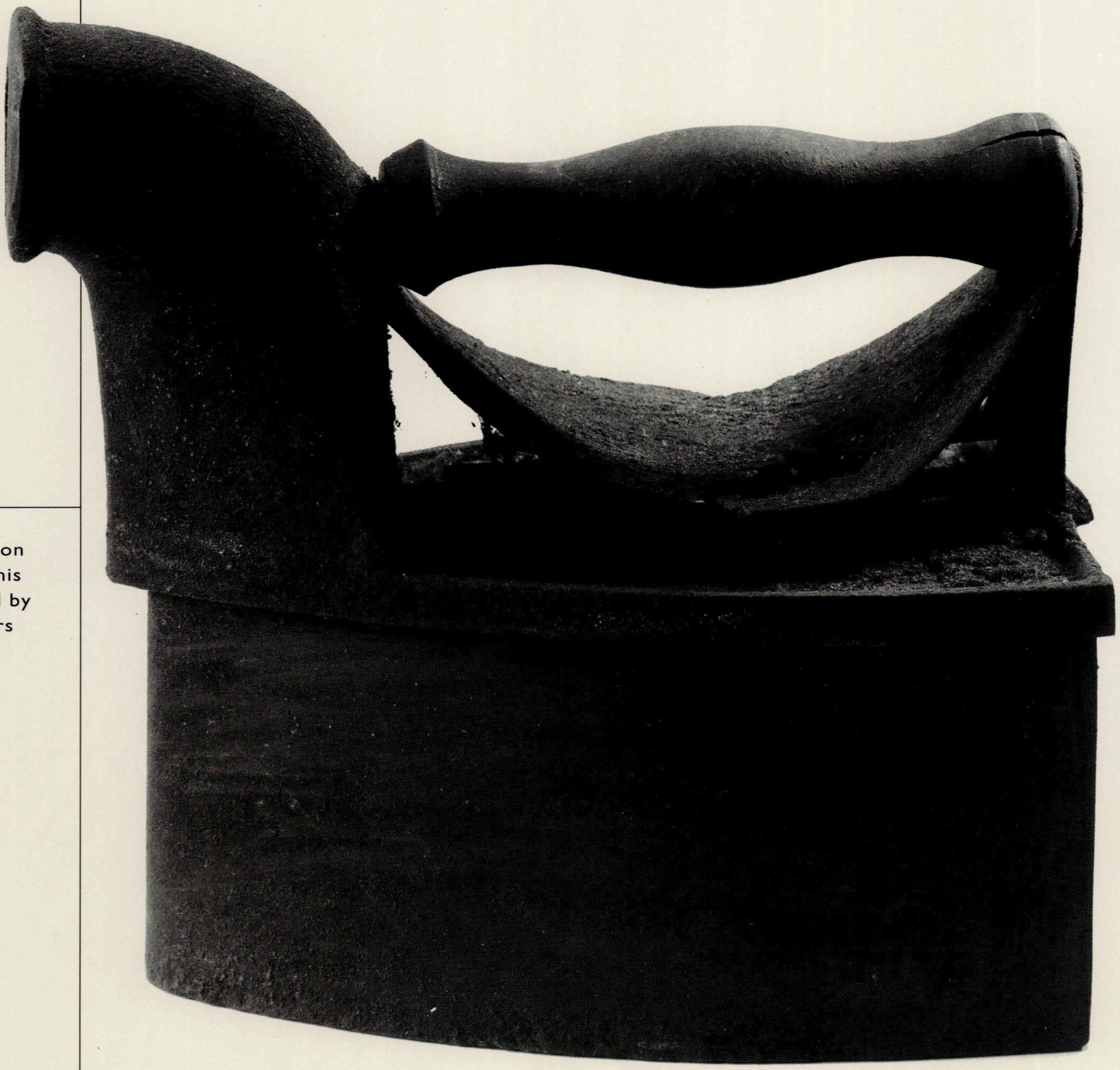

Made of cast iron in the 1880s, this **iron** is heated by charcoal embers placed inside.

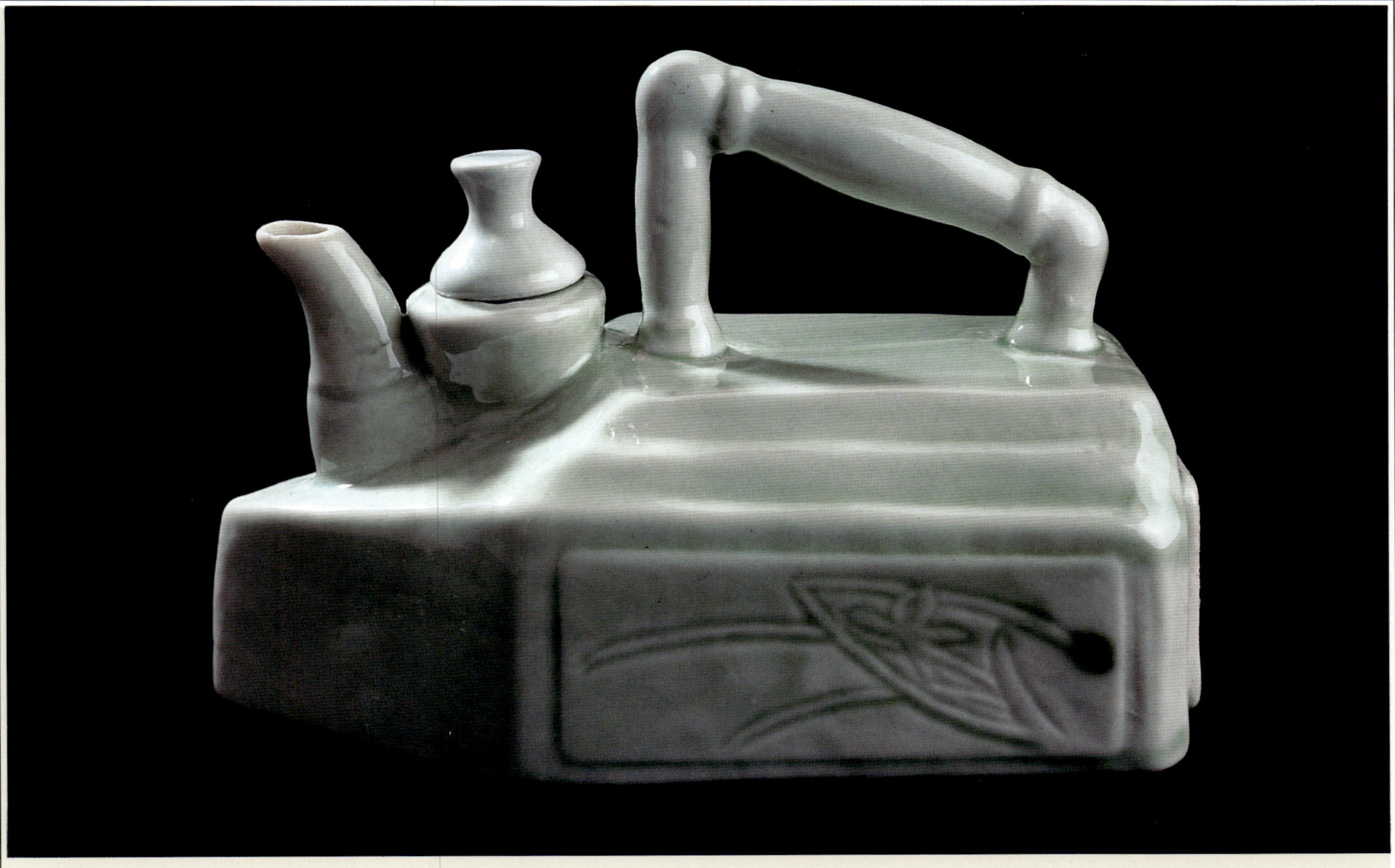

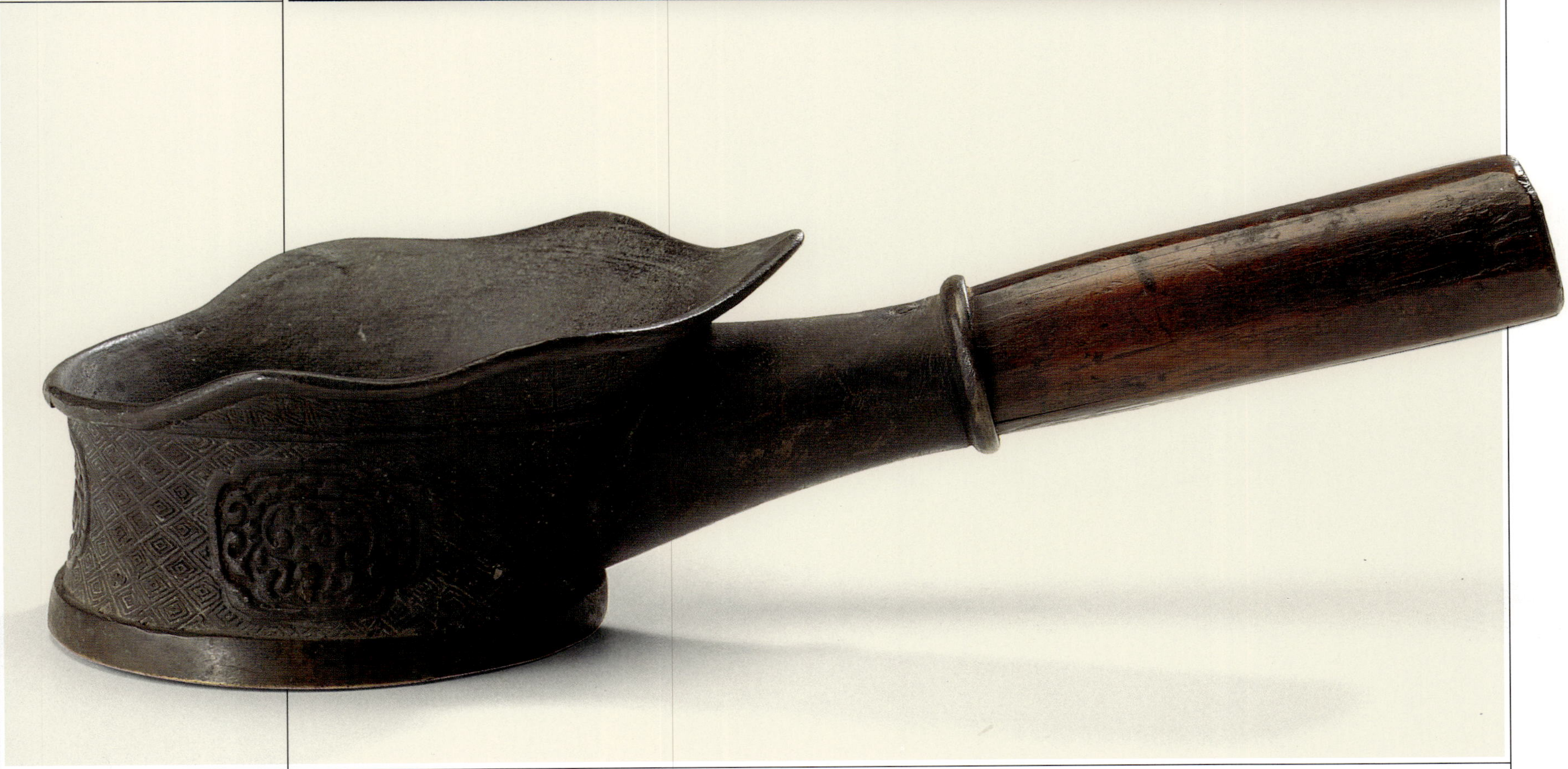

Top **Ceramic iron** with green glaze, used for silk, dating from the turn of the century, with lidded funnel for hot water. *Bottom* **Flat-iron** used by the professional tailor to flatten seams and smooth creased fabrics. The receptacle to receive the charcoal with a socket for the wooden handle is cast out of one piece of bronze, length, 26 cm.

DAILY ROUND

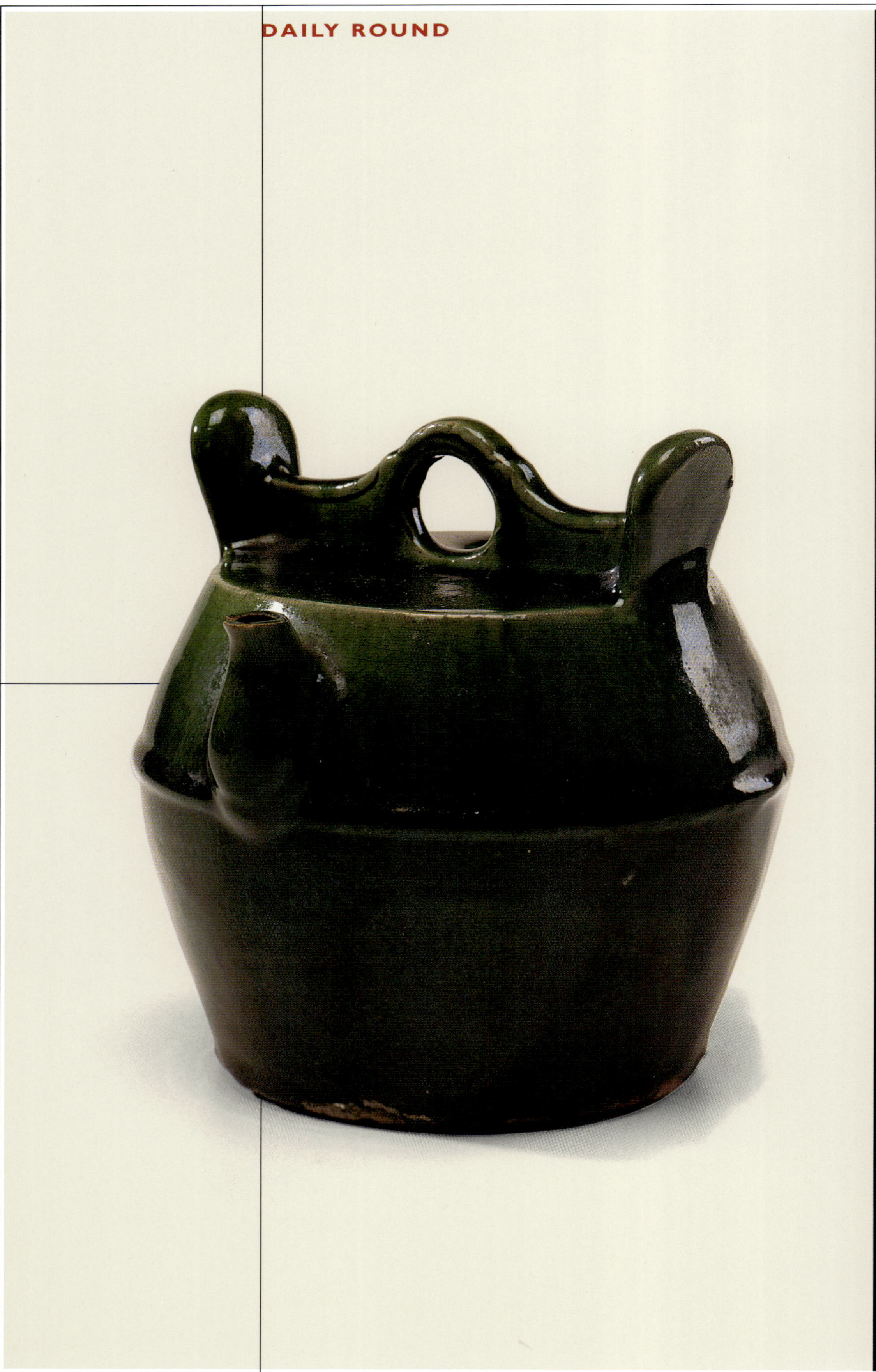

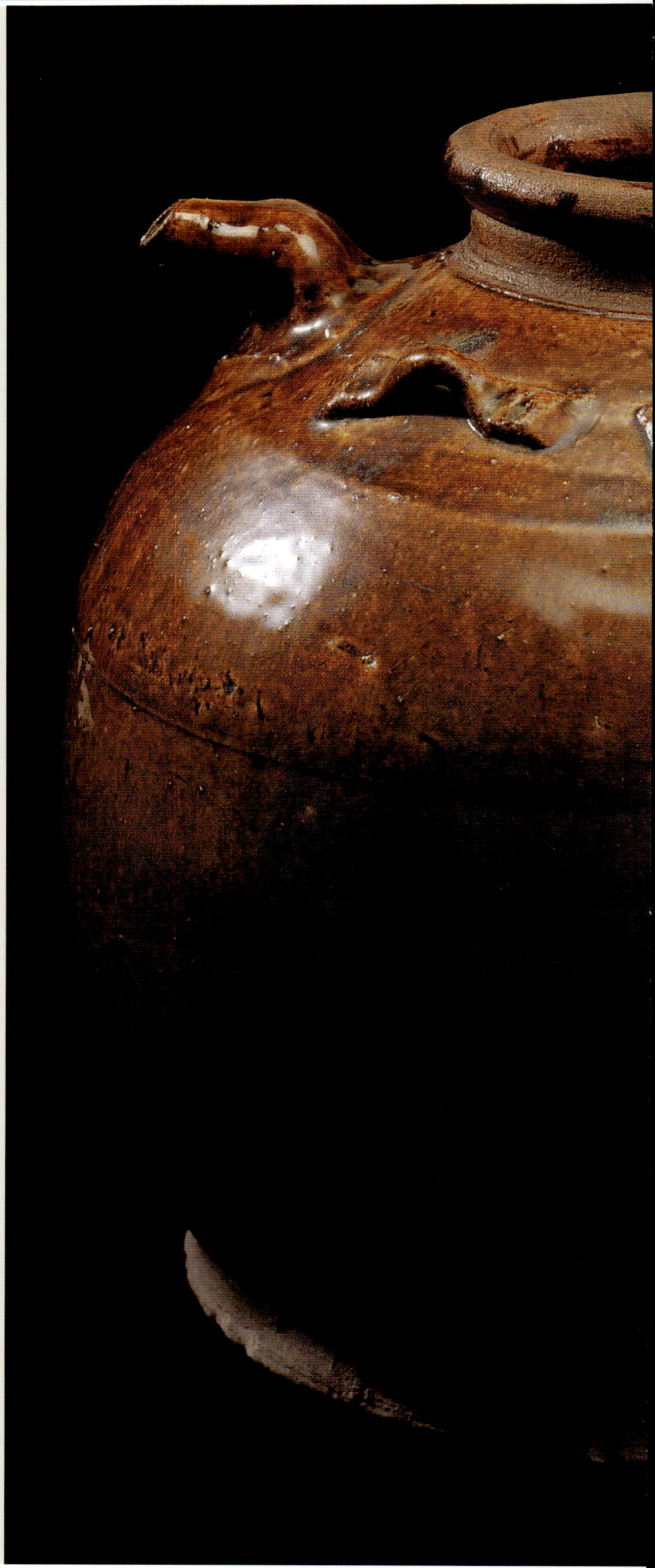

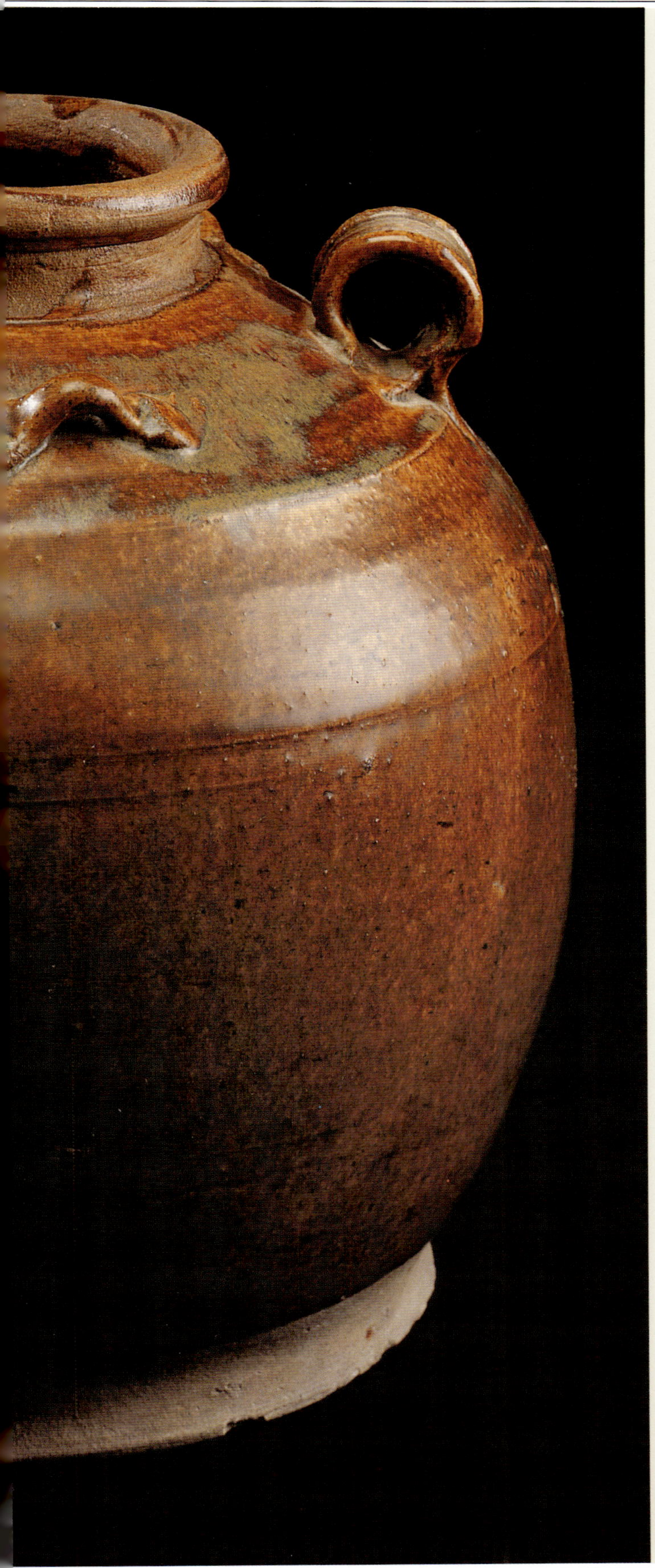

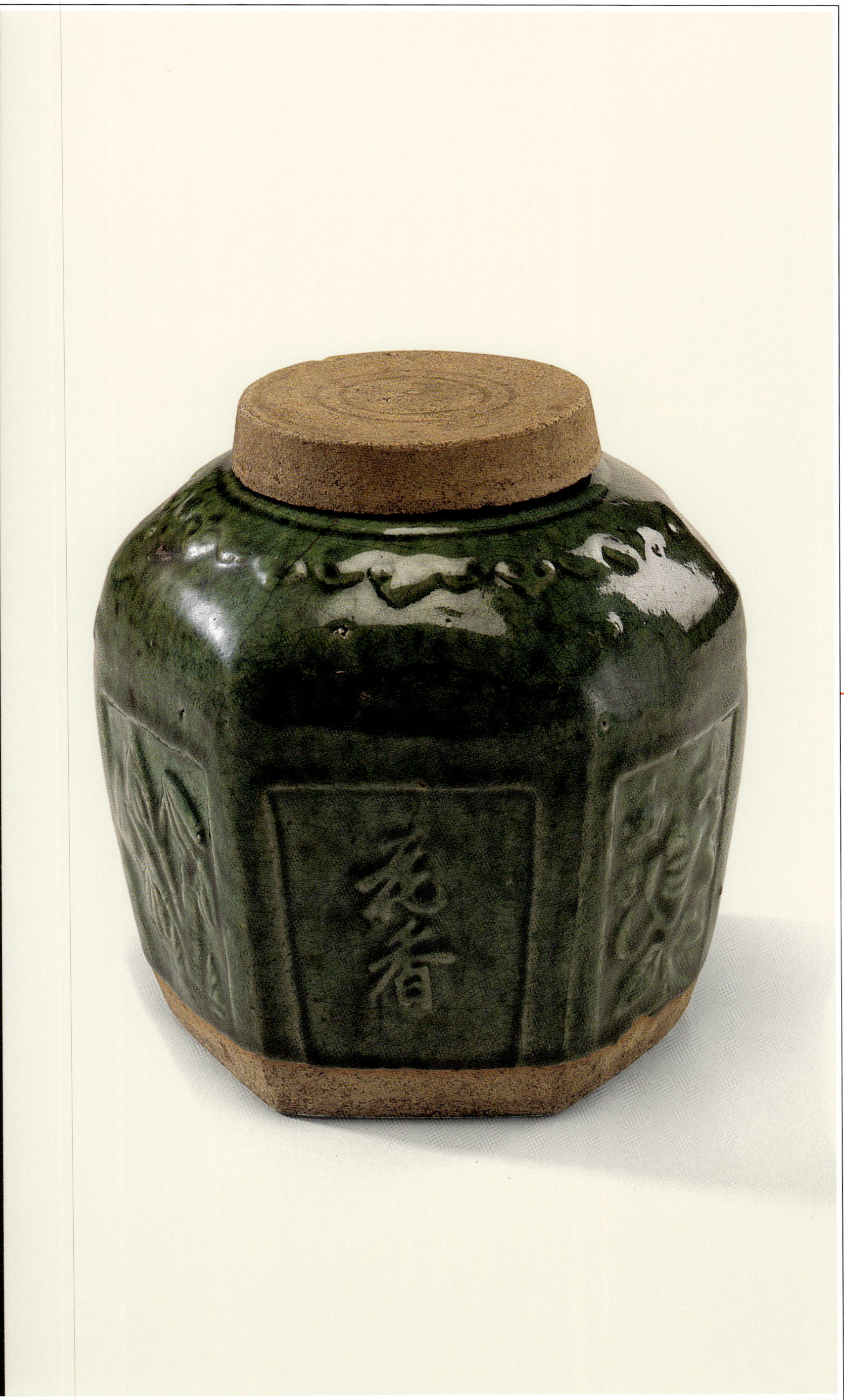

Left to right **Farmer's teapot** from the potteries of Shekwan, near Canton, height 22 cm. **Glazed earthenware jar** for pickles with loops for receiving a rope to tie down lid, height 43 cm. **Glazed terracotta jar** with moulded flowers and Chinese characters (*huaxiang*, "flower scent") in low relief, and with unglazed clay cover meant to be broken, height 18 cm.

DAILY ROUND

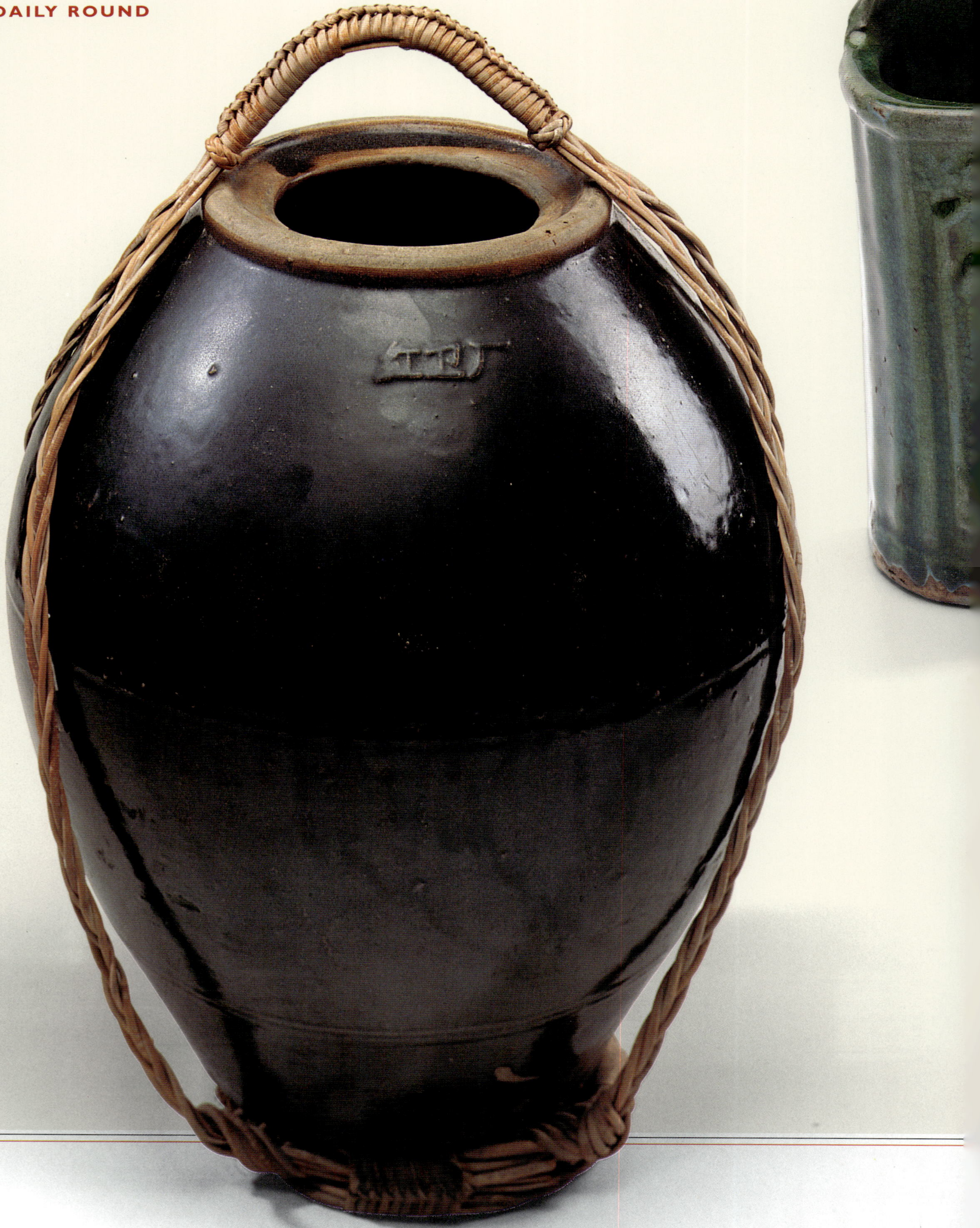

Earthenware jar with willow twig handle, height 50 cm.

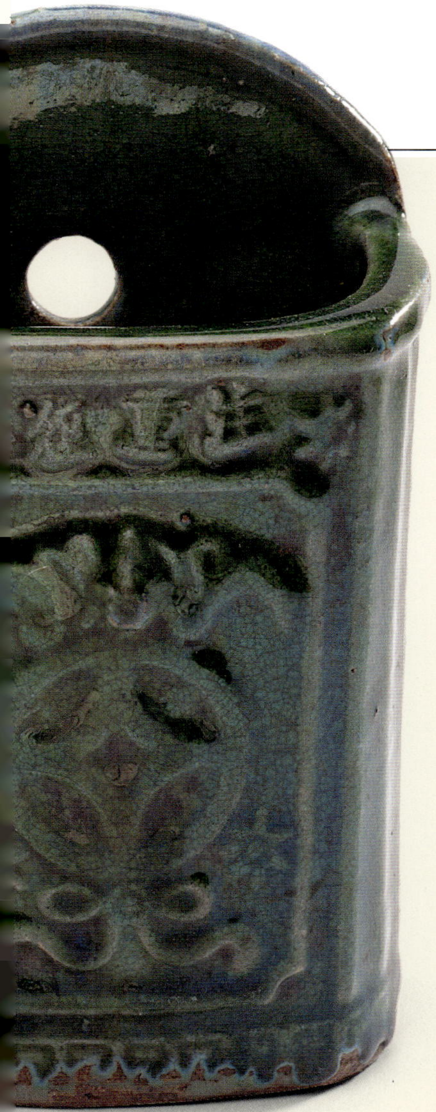

Glazed terracotta holder for chopsticks with hole for a string or peg for mounting it on wall, height 22 cm.

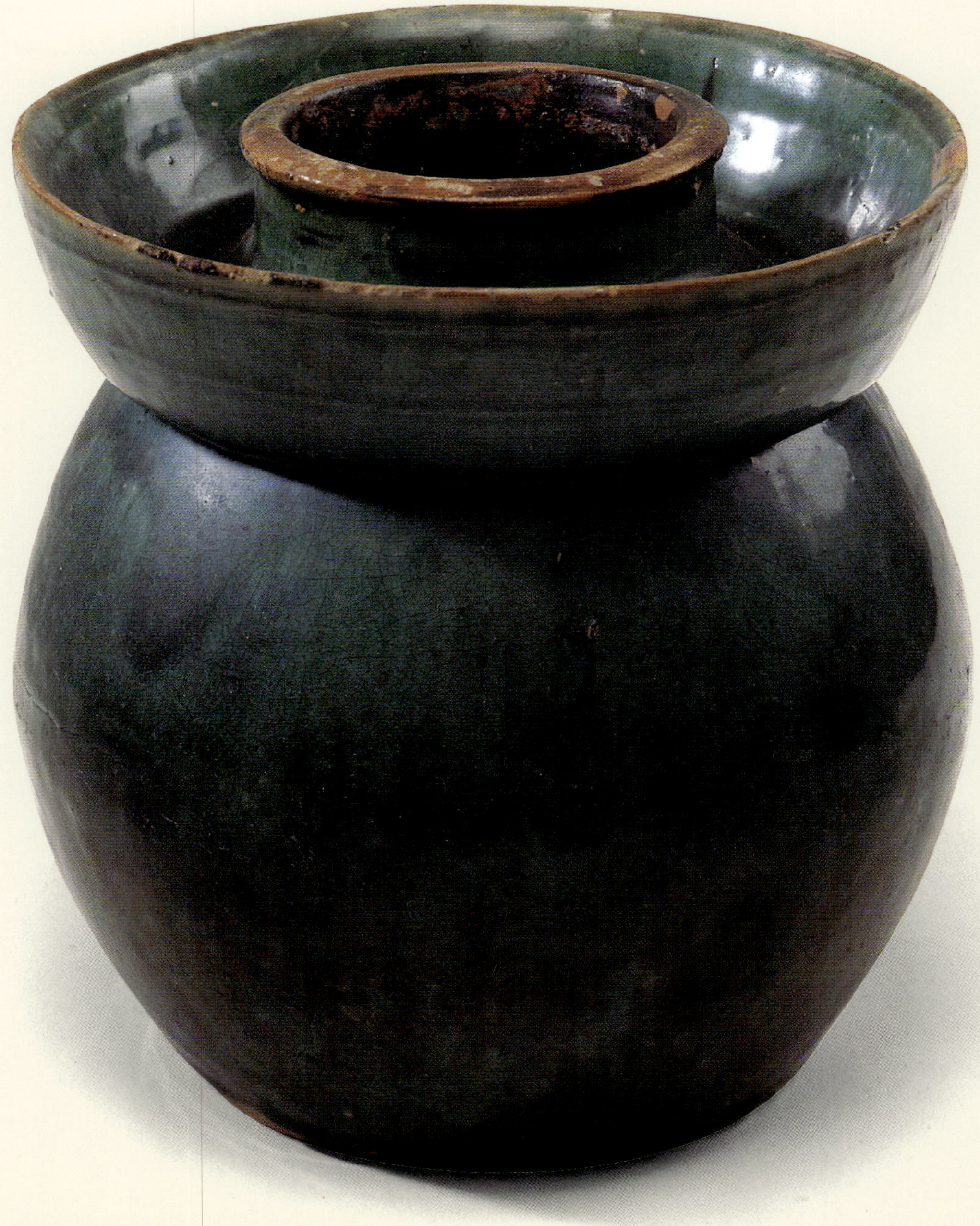

Glazed clay jar for preserving salted cabbage with a second rim forming a gutter that was filled with water. By placing an inverted bowl over the top with its rim submerged in the water, the jar was closed airtight, and yet any gases of fermentation which might form in the jar could easily escape, bubbling up through the water, height 40 cm.

DAILY ROUND

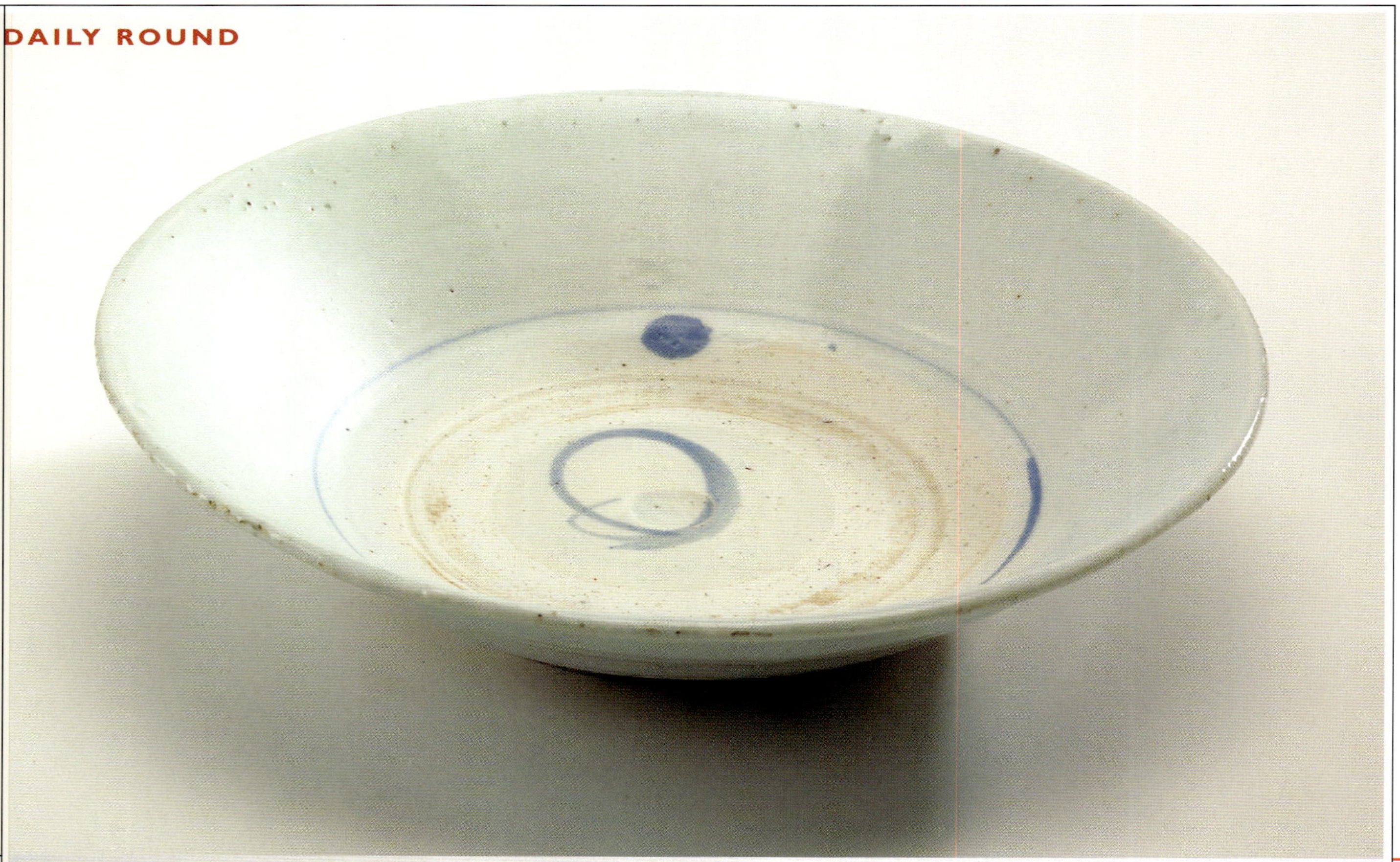

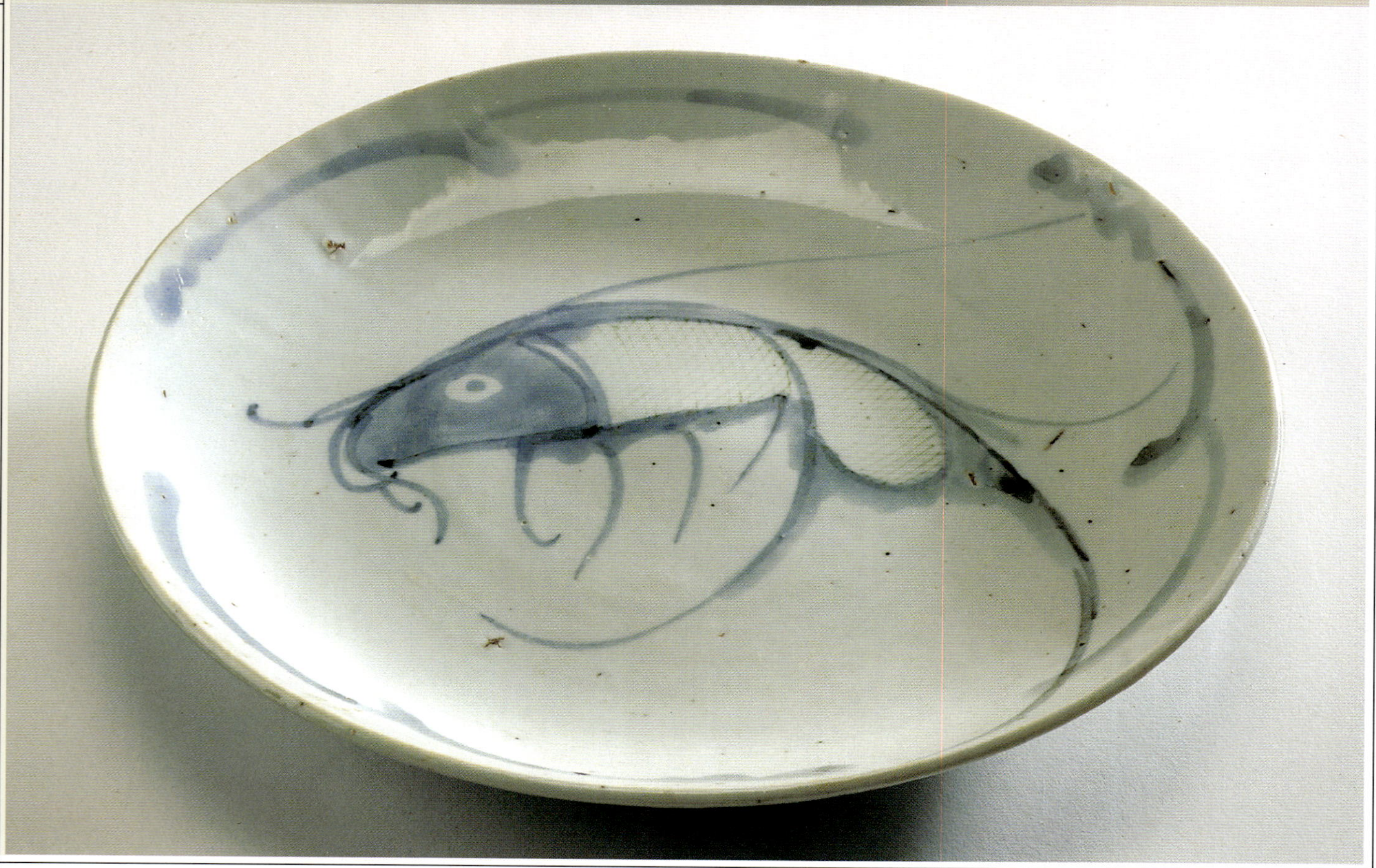

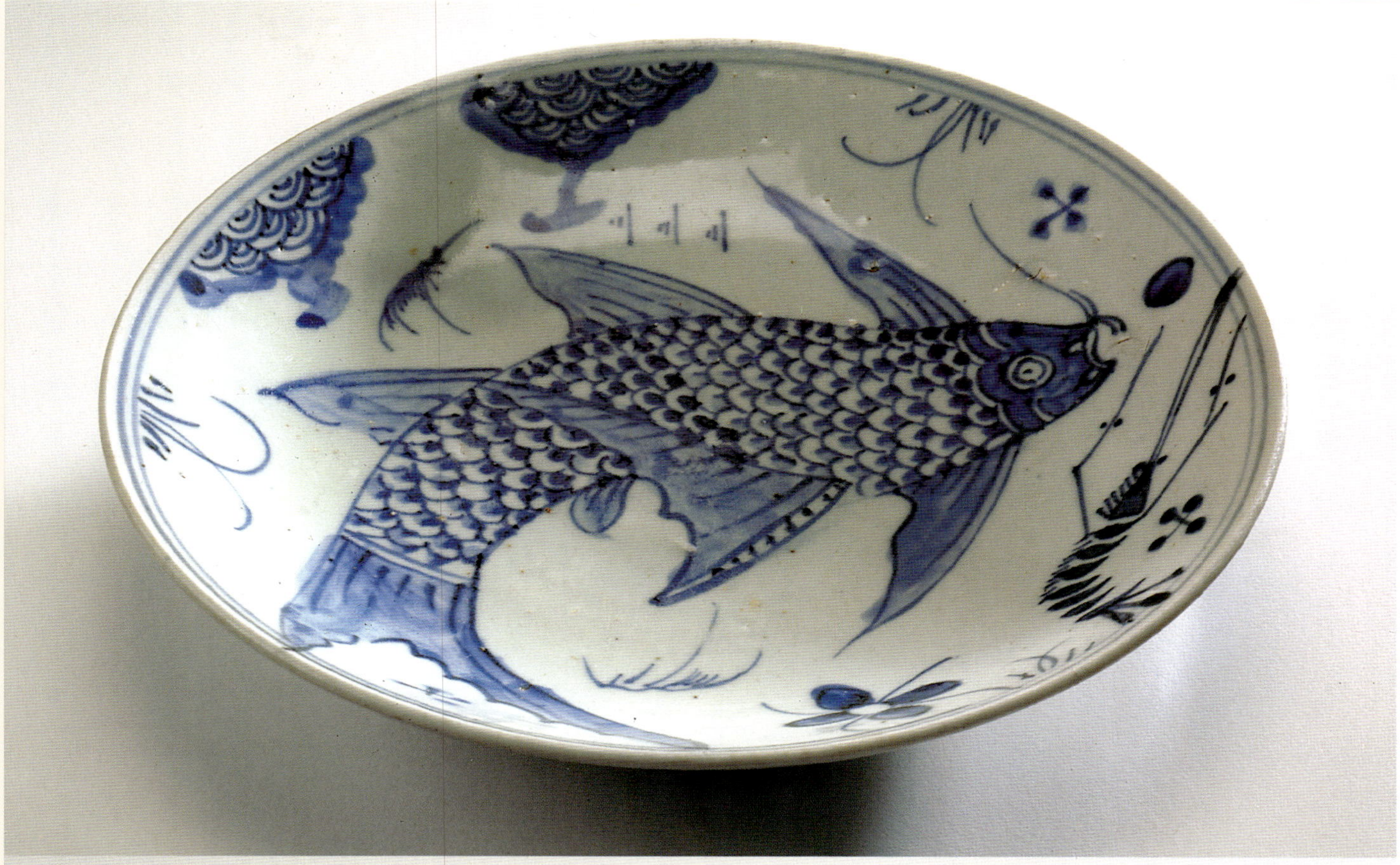

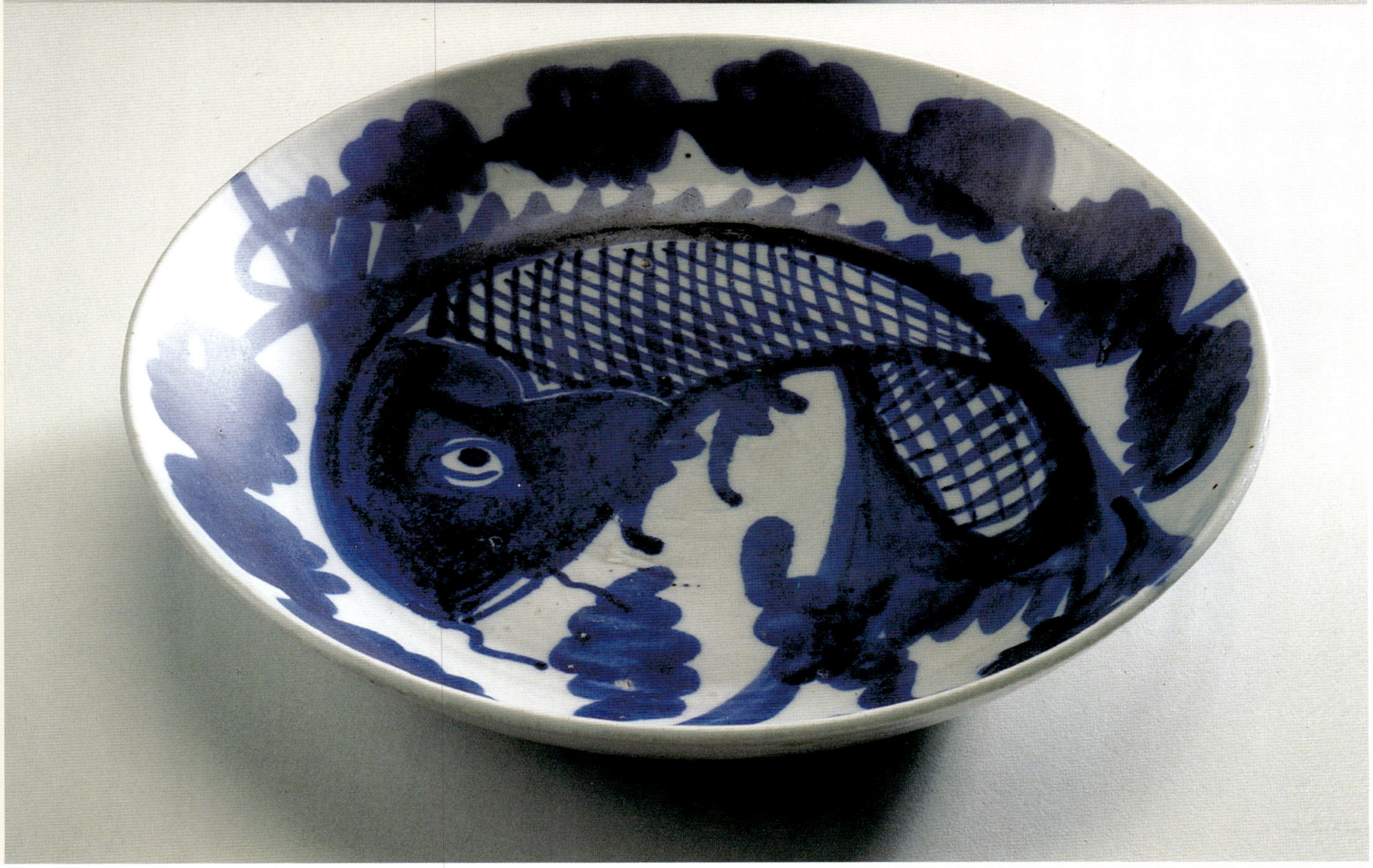

Four blue and white ceramic plates, three with fish motif, signifying abundance.

DAILY ROUND

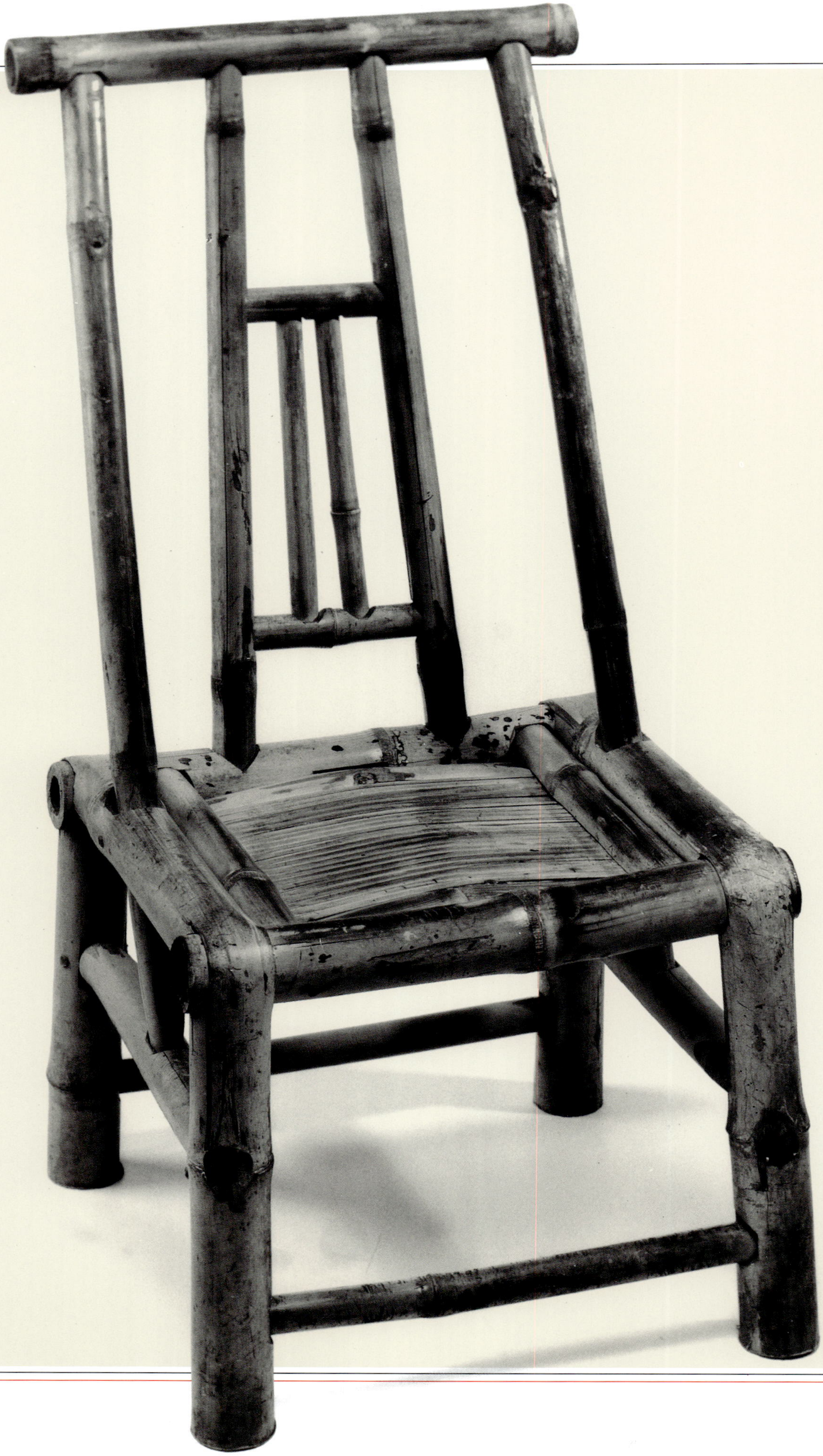

Bamboo chairs, made by bending two bamboo tubes twice at right angles into a U, with each U forming one pair of legs; two shorter bamboo tubes are then fitted horizontally into the bends and the seat is formed of bamboo slats. The side rungs are of thick enough bamboo to receive the slanting arms of the backrest. Heights 60 cm *(left)* and 70 cm *(right)*.

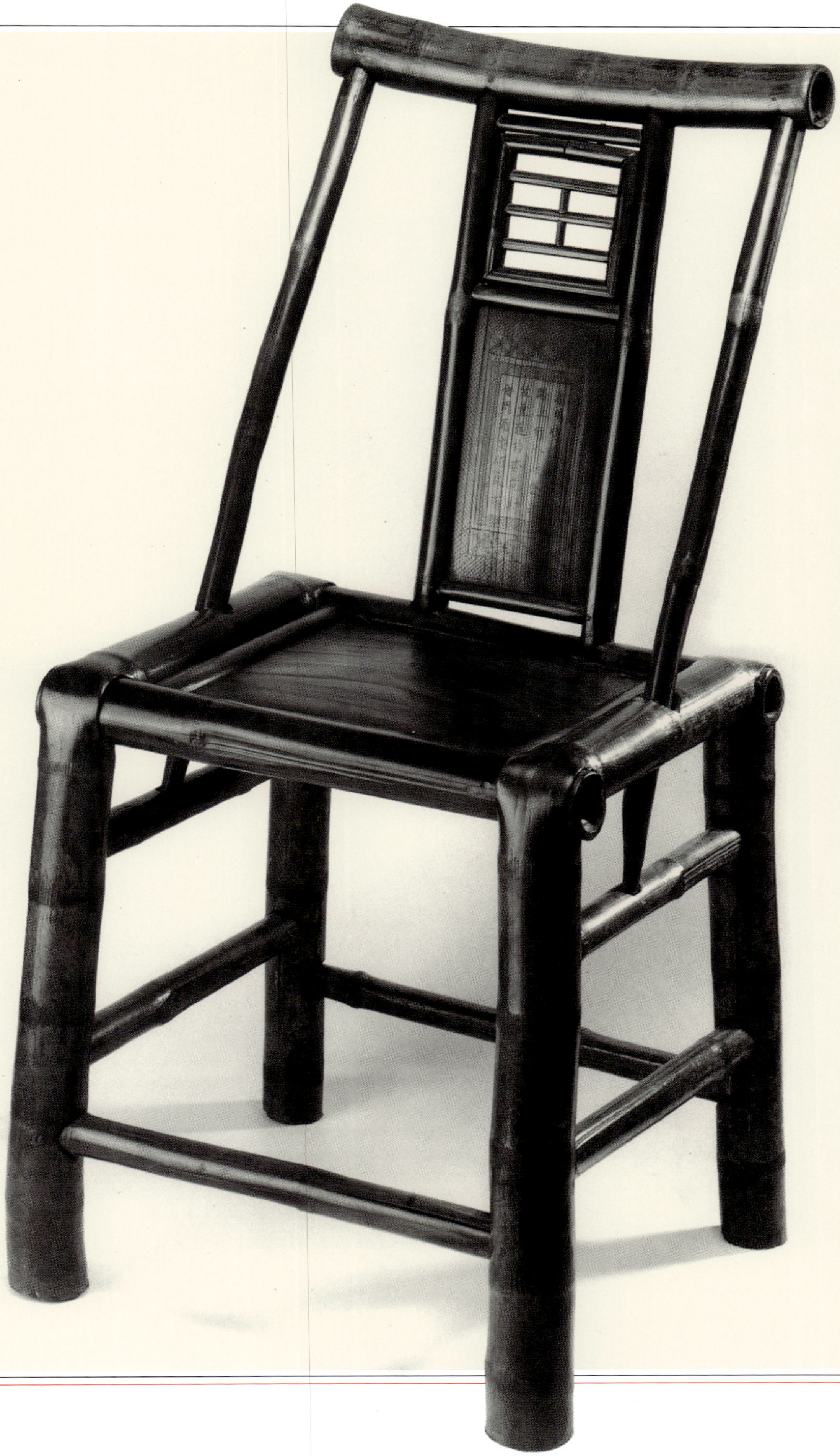

DAILY ROUND

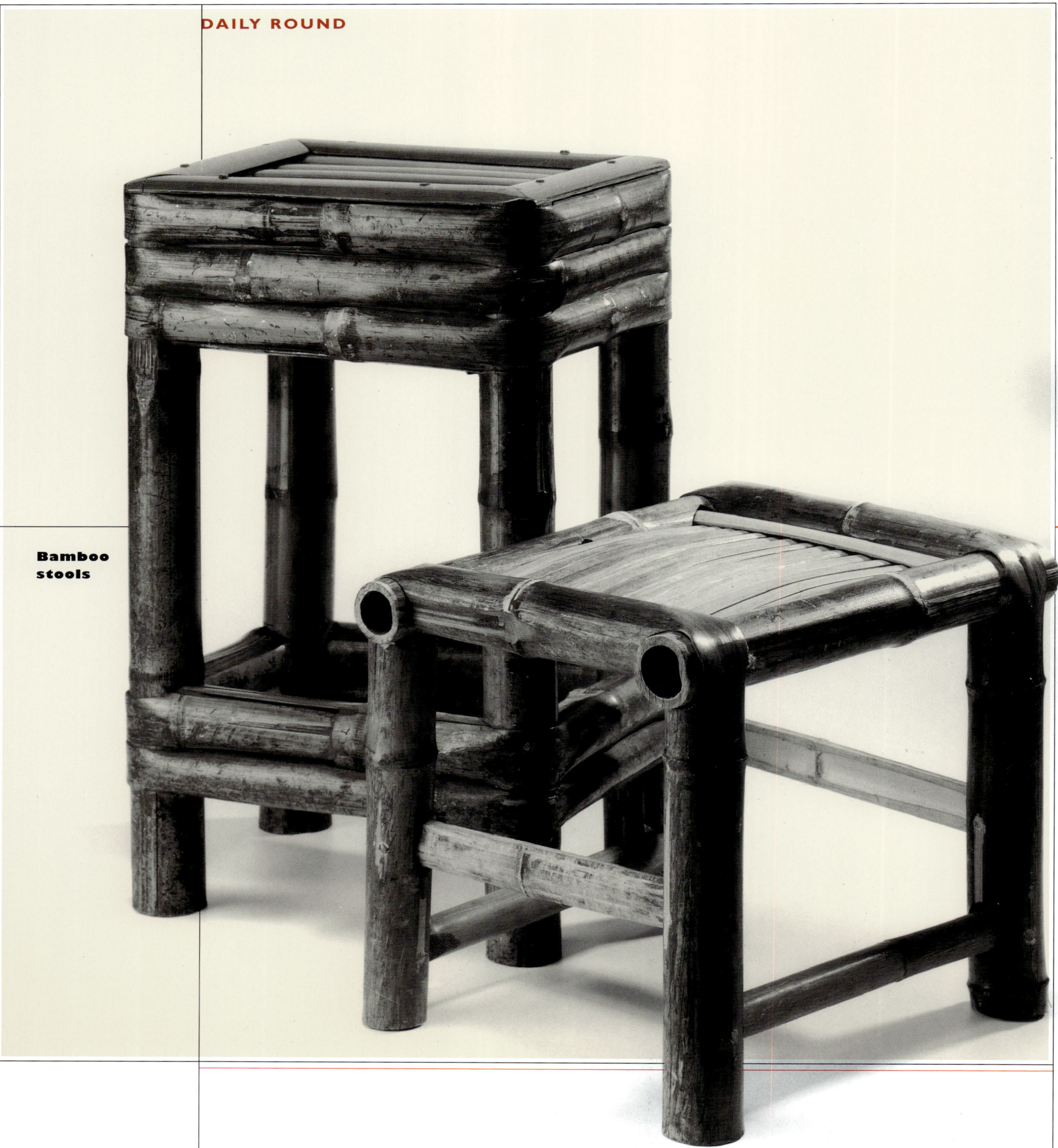

Bamboo stools

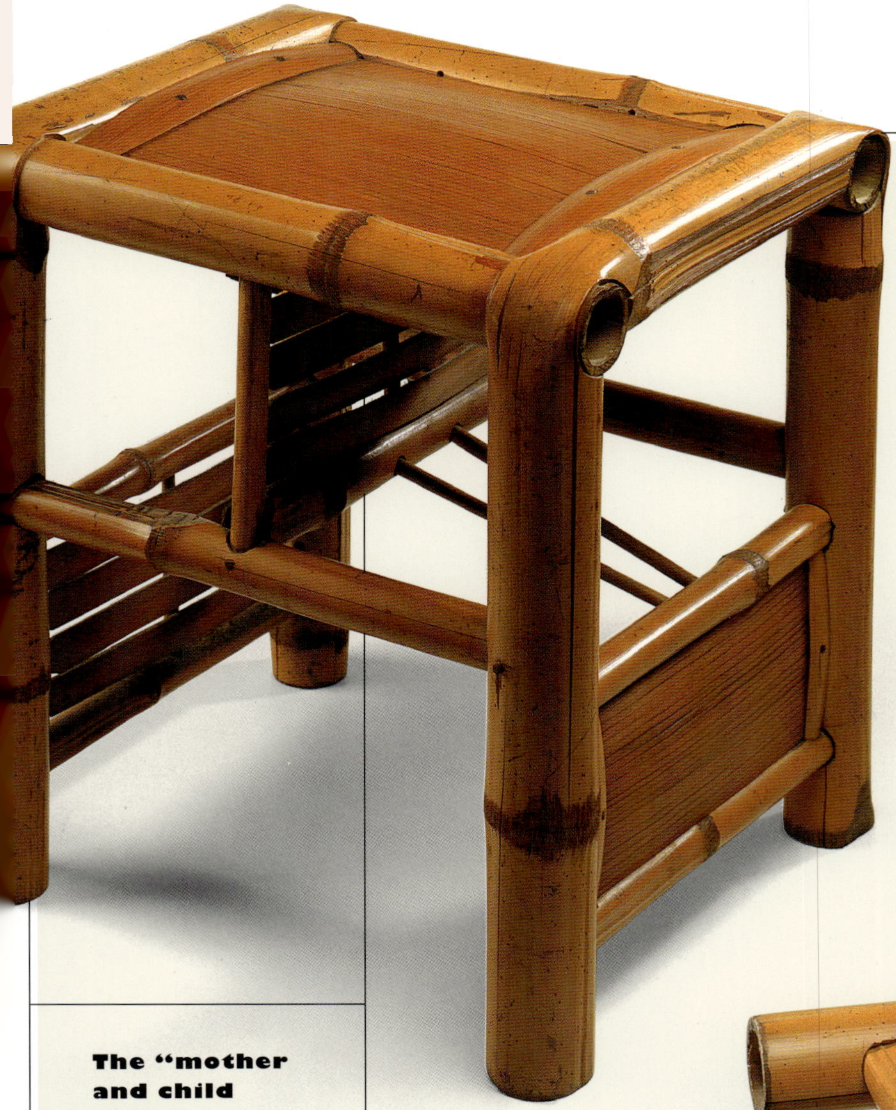

The "mother and child chair", when stood on its side, is turned into penned baby's chair with tabletop of slatted bamboo, height 45 cm.

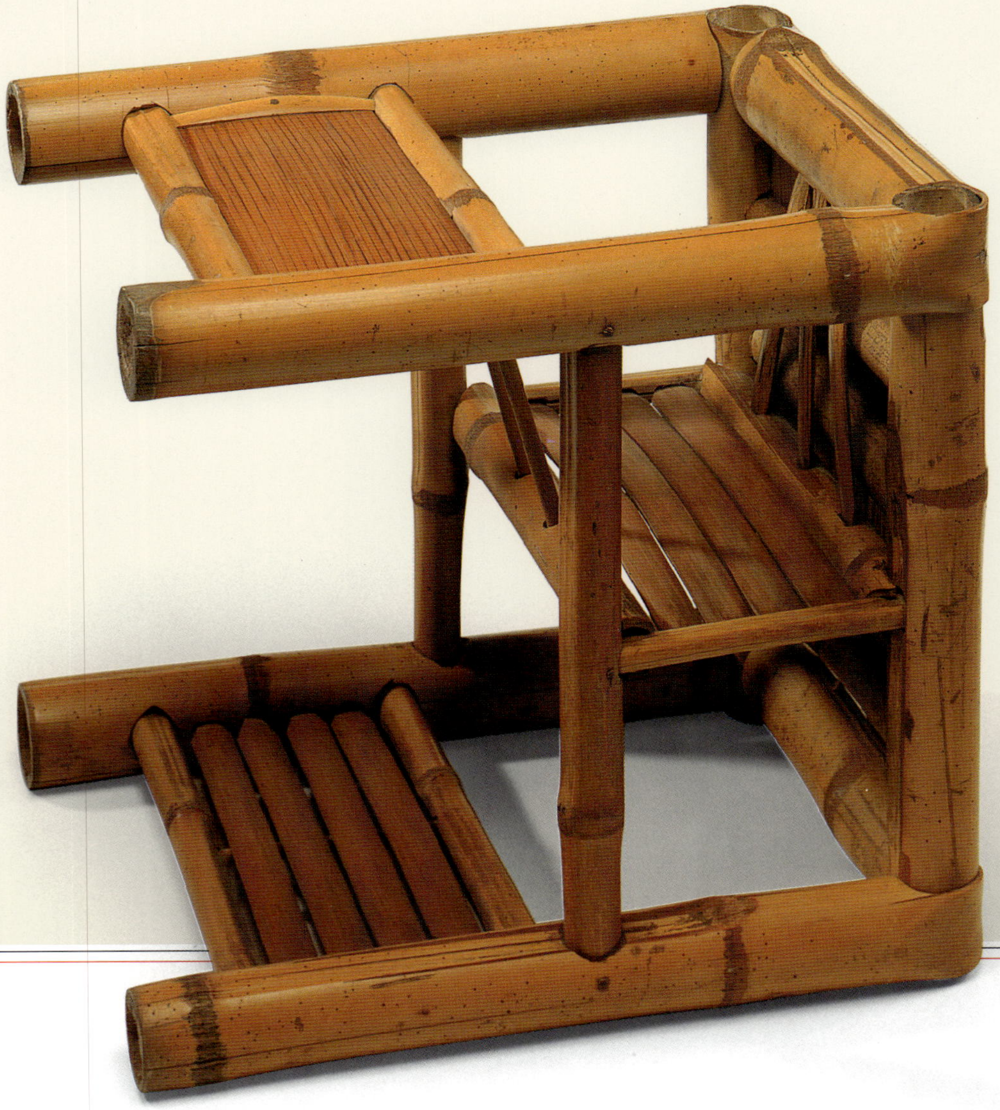

DAILY ROUND

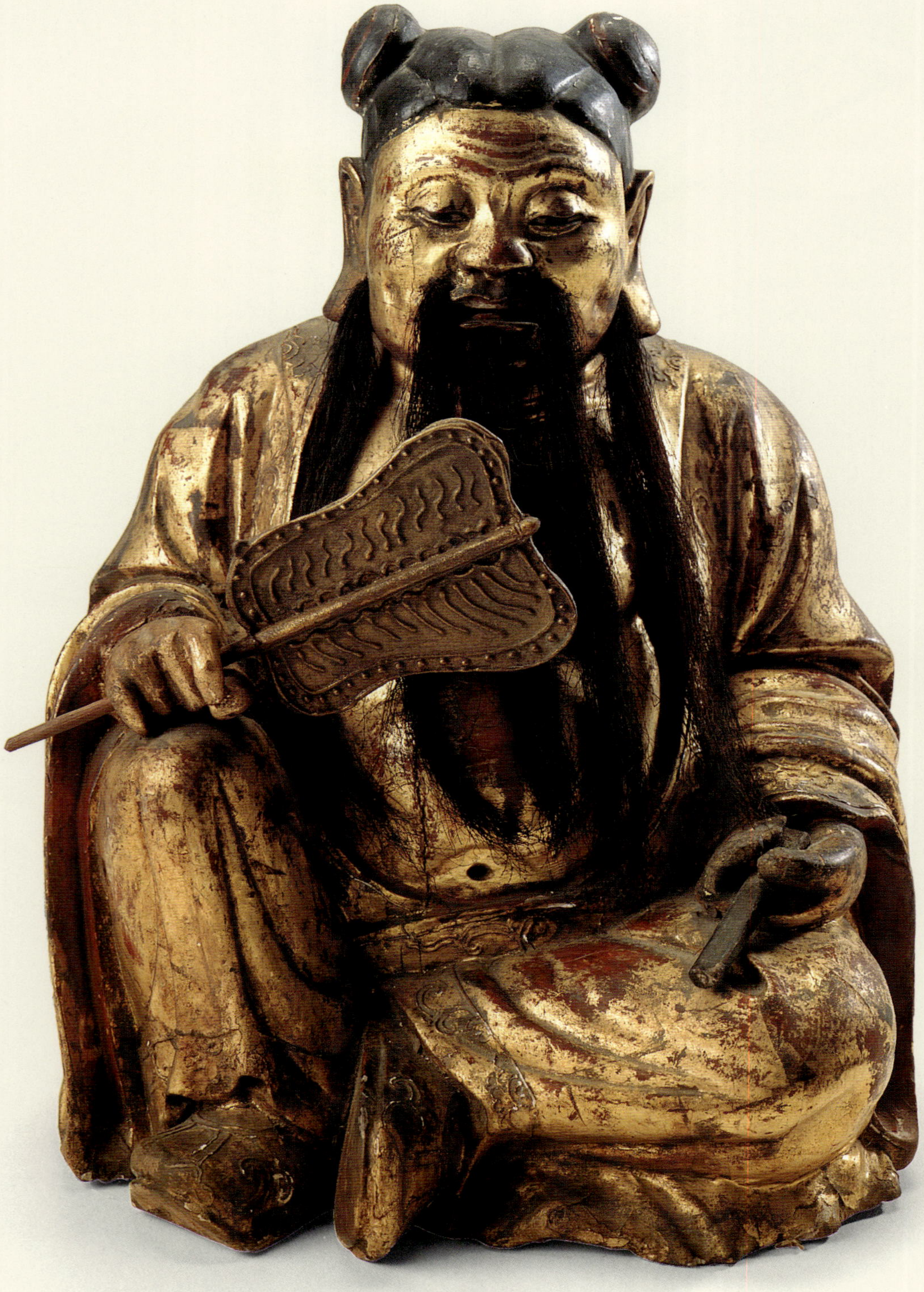

Carved wooden figure of God of Foundries, with fan for fanning flames, height 26 cm.

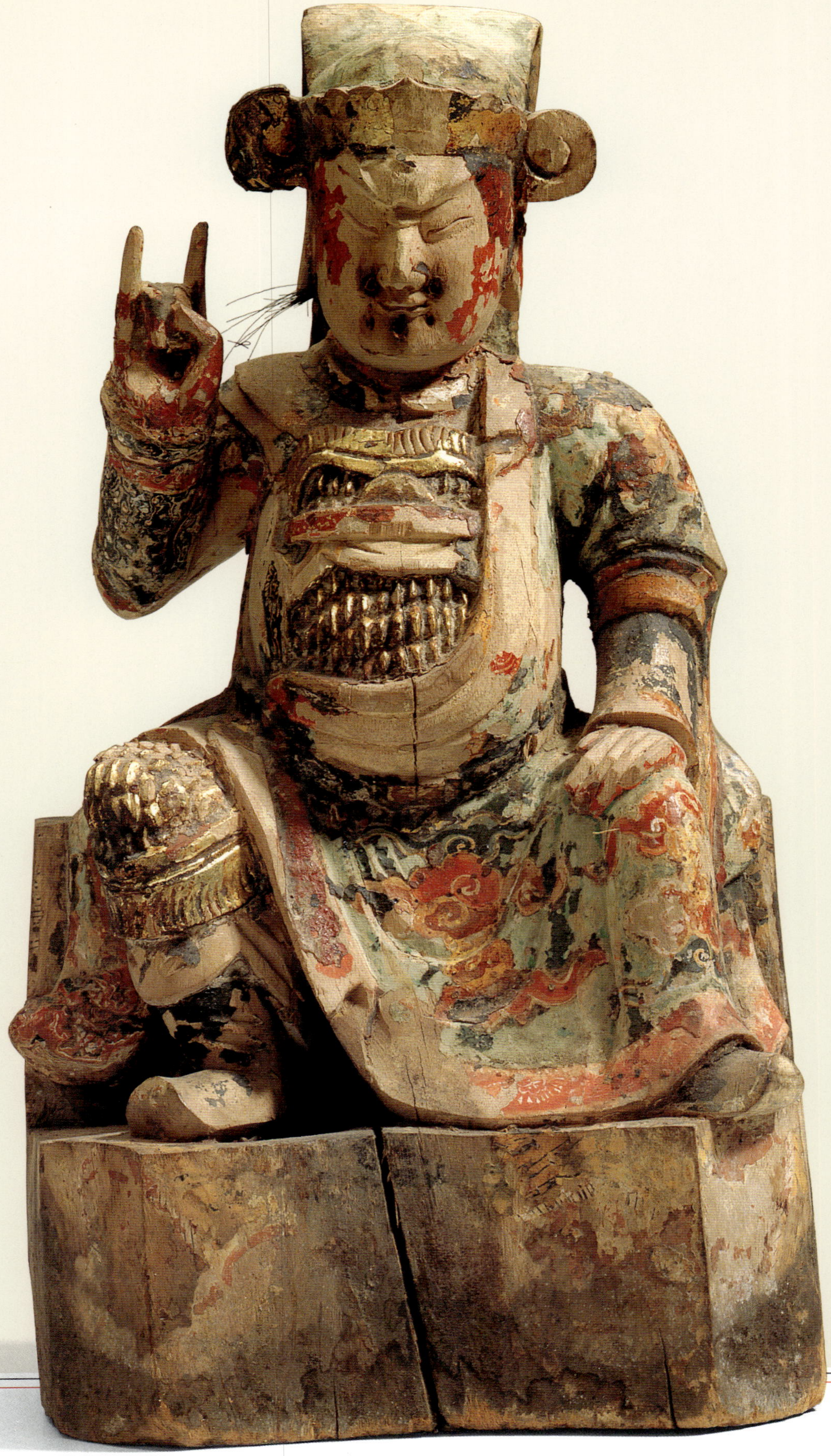

Gilt and painted wooden sculpture from Hunan province, of *jiashen,* anscestral god, commonly housed in temple to local deity, with big square hole in his back for lodging the deceased's dates of birth and death, grains and some small belongings, height 25 cm.

DAILY ROUND

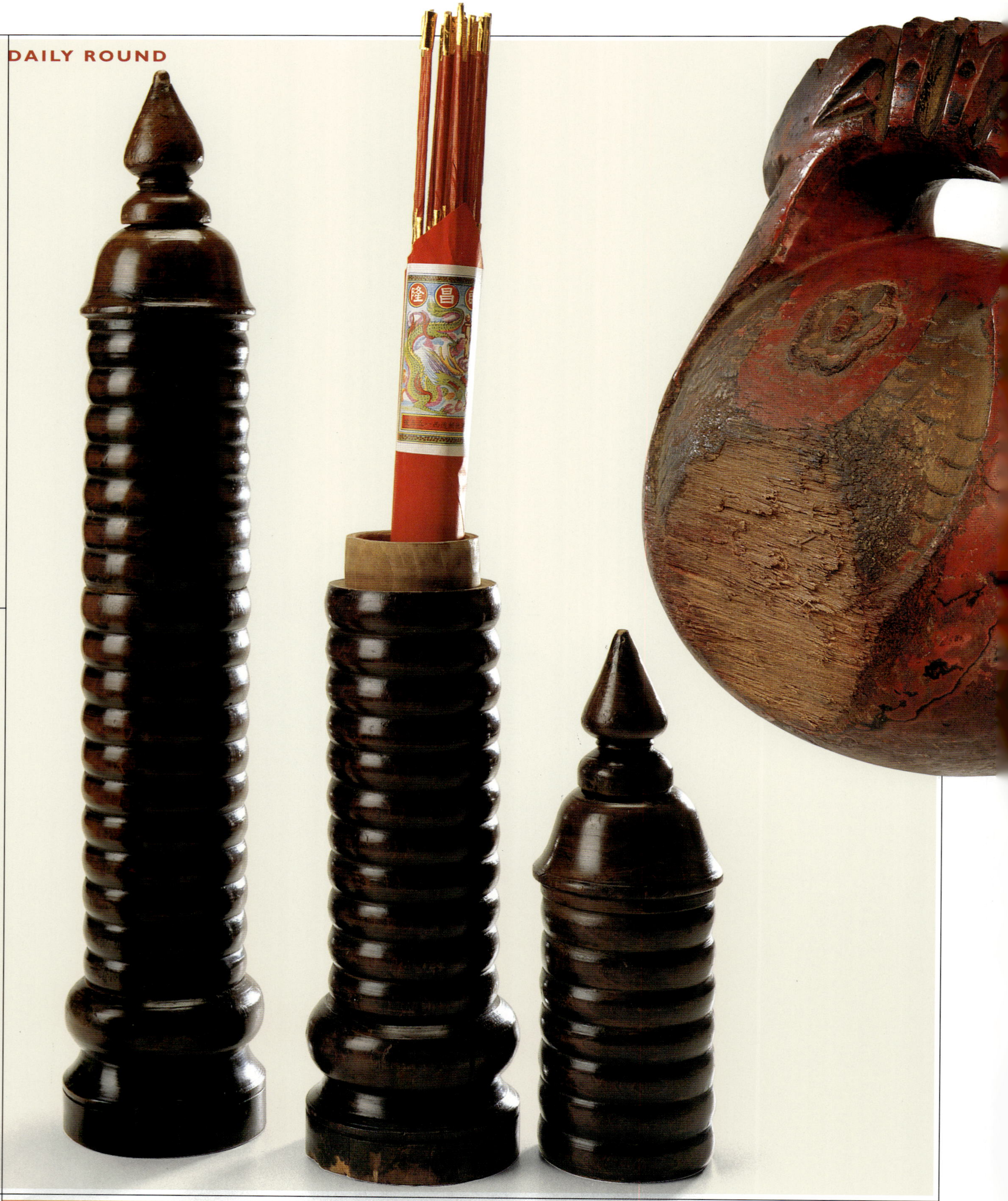

Left to right **Wooden incense holders** with incense. Hollow wooden "gong" with a stick like the *muyu*, "wooden fish", beaten by Buddhist monks to keep time while chanting sutras, height 24 cm. **Ceramic wick lamps** for ordinary domestic use and for placing on altar tables.

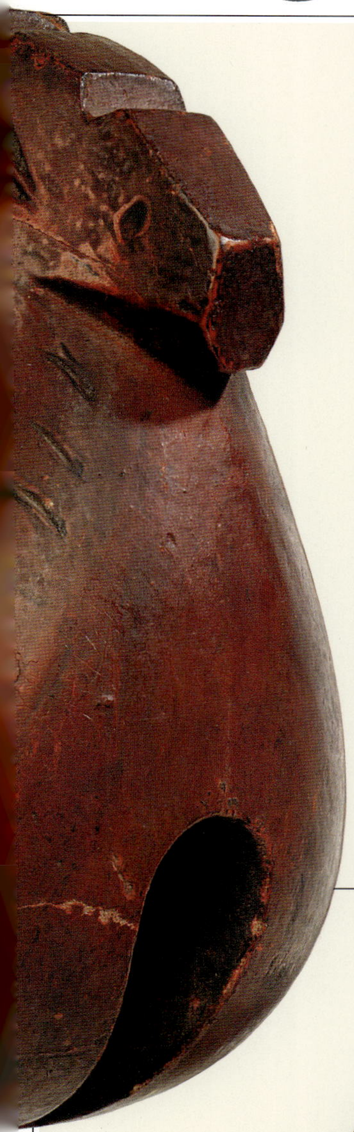

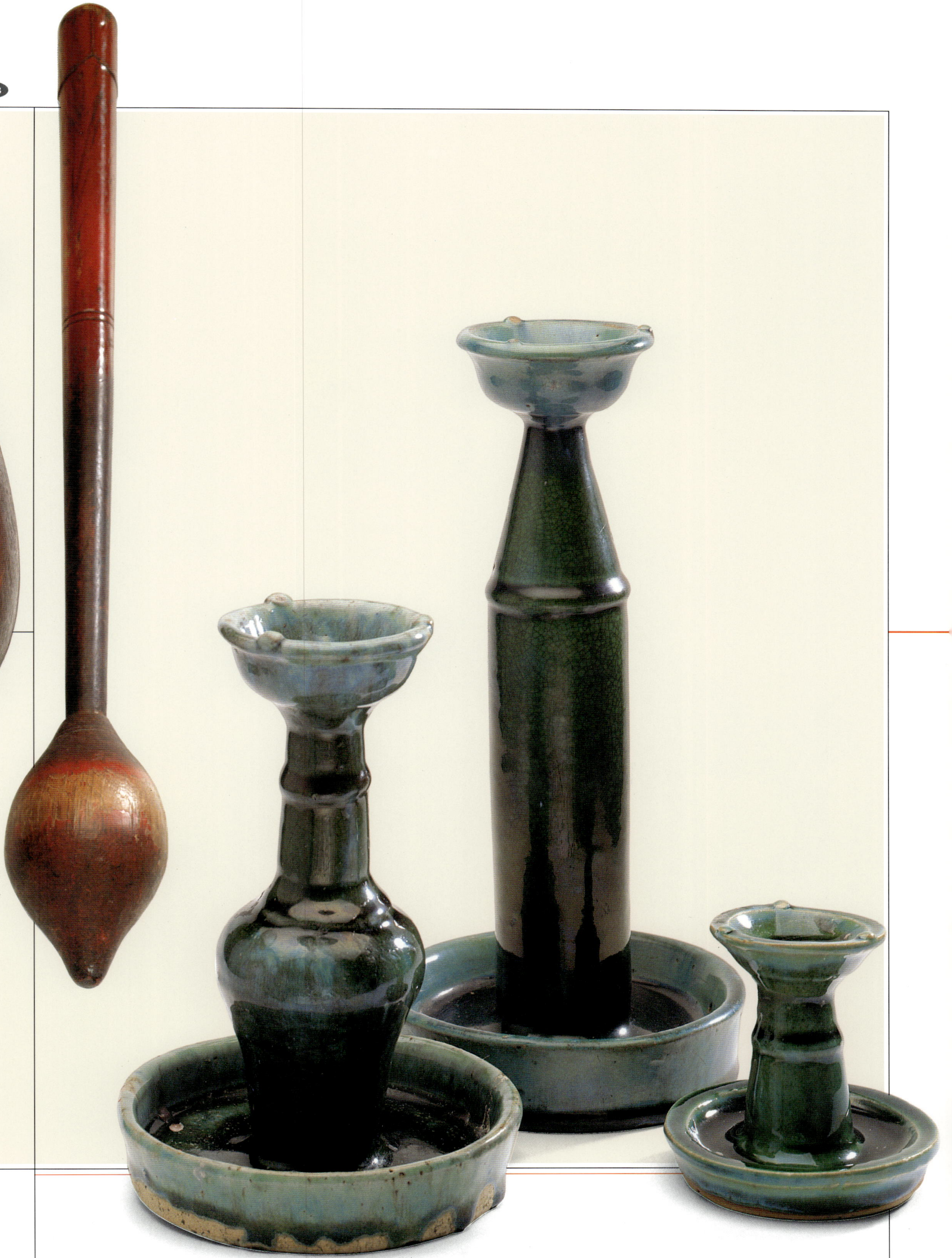

DAILY ROUND

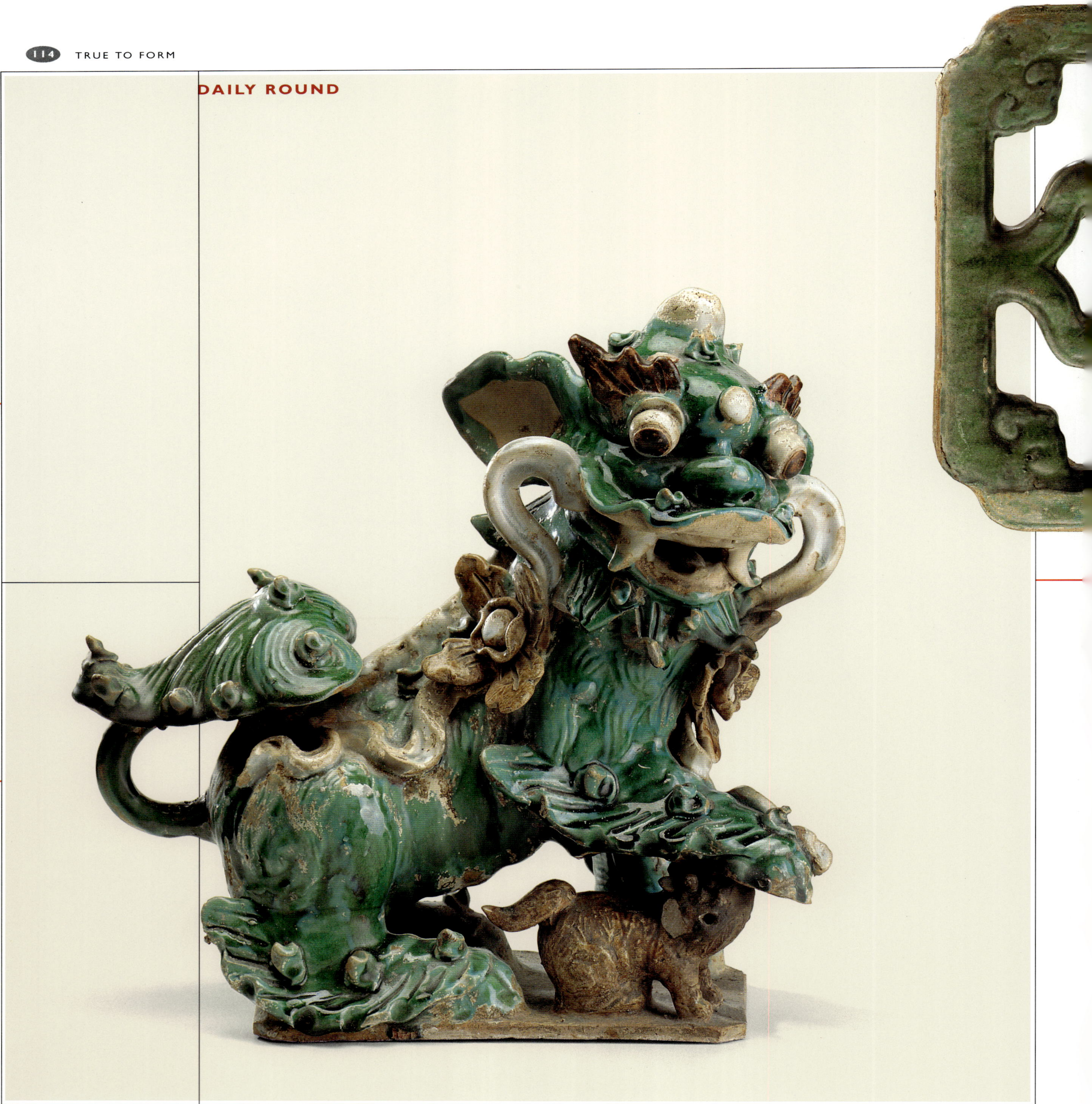

Lion and fish, part of a temple roof ridge pantheon in Hong Kong's New Territories, in glazed Shekwan pottery, height 42 cm and 60 cm.

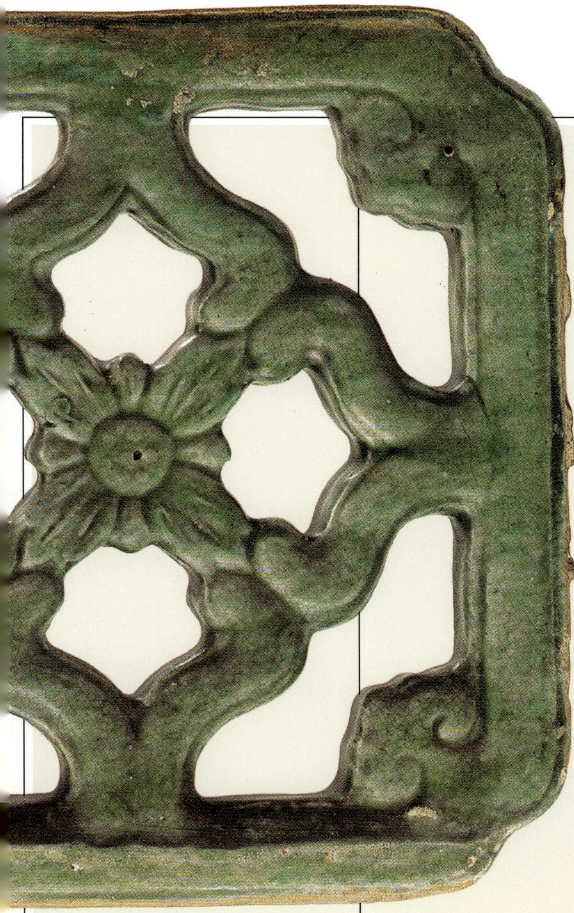

Ceramic air tile in the green glaze of Shekwan ware, 30 cm square.

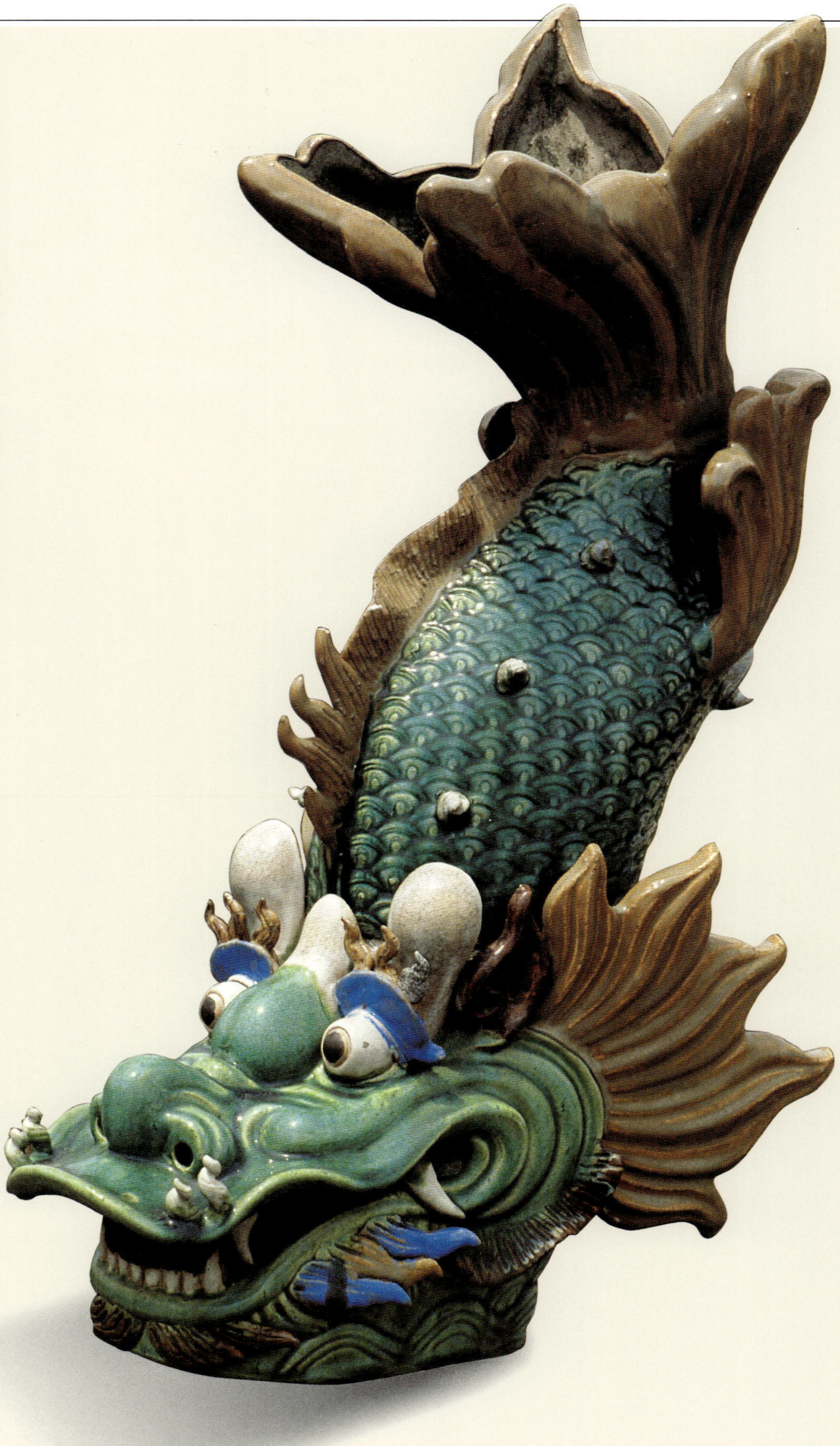

DAILY ROUND

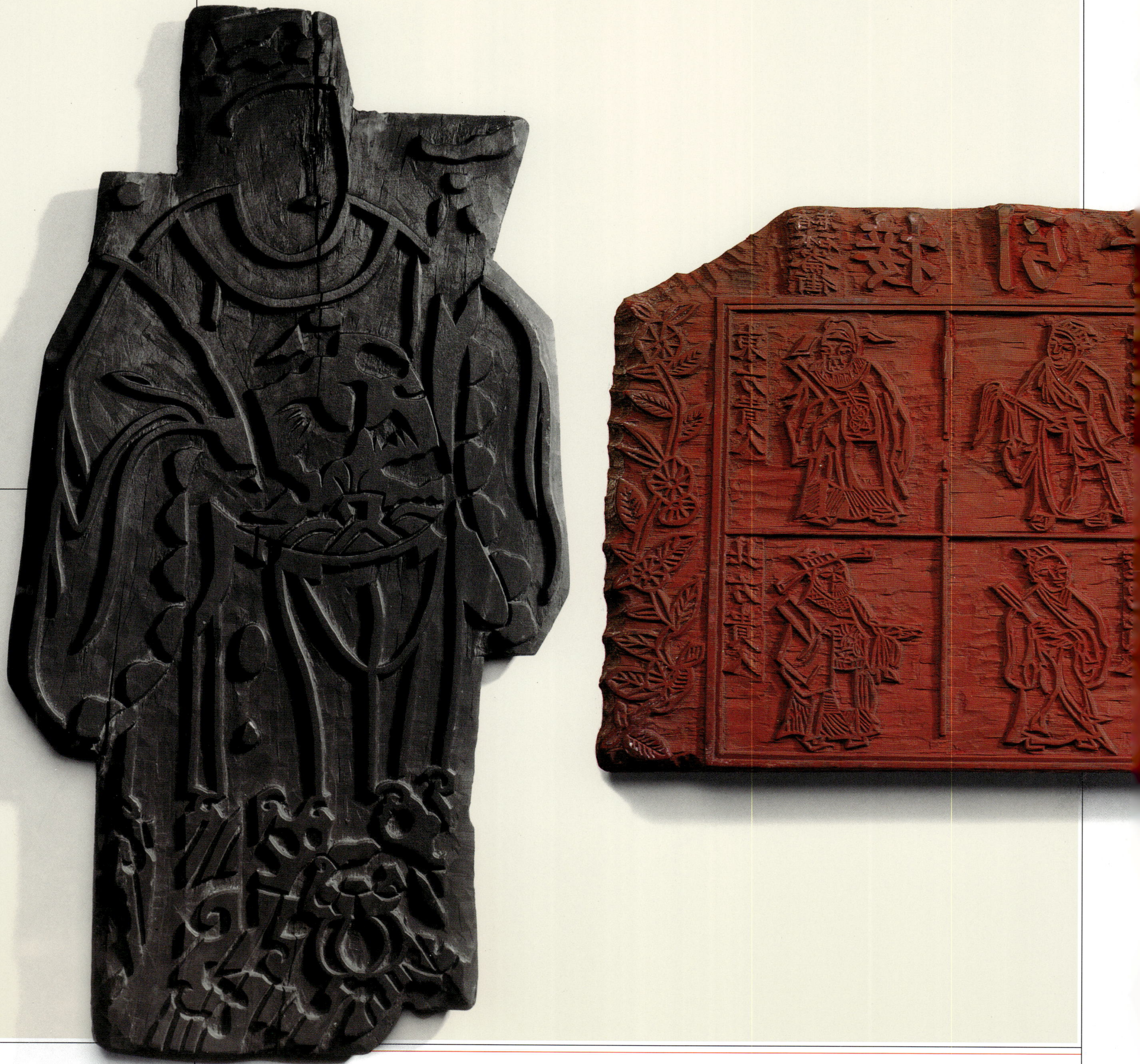

Wooden block for printing paper charms, 60 cm long, flanked by pair of wooden blocks of door gods cut out in reverse for printing, height 50 cm. Copies are taken by inking the block, covering it with paper, and rubbing the paper with a stiff, dry brush.

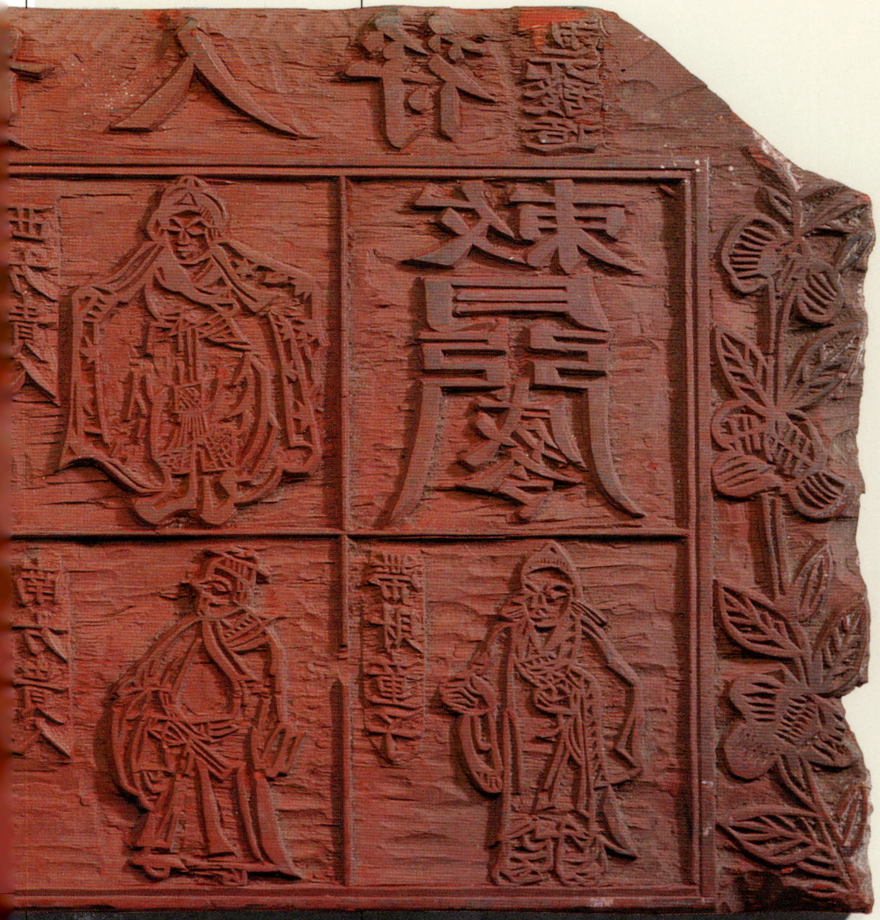

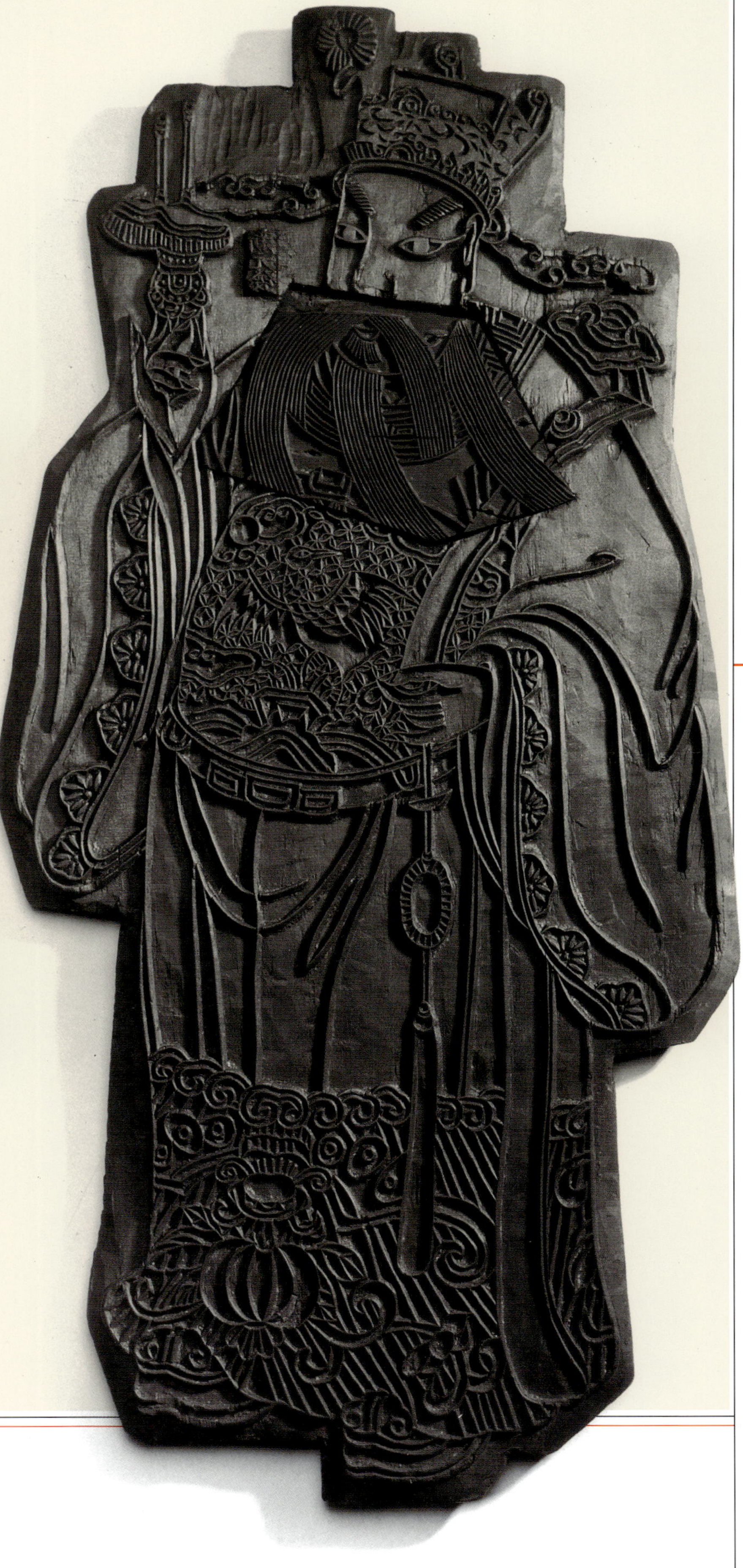

Wood block prints of pair of door gods, popularly mounted at entrances during the Lunar New Year to protect those inside against evil spirits.

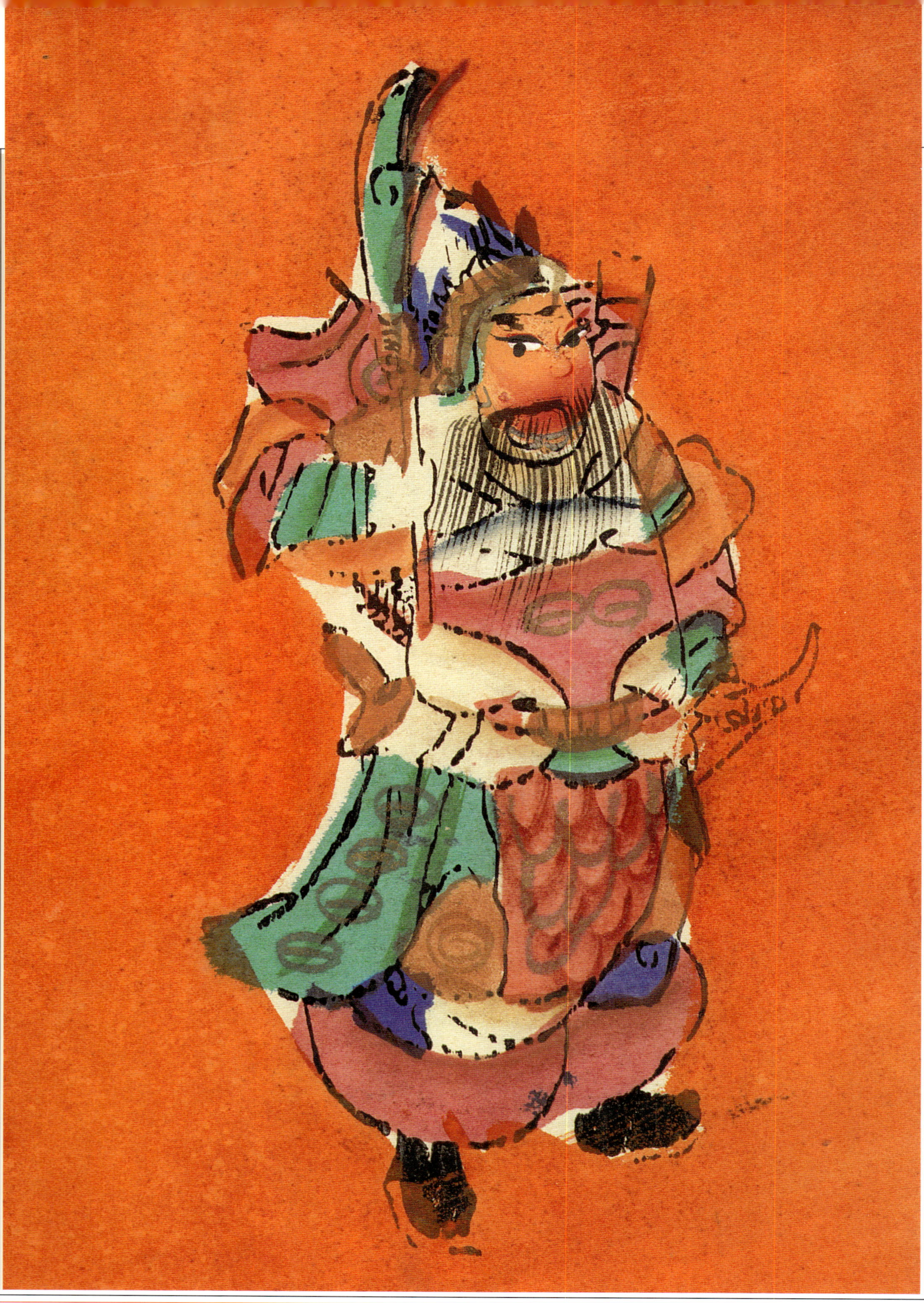

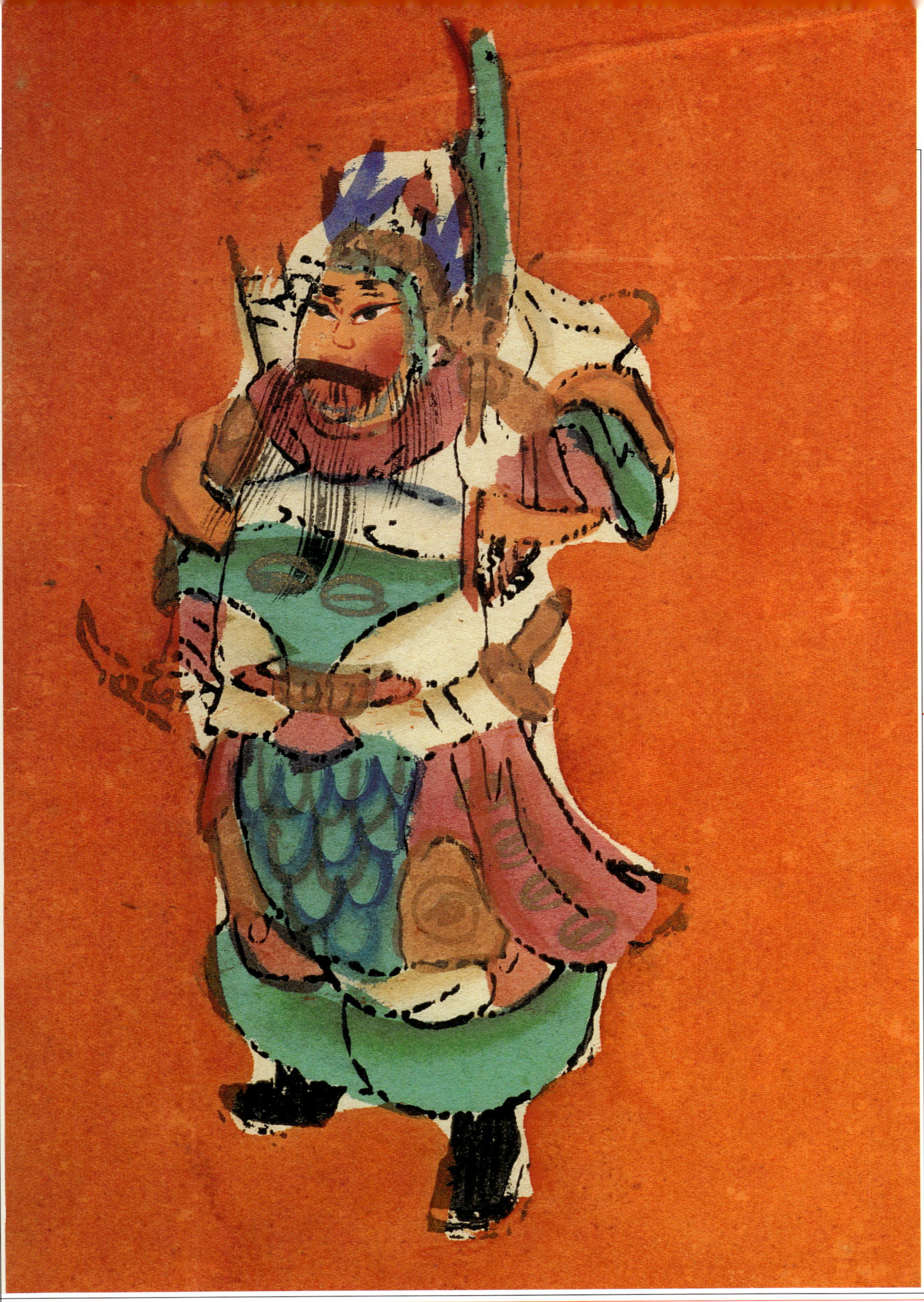

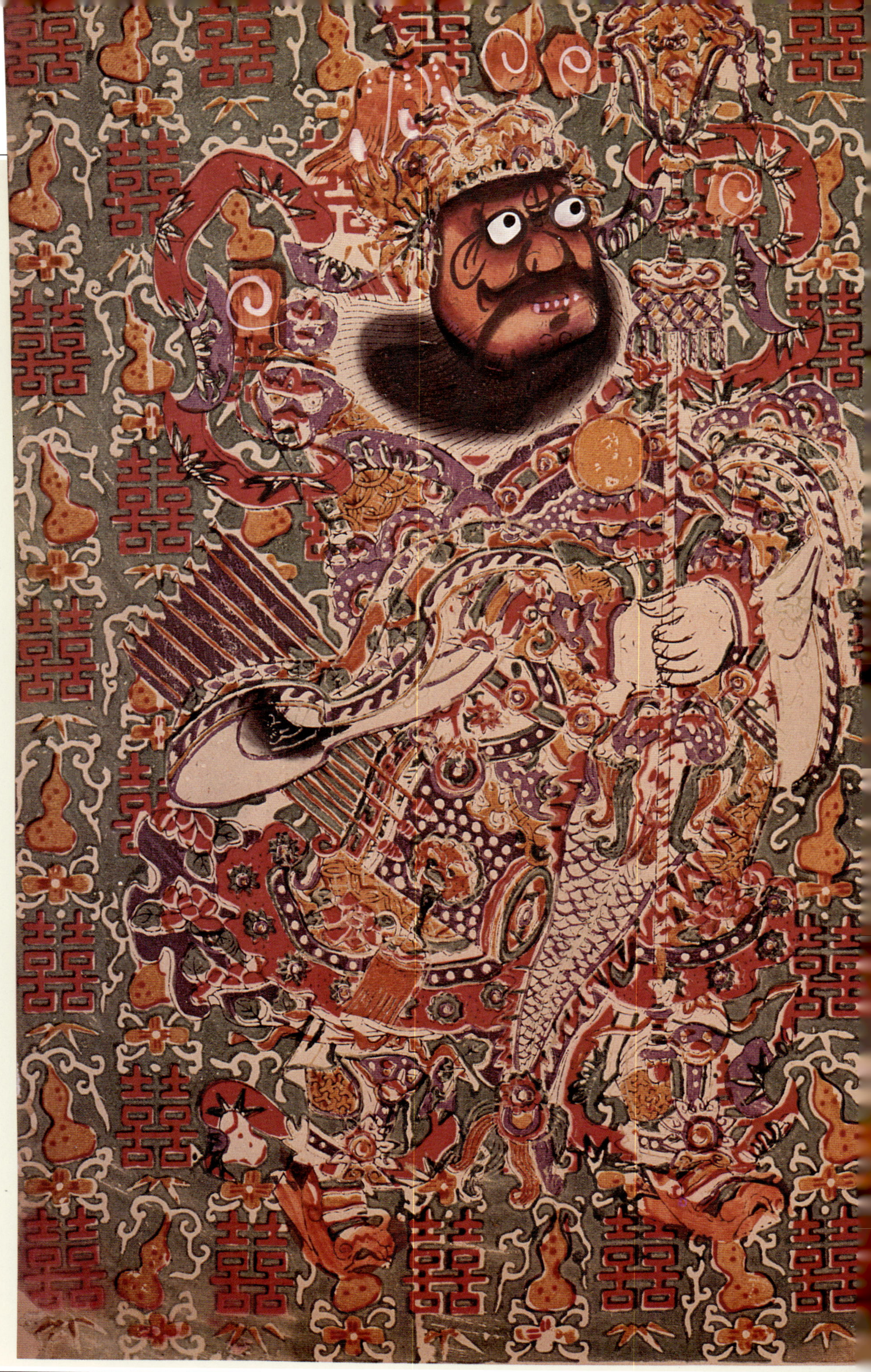

Pair of door gods surrounded by red "double happiness" characters and images of the bottle gourd, whose many seeds represent multitudes of children. With such motifs, the prints could well have decorated a newly married couple's first home.

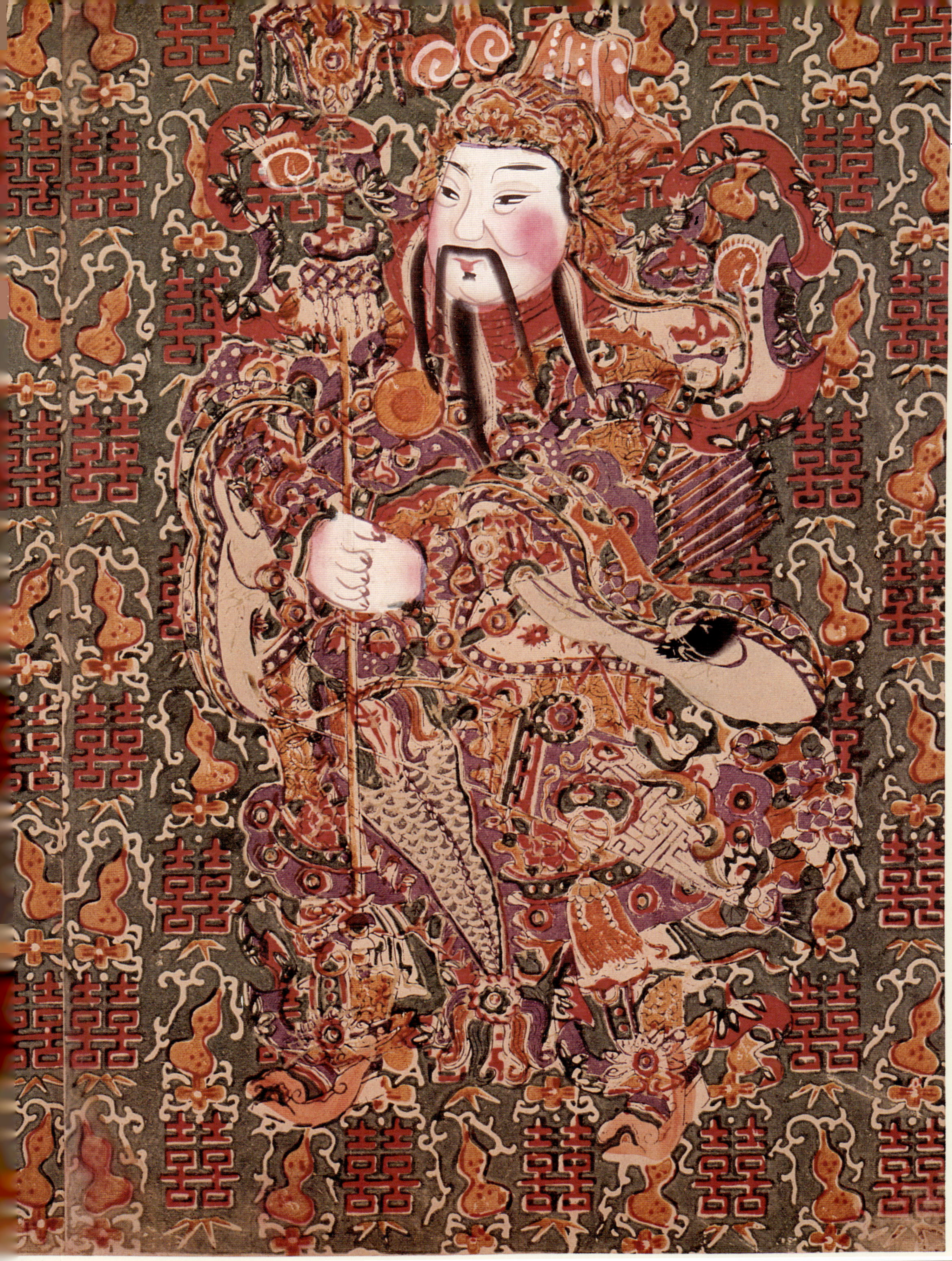

Left and right **Door paper cuts** inscribed with the characters for "peace" to be pasted on lintel of door, with cut part floating free like a curtain, to welcome the New Year, Such paper cuts come in red or gold, in sets of five, six, seven and nine, and are changed once a year.

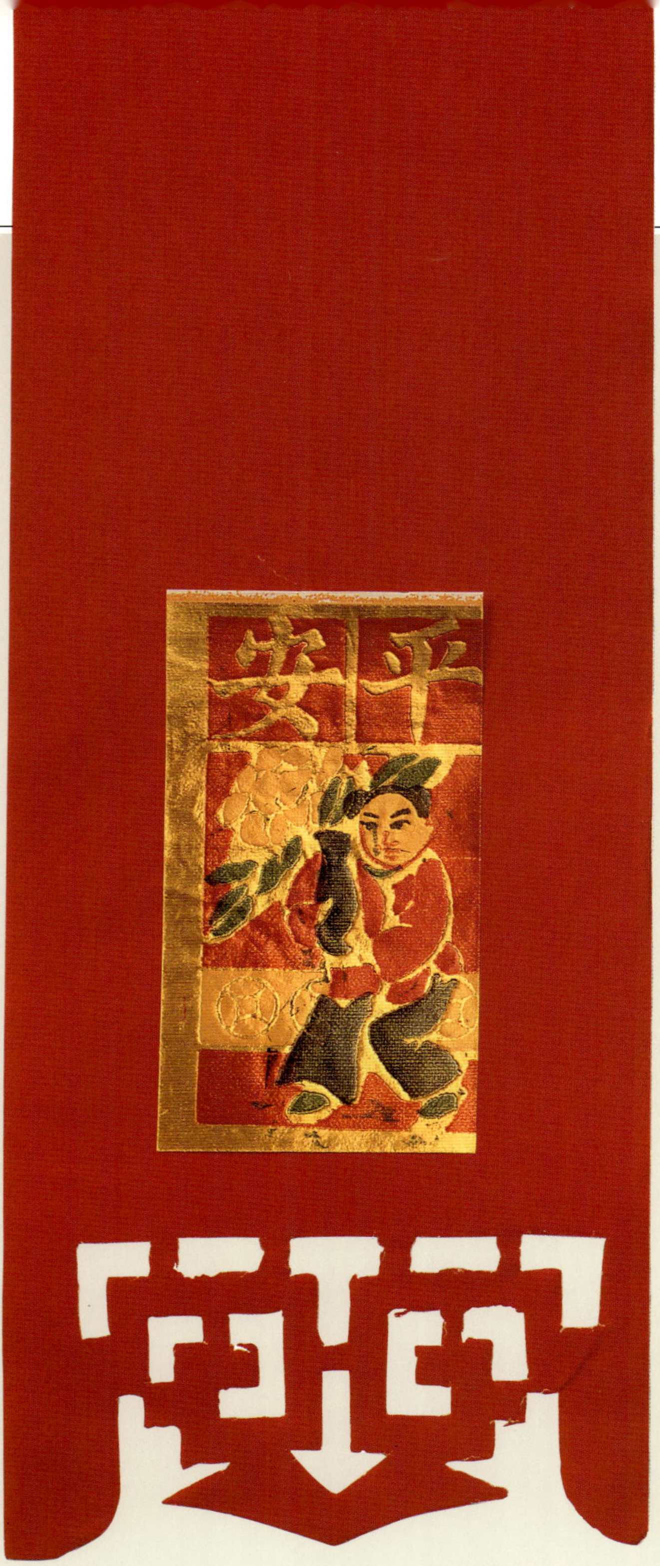

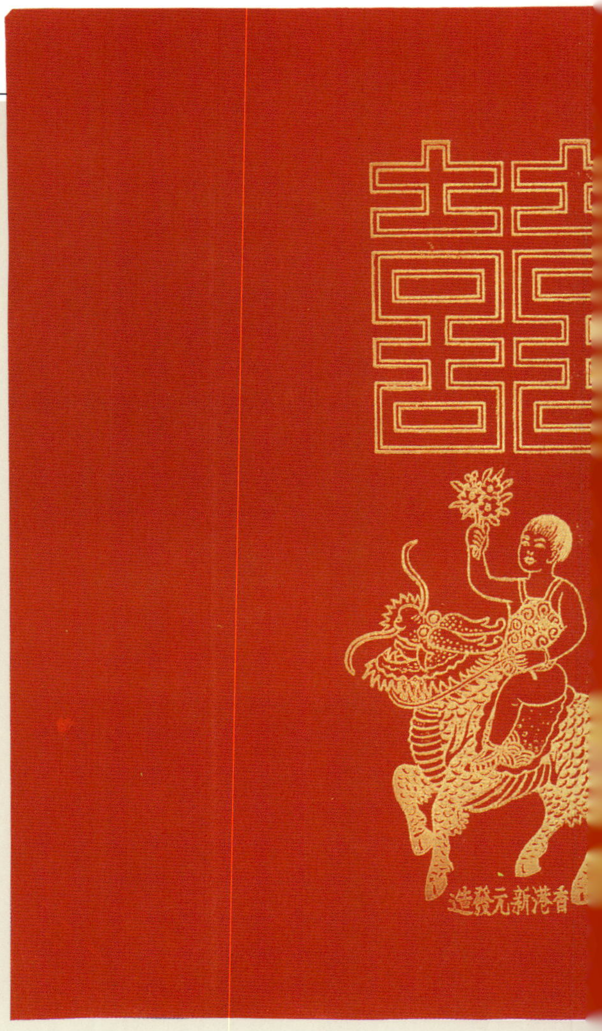

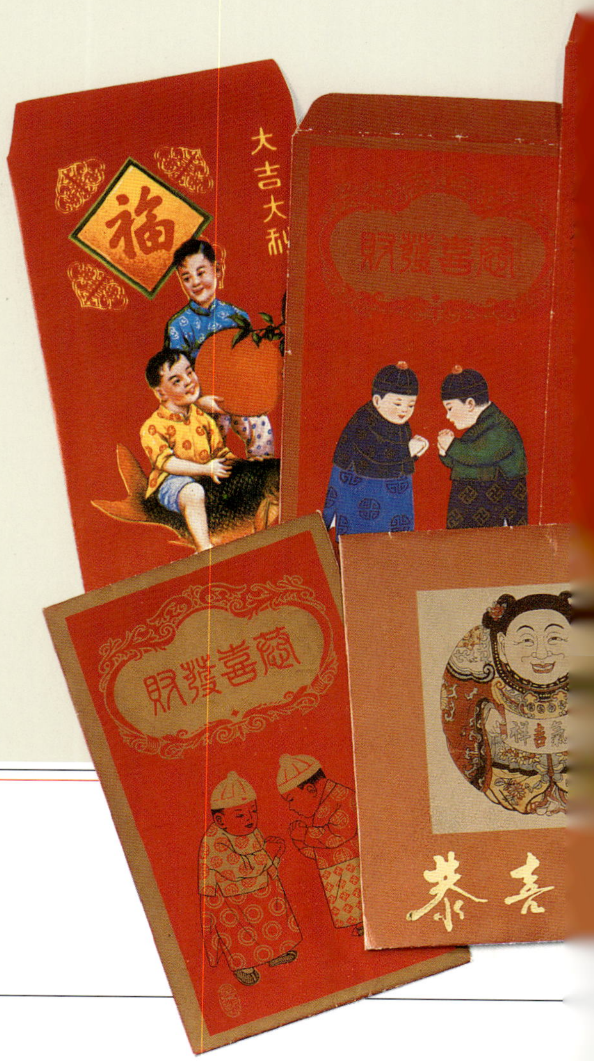

Centre bottom **Red packets** for Lunar New Year gifts of money (*yasuiqian*,"money to hold down the year," or *laisee* in Cantonese).

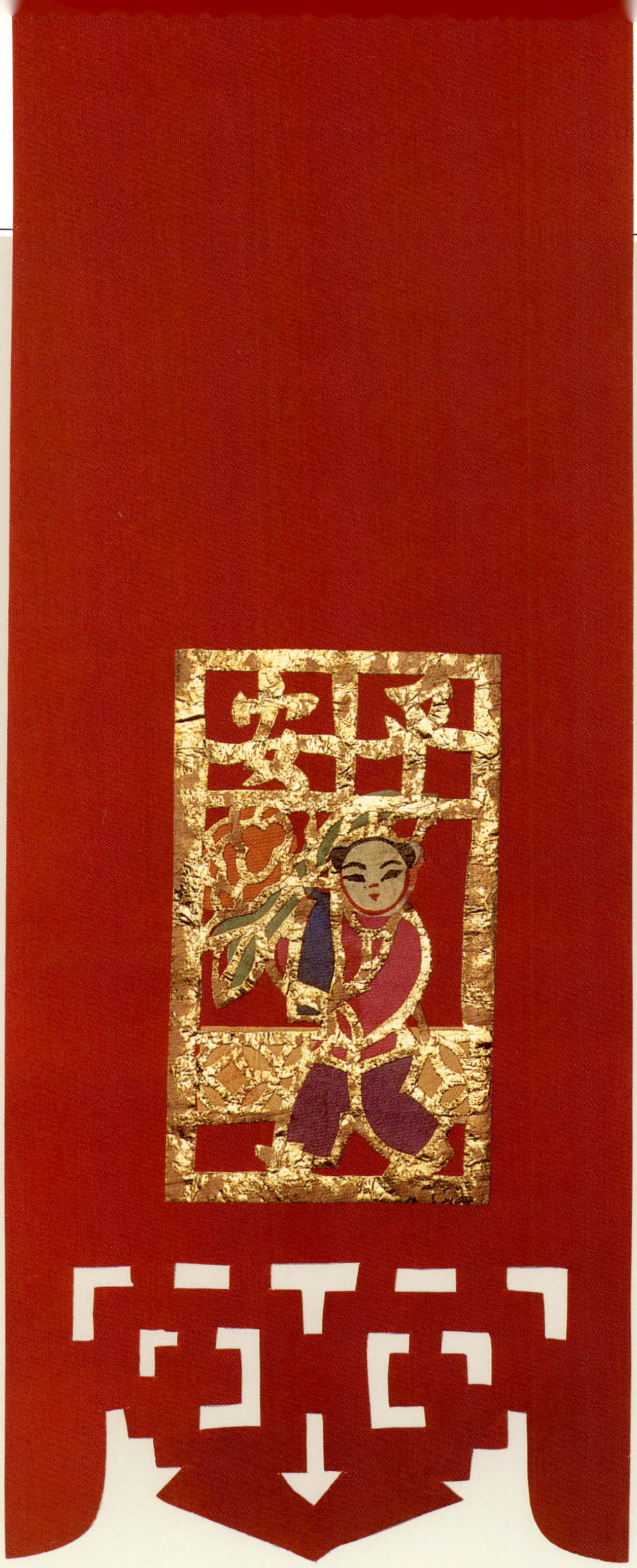

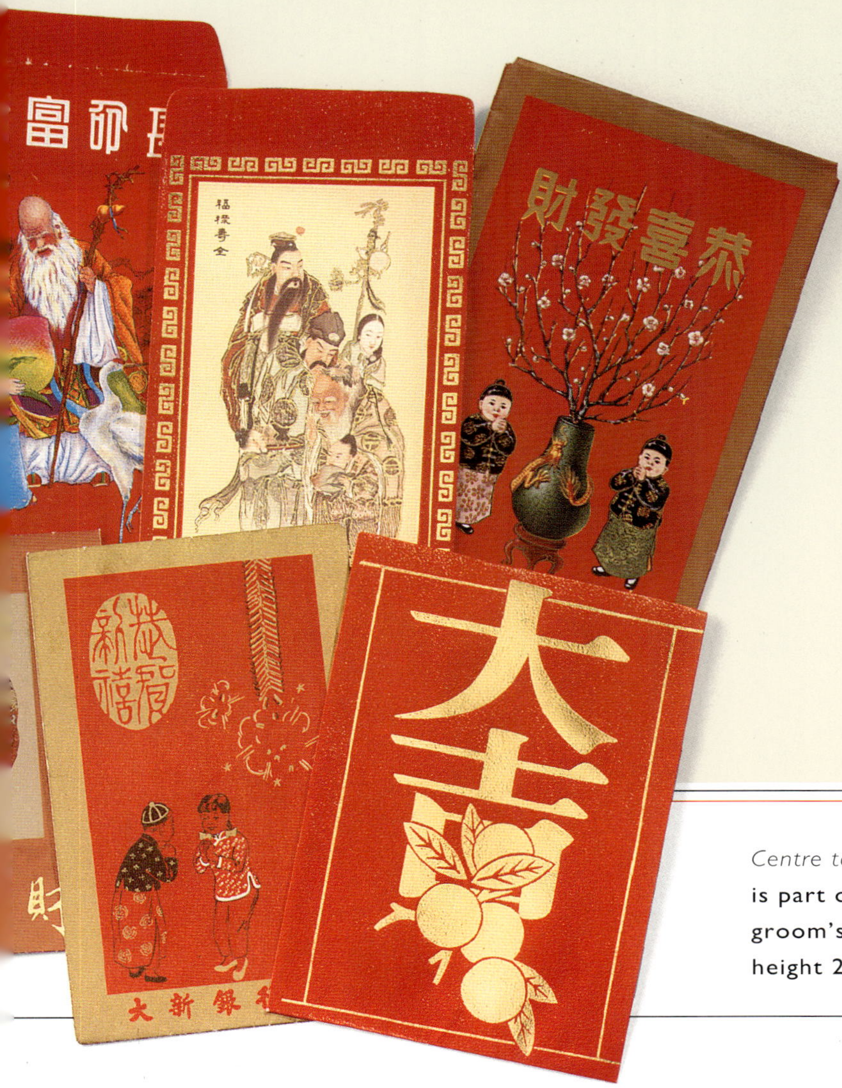

Centre top **Printed with the character for "double happiness",** this is part of a blank wedding invitation on which to inscribe names of groom's and bride's families, and time and place of wedding banquet, height 21 cm.

DAILY ROUND

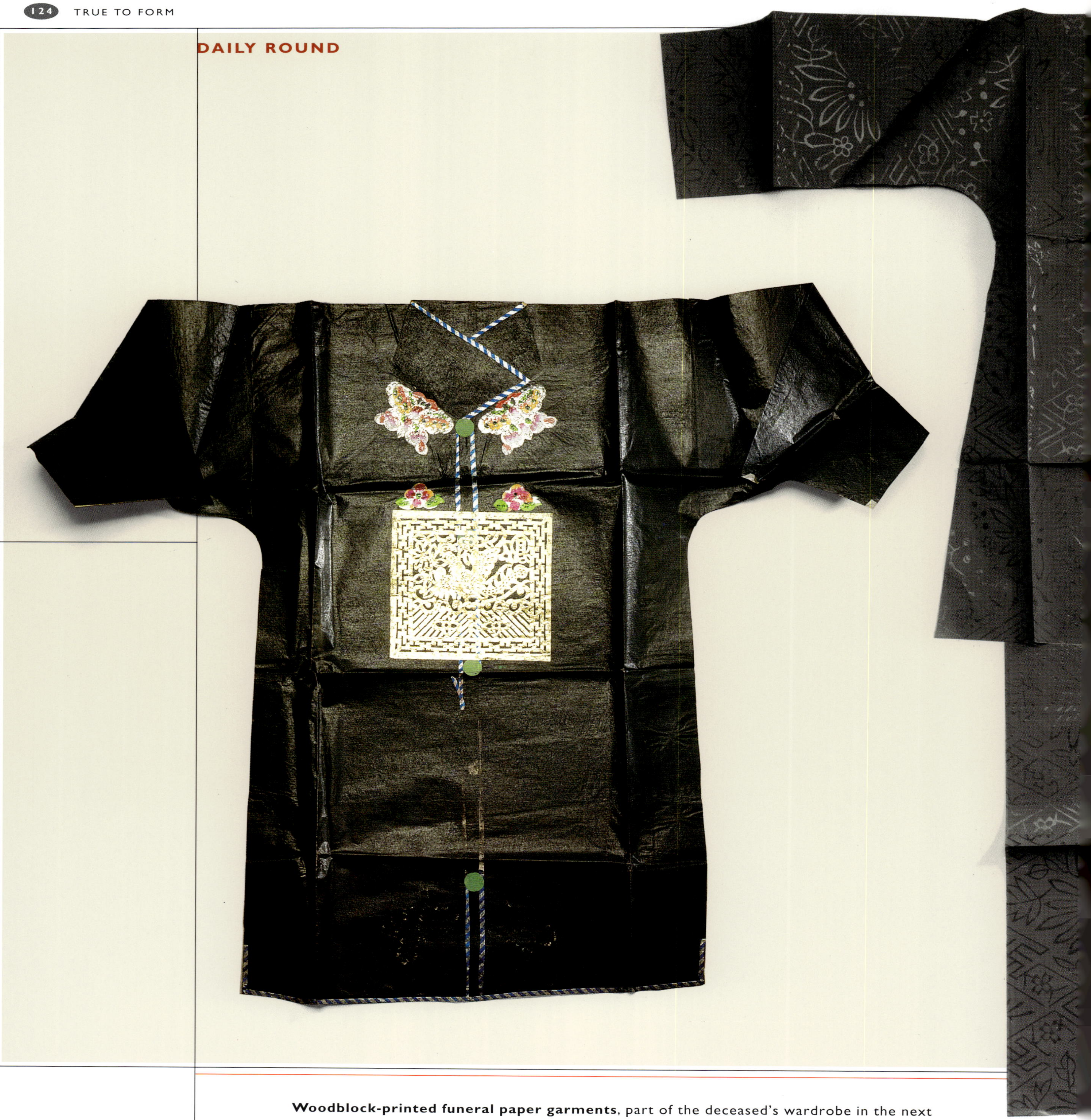

Woodblock-printed funeral paper garments, part of the deceased's wardrobe in the next life, full-length, the left embellished with rank badge (mandarin square) signifying official status.

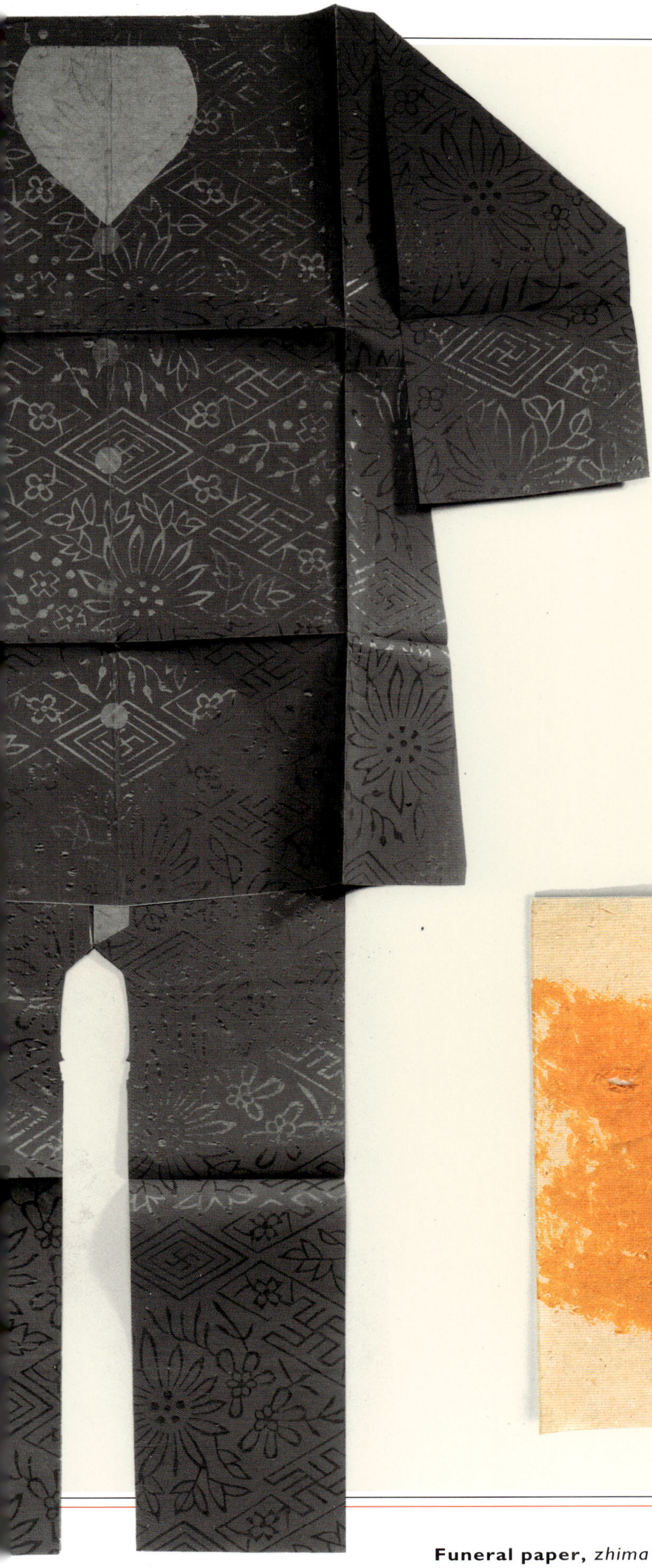

Funeral paper, *zhima* in Chinese, for folding into ingots and throwing into sea during the Tianhou (the Queen of Heaven, the seafarers' goddess) Festival, 11 cm square.

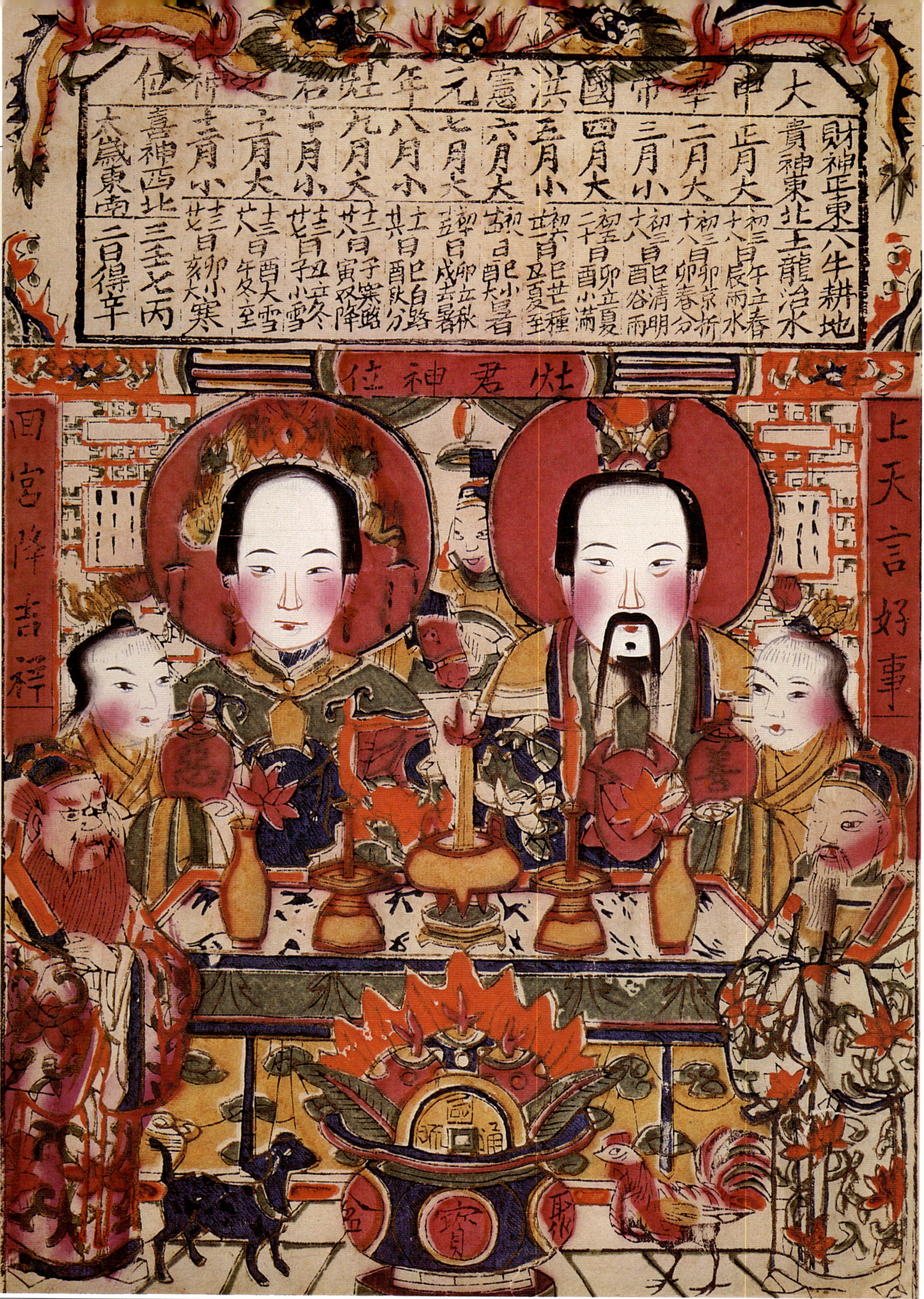

Woodcut print, dated 1916, of almanac and Kitchen God (pictured with his wife and sons), who is propitiated in the last month of the lunar year with sacrifices of sweetmeats and spirit money so that when he ascends to heaven, he will report only the good goings-on in the households where his image is hung. The picture is burnt and a new one pasted up after the new year, height 40 cm.

五 TOOLS OF THE TRADE

TOOLS OF THE TRADE

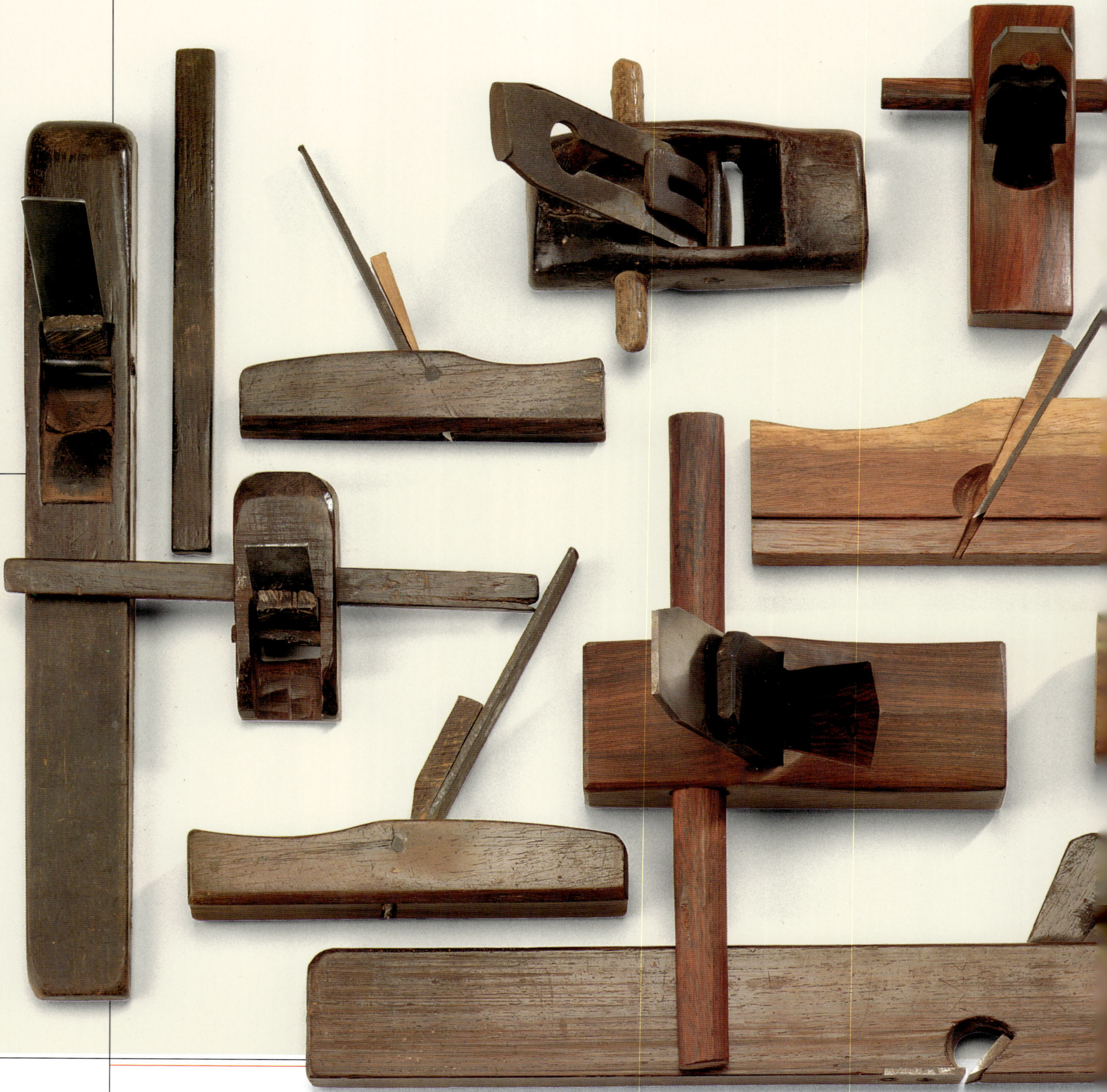

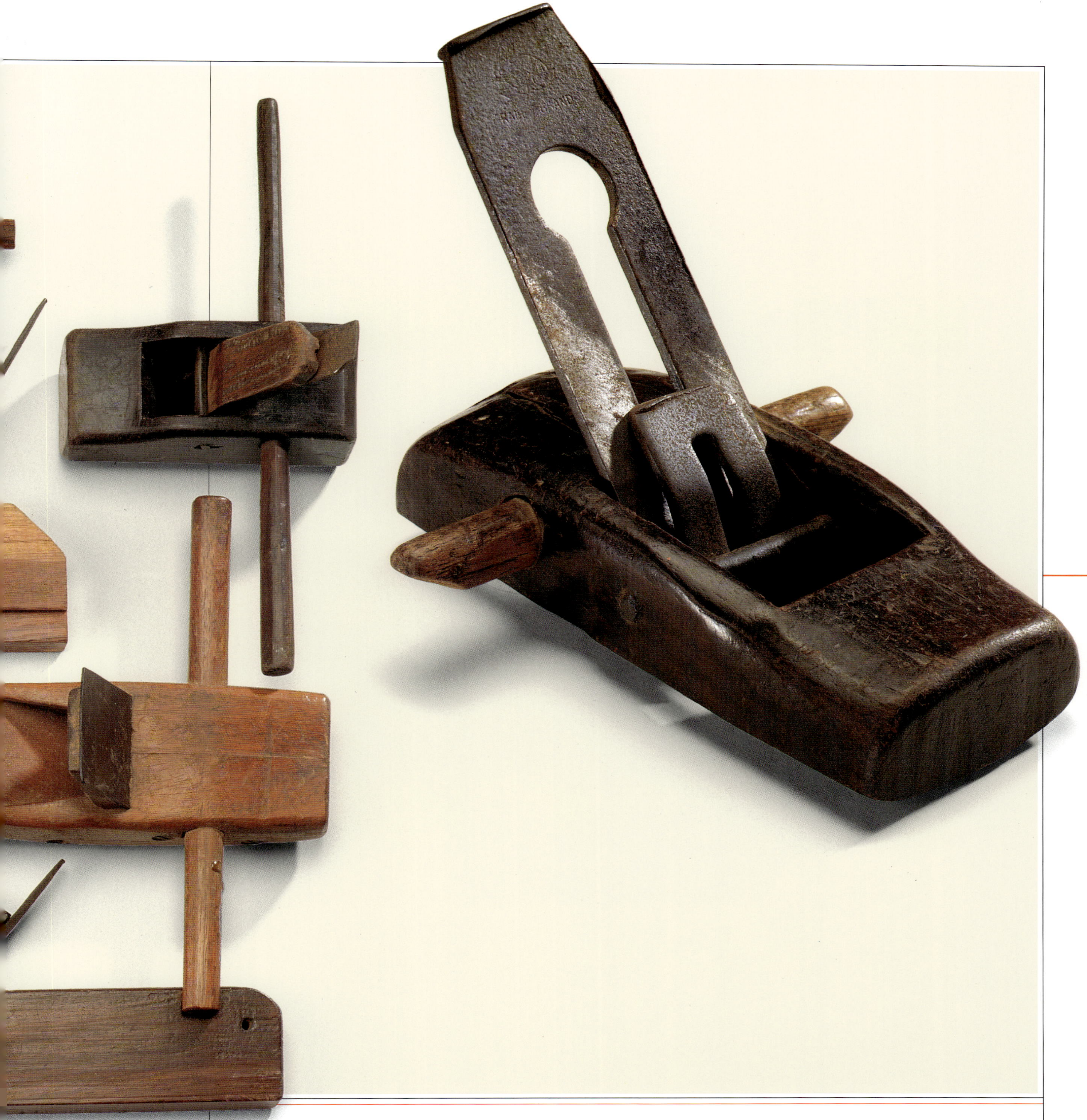

Carpenter's planes for all-round work with cross-handles slotted into a groove behind the plane, and rabbet-planes *(bottom left)*. Chinese carpenter planes are pushed away from the body and held by the handle if they have any, or else with one hand at one end and the other near the opposite end.

TOOLS OF THE TRADE

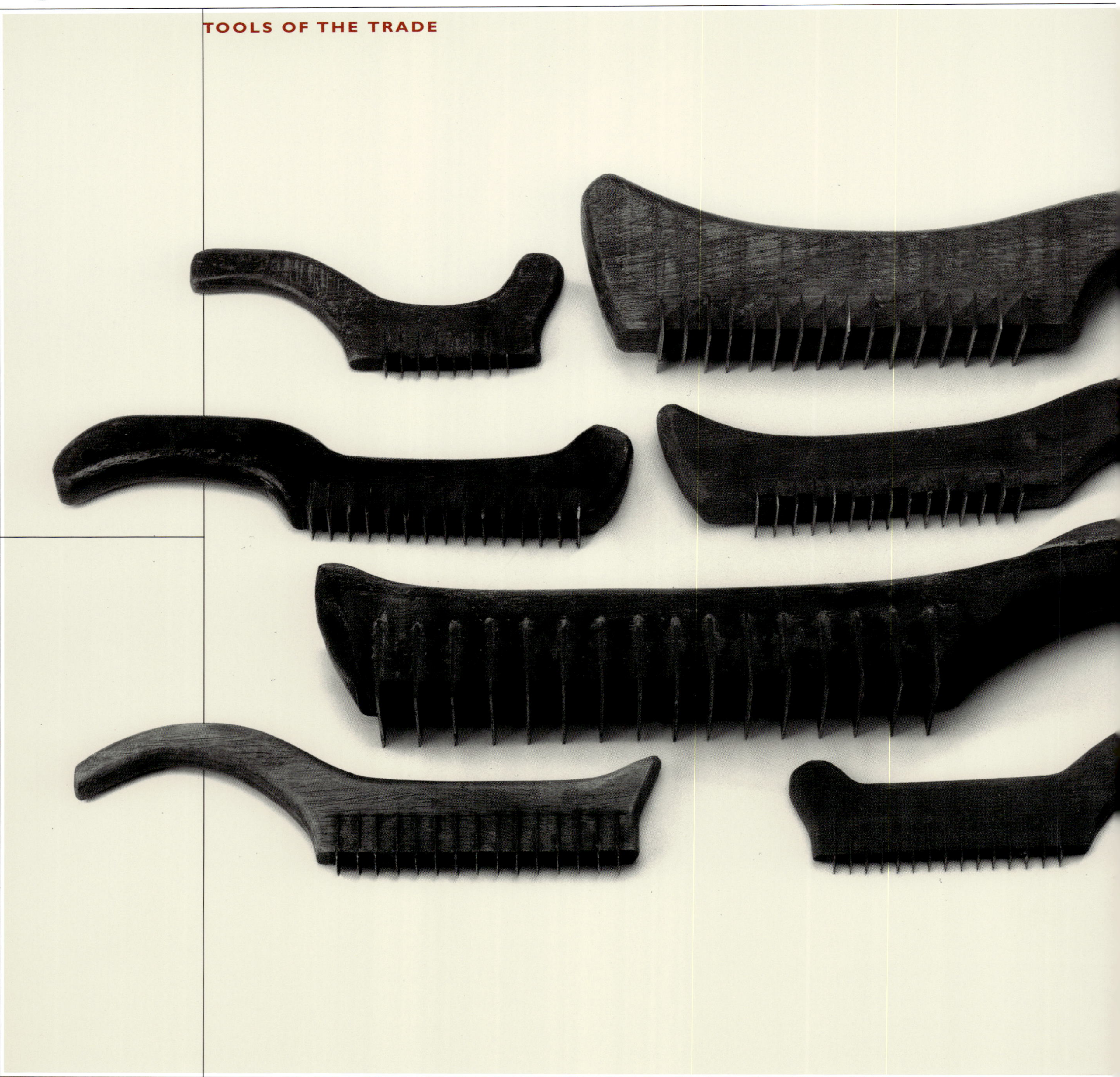

Top **Carpenter's wood scrapers,** fine- or coarse-toothed according to requirements.
Right **Carpenter's chisels, rasps and gouge**.

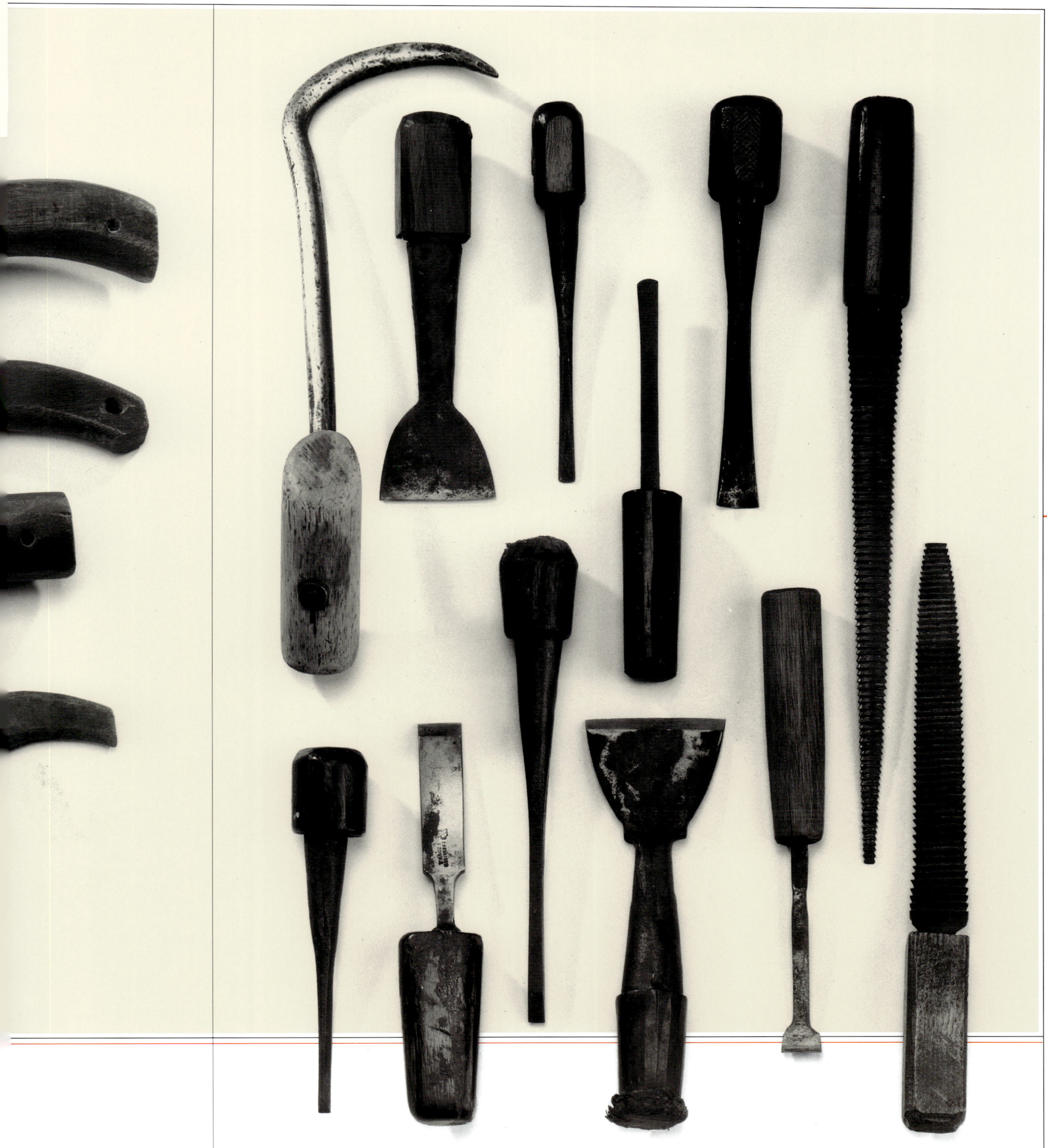

TOOLS OF THE TRADE

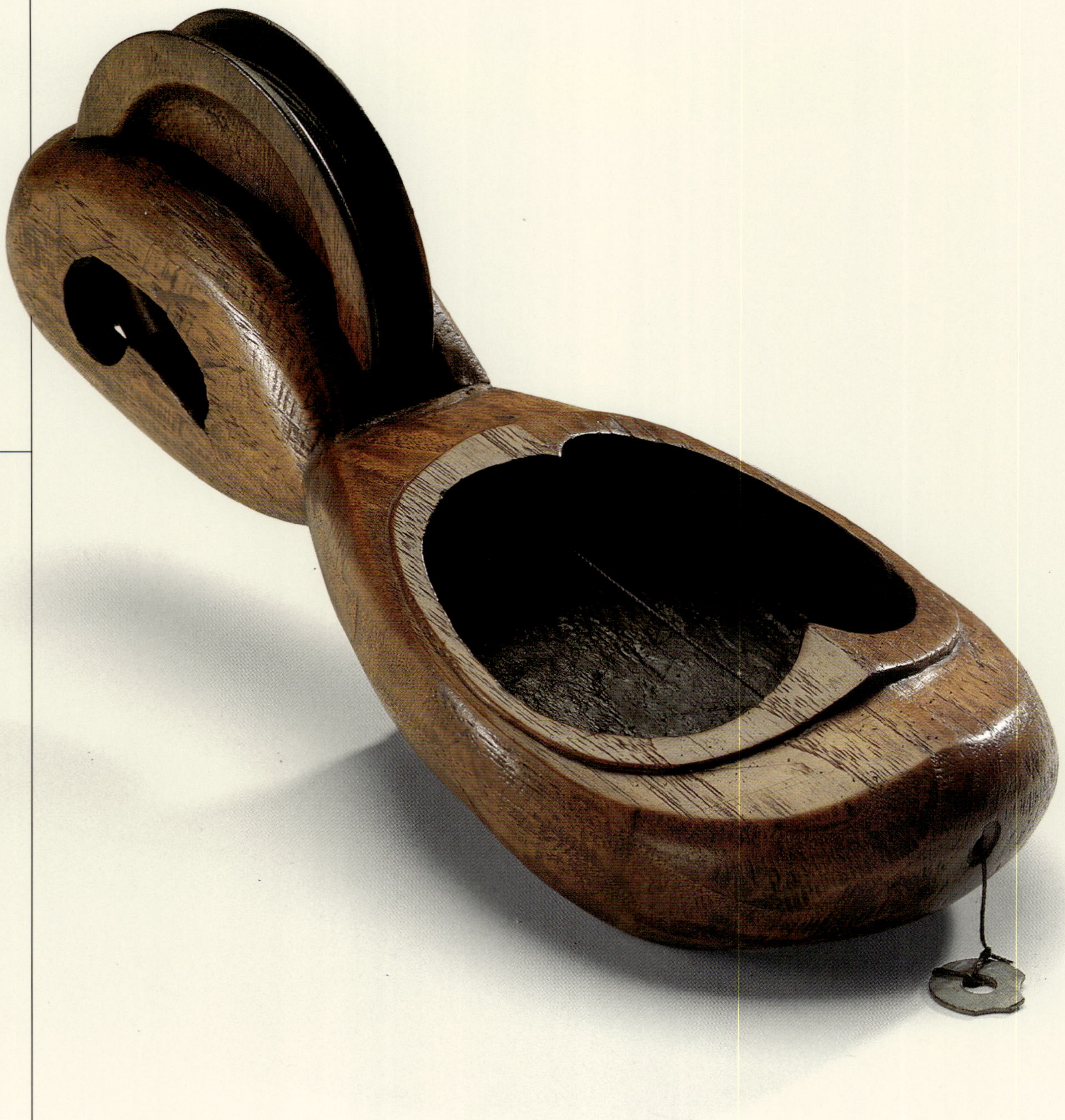

Carpenter's line marker with inkwell, handle and string. The string is run out through the inkwell and stretched taut over the place to be marked. Then it is picked up with thumb and forefinger and let go, snapping a black line along its path, length 22 cm.

Ship's fender in rattan,
height 60 cm.

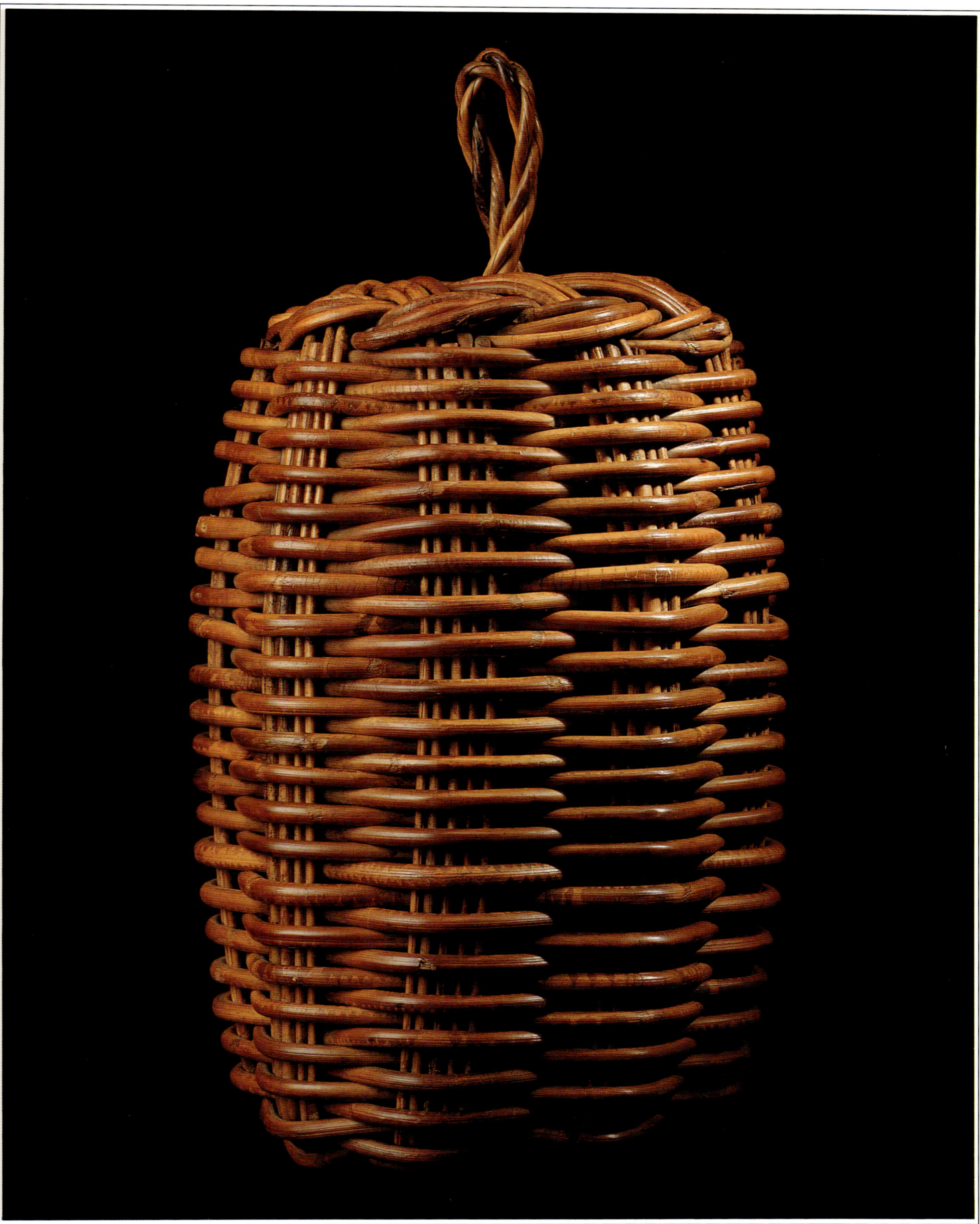

TOOLS OF THE TRADE

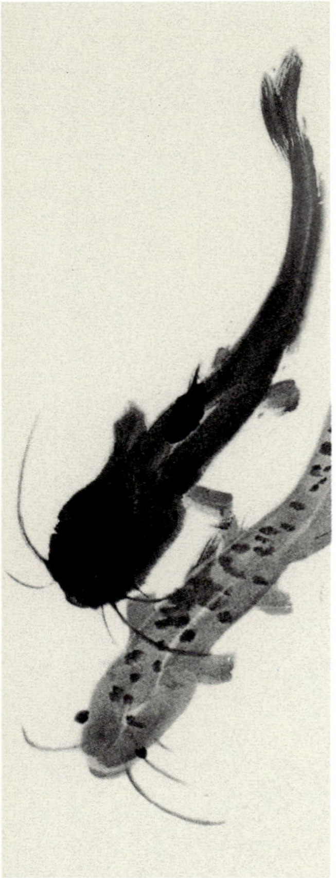

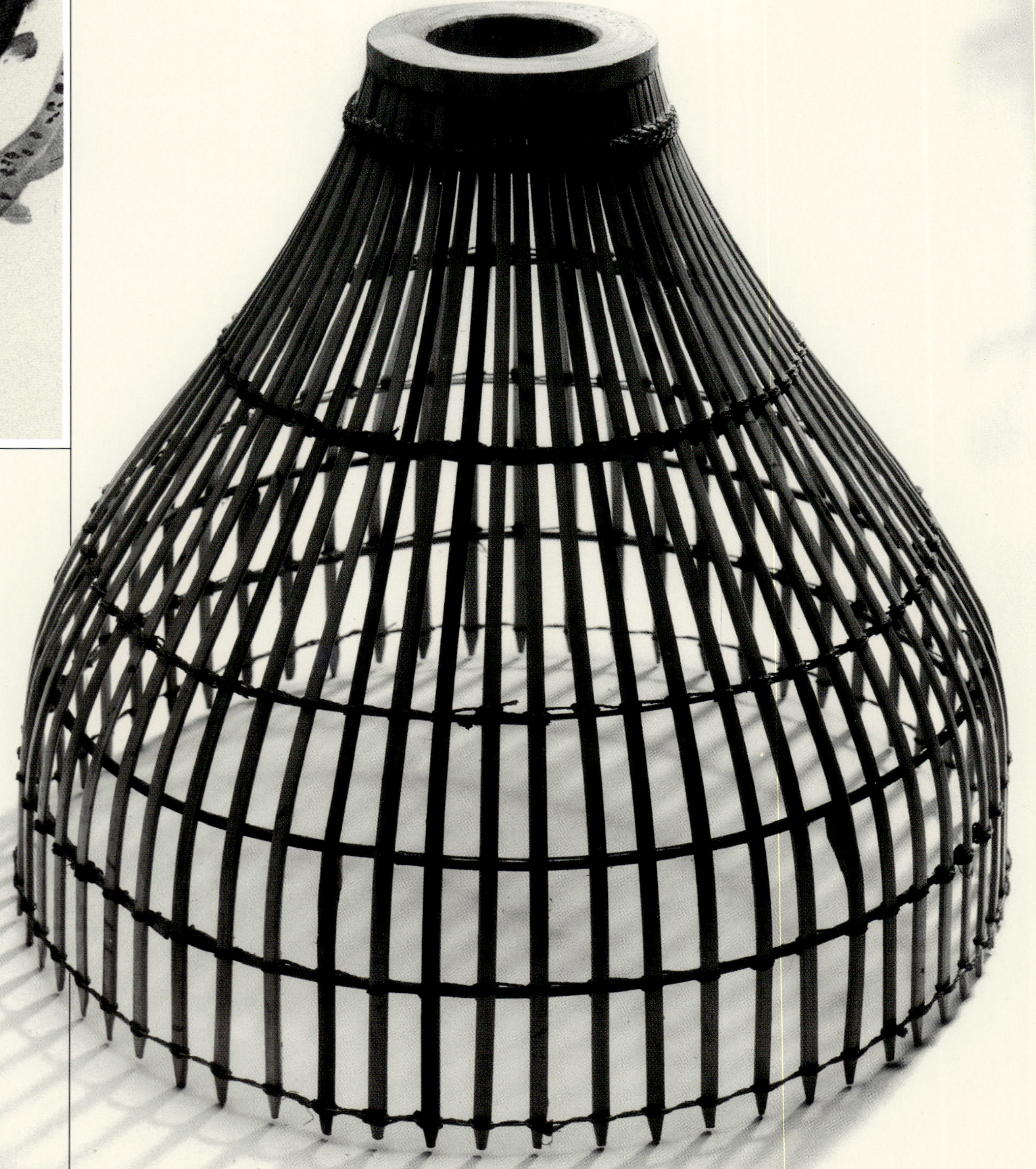

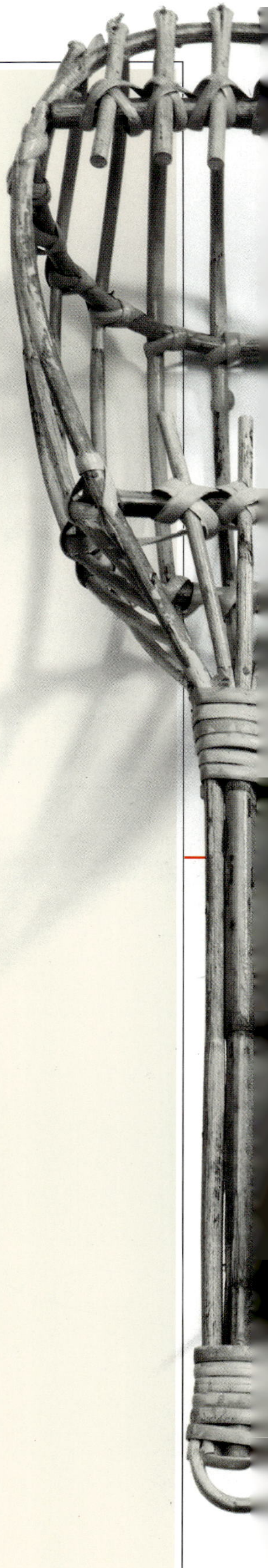

Wicker hood of bamboo splints for stabbing into swamp lands or rice fields with top opening through which fisherman's hand reaches to remove trapped fish, height 35 cm.

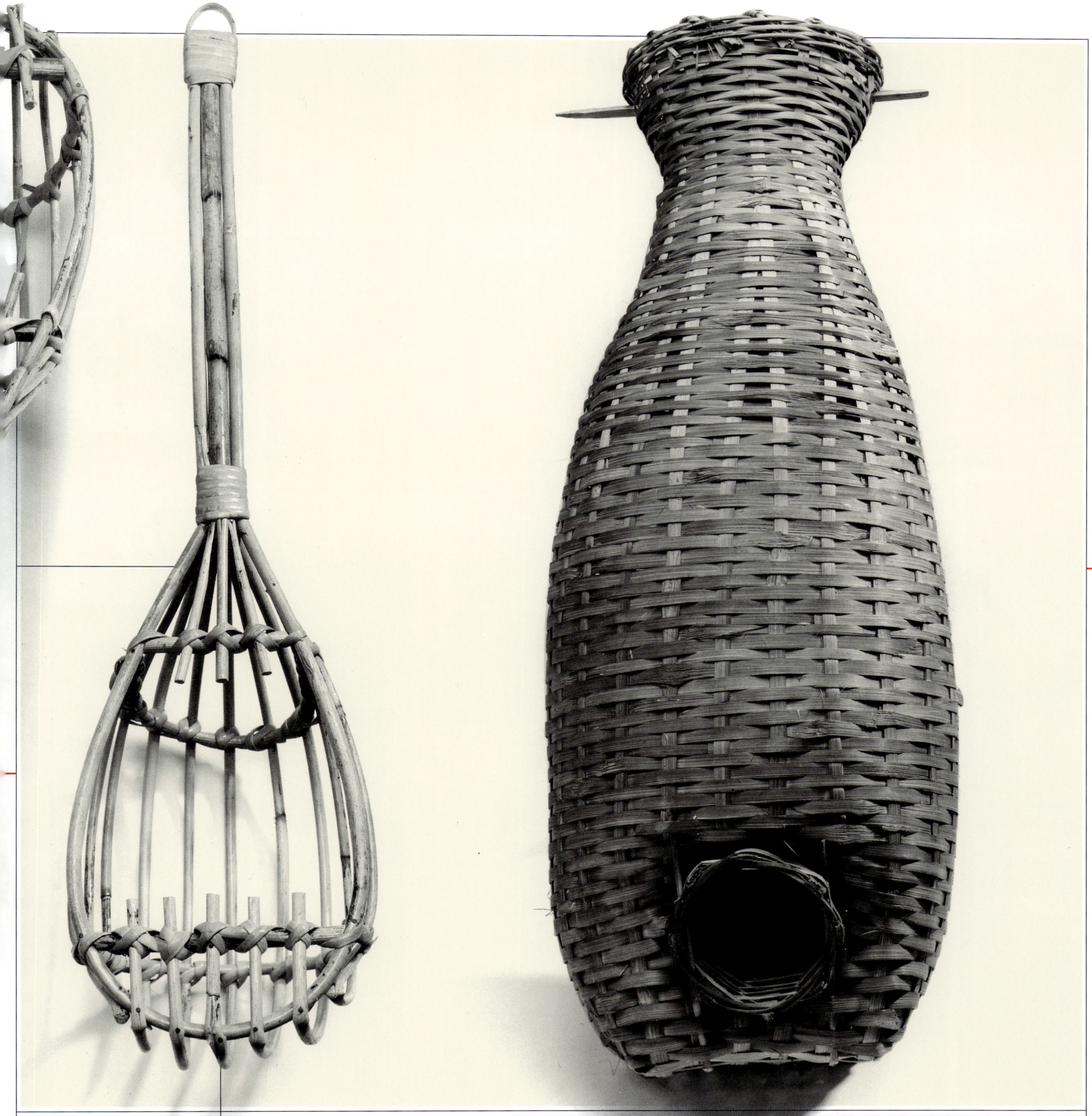

Left **Fish scoops of willow**. *Right* **Bamboo shellfish trap** from Canton with opening to a narrowing tunnel with spokes inside to prevent fish from escaping. Pulling out the twig at the other end releases the catch, length 50 cm.

TOOLS OF THE TRADE

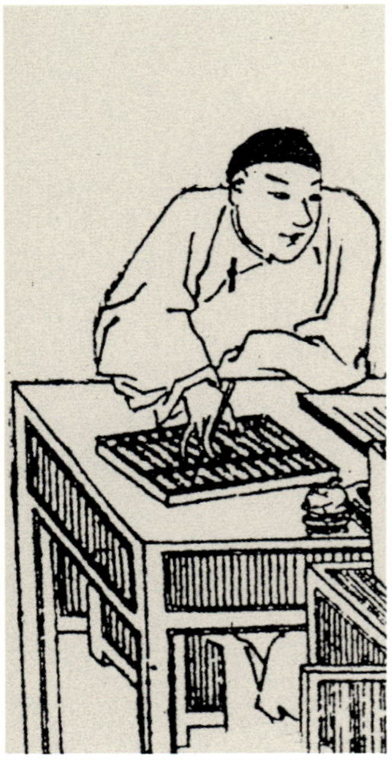

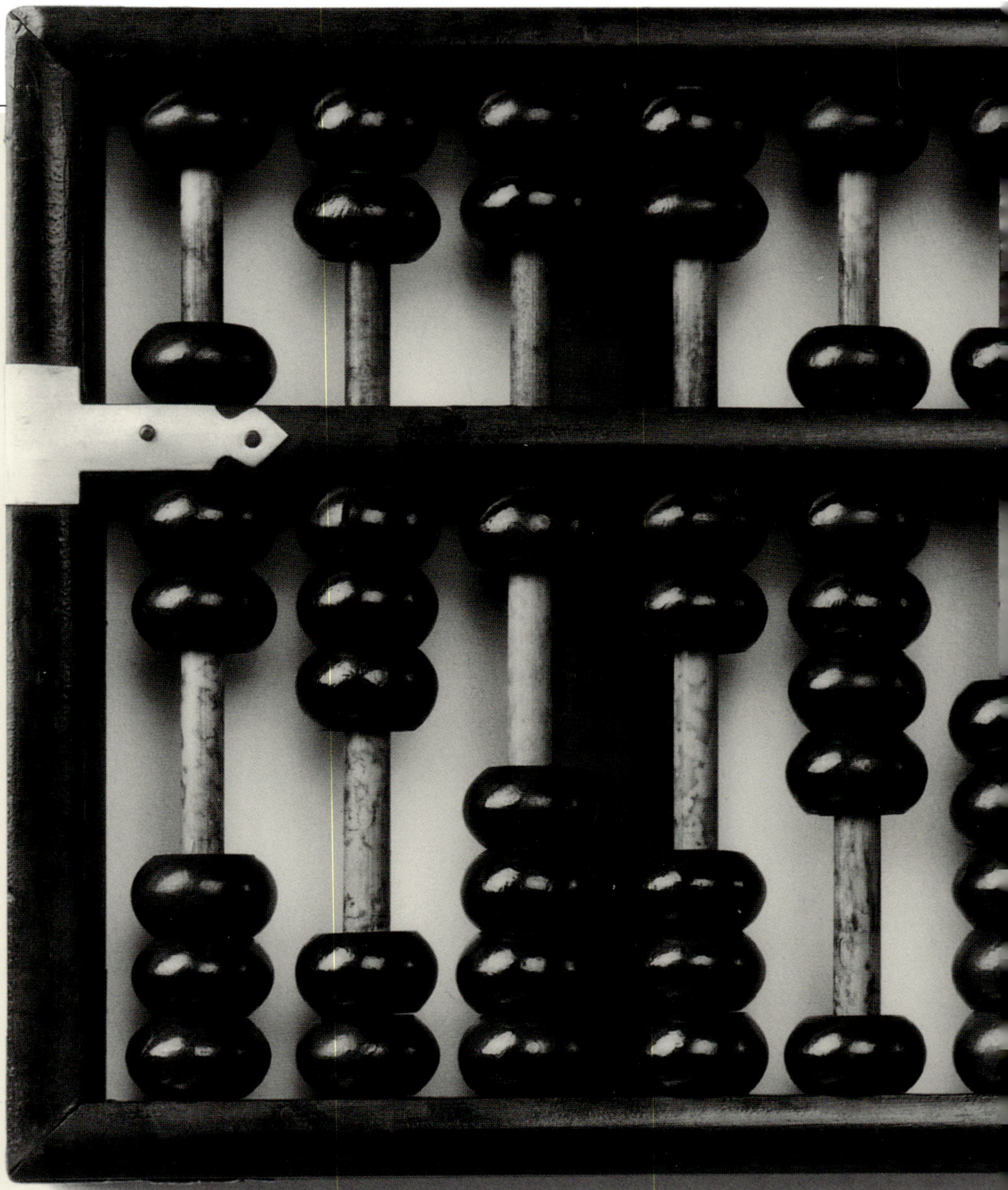

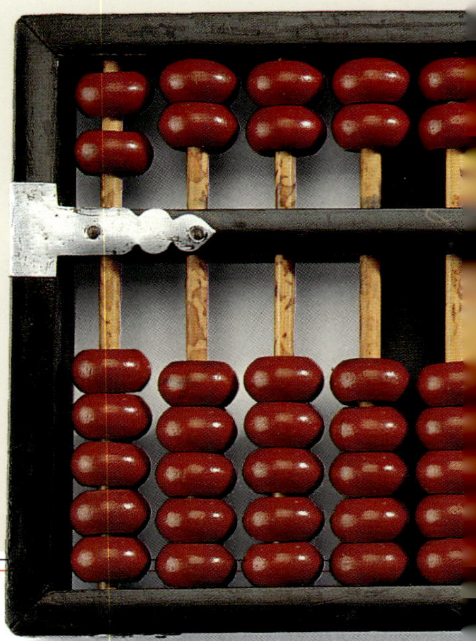

Wooden abacus
Top Taken separately, the beads are set to read, from right to left, 9, 8, 4, 5, 2, 3, 6, 5, 9, 2, 1, 3, 7, length 40 cm.

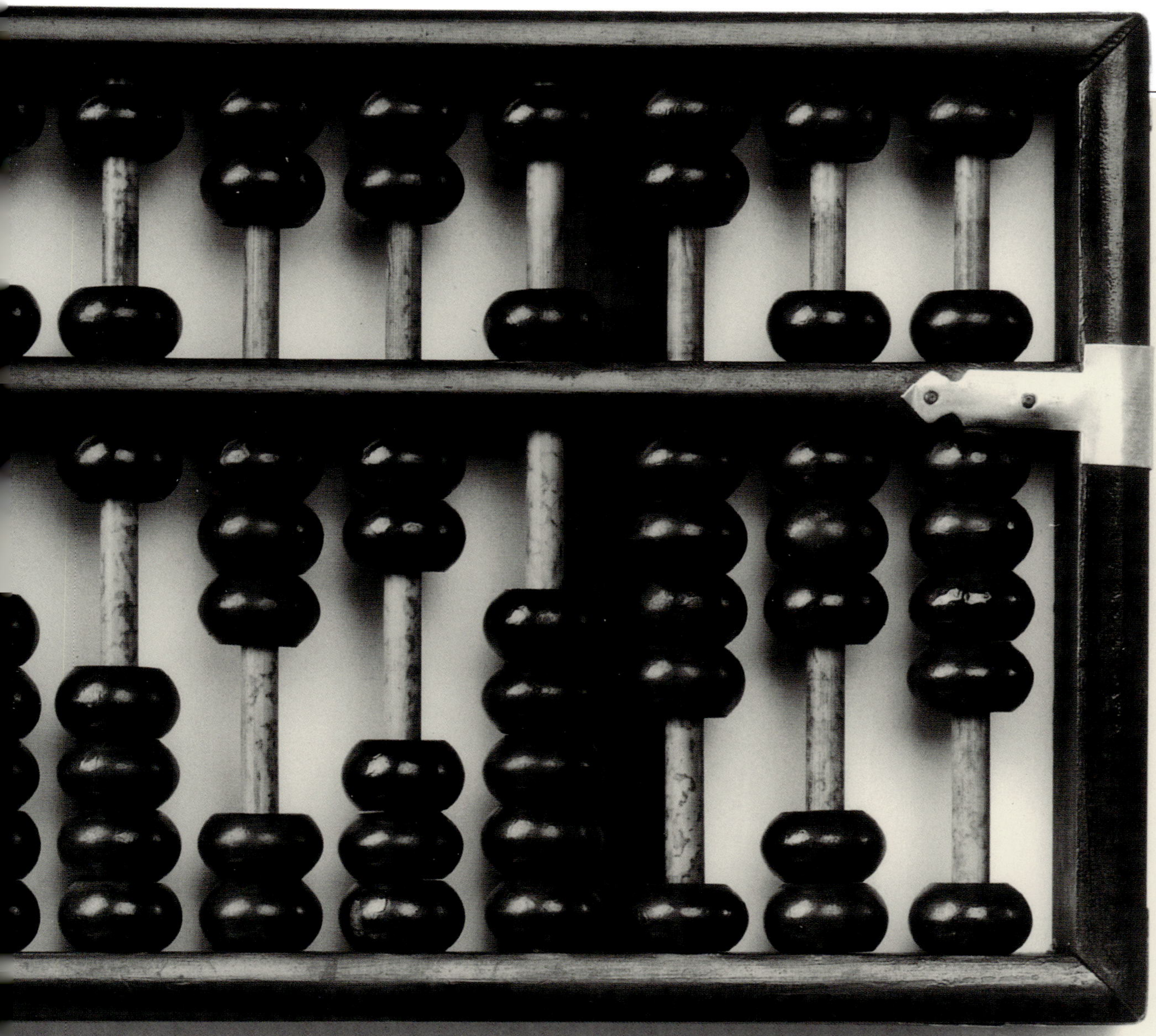

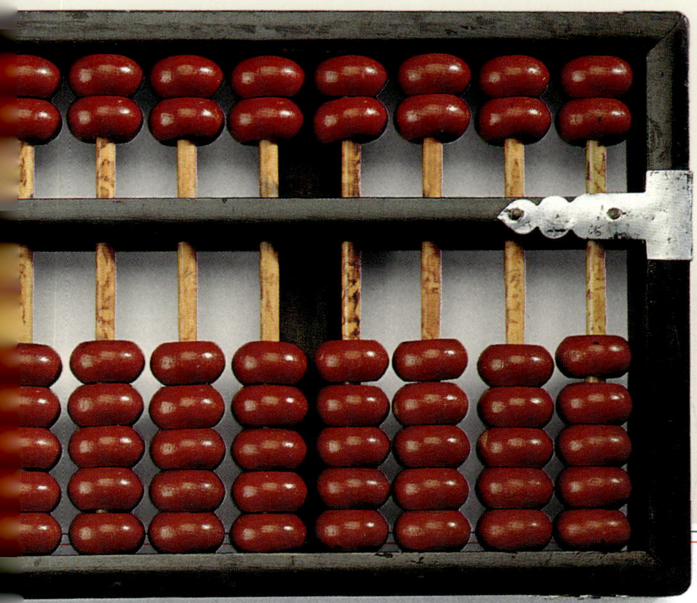

TOOLS OF THE TRADE

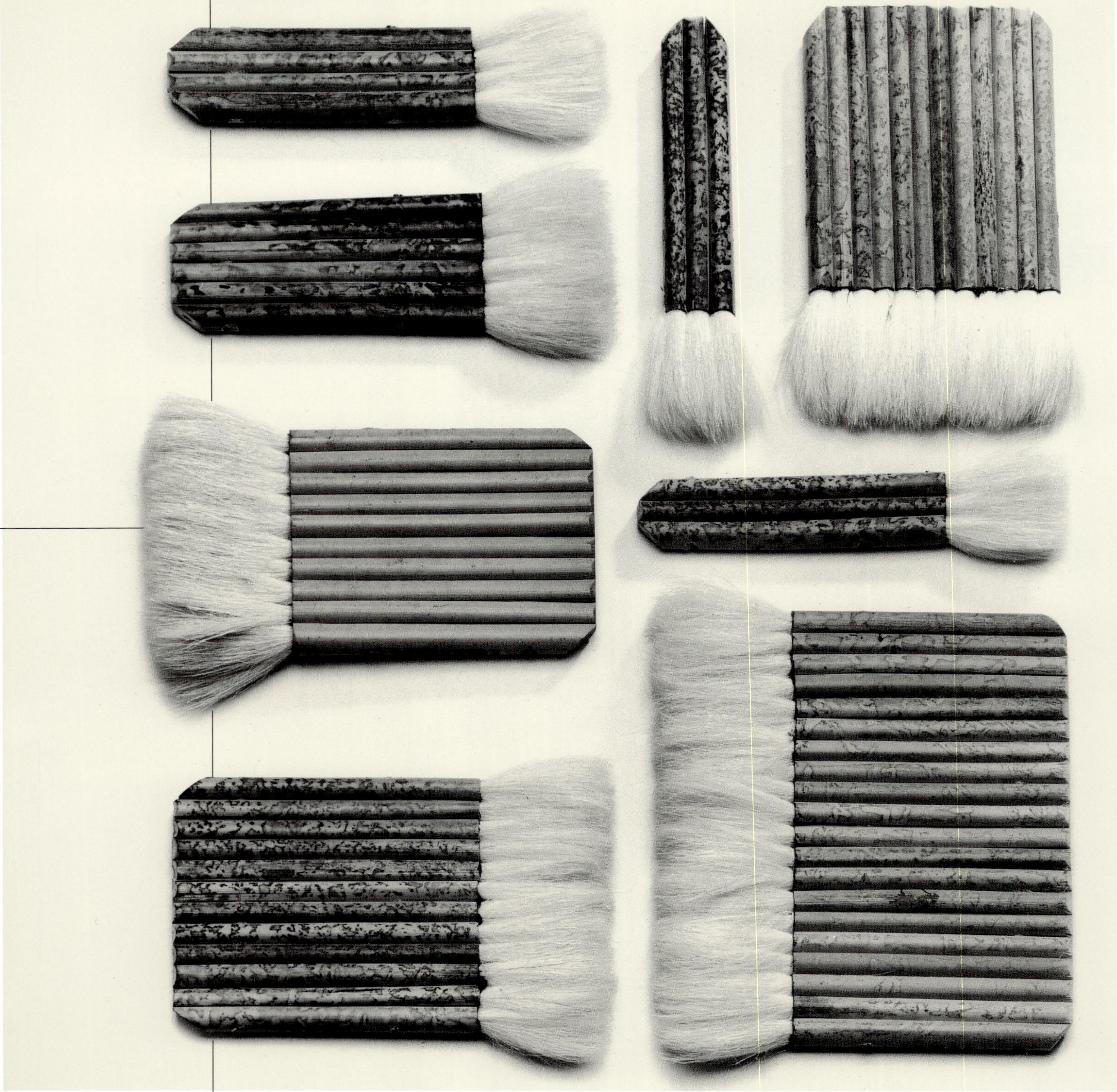

Bamboo brushes used in painting and papering walls, for applying glue and in mounting scrolls or pictures.

六 PASTIMES

PASTIMES

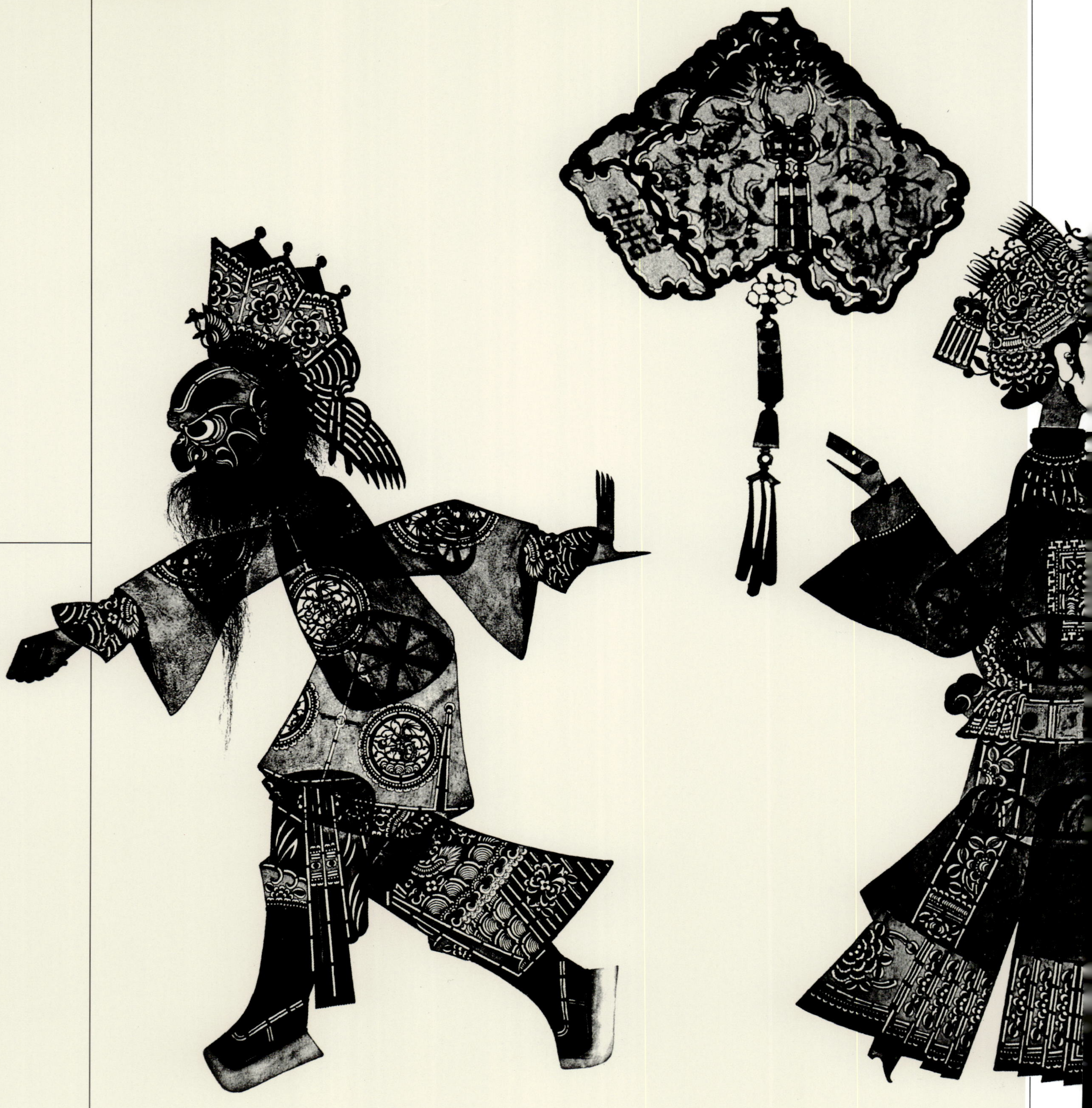

Shadow puppets cut out of leather with articulated joints held together by string or wire. Scenes from ancient legends and historical romances are acted out in front of a lamp and the images projected on a screen, usually a white cloth or sheet of white paper stretched between two bamboo poles.

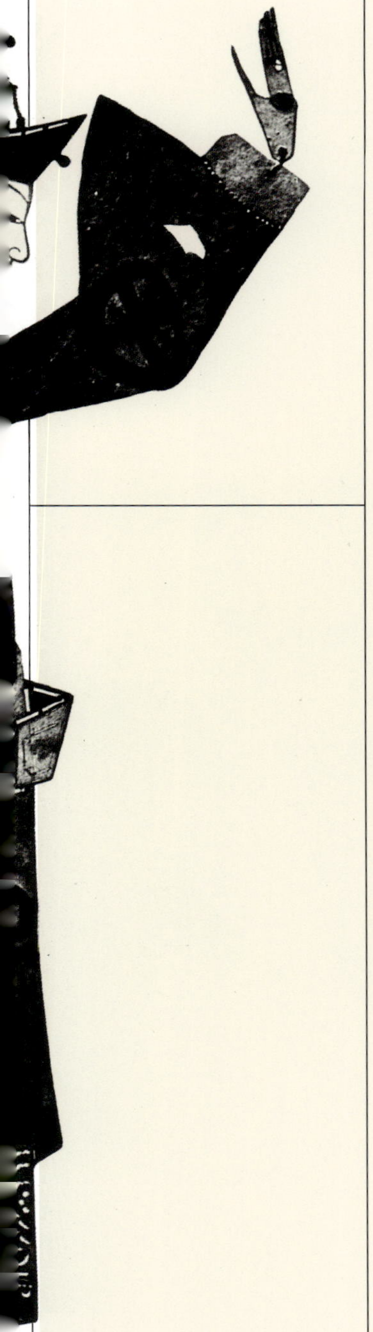

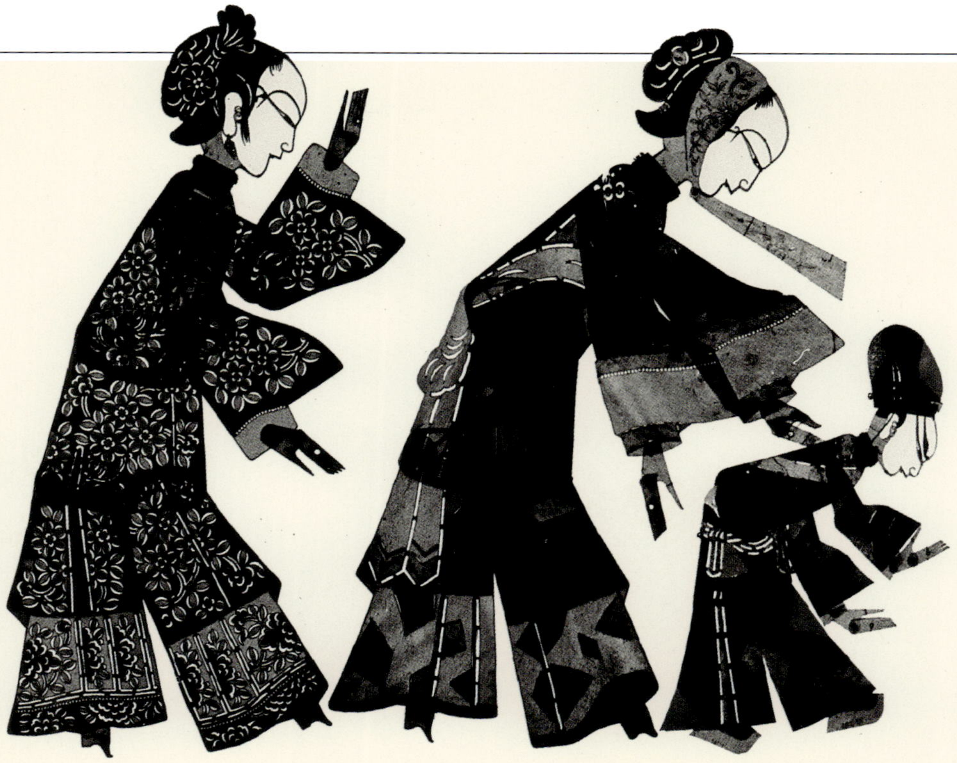

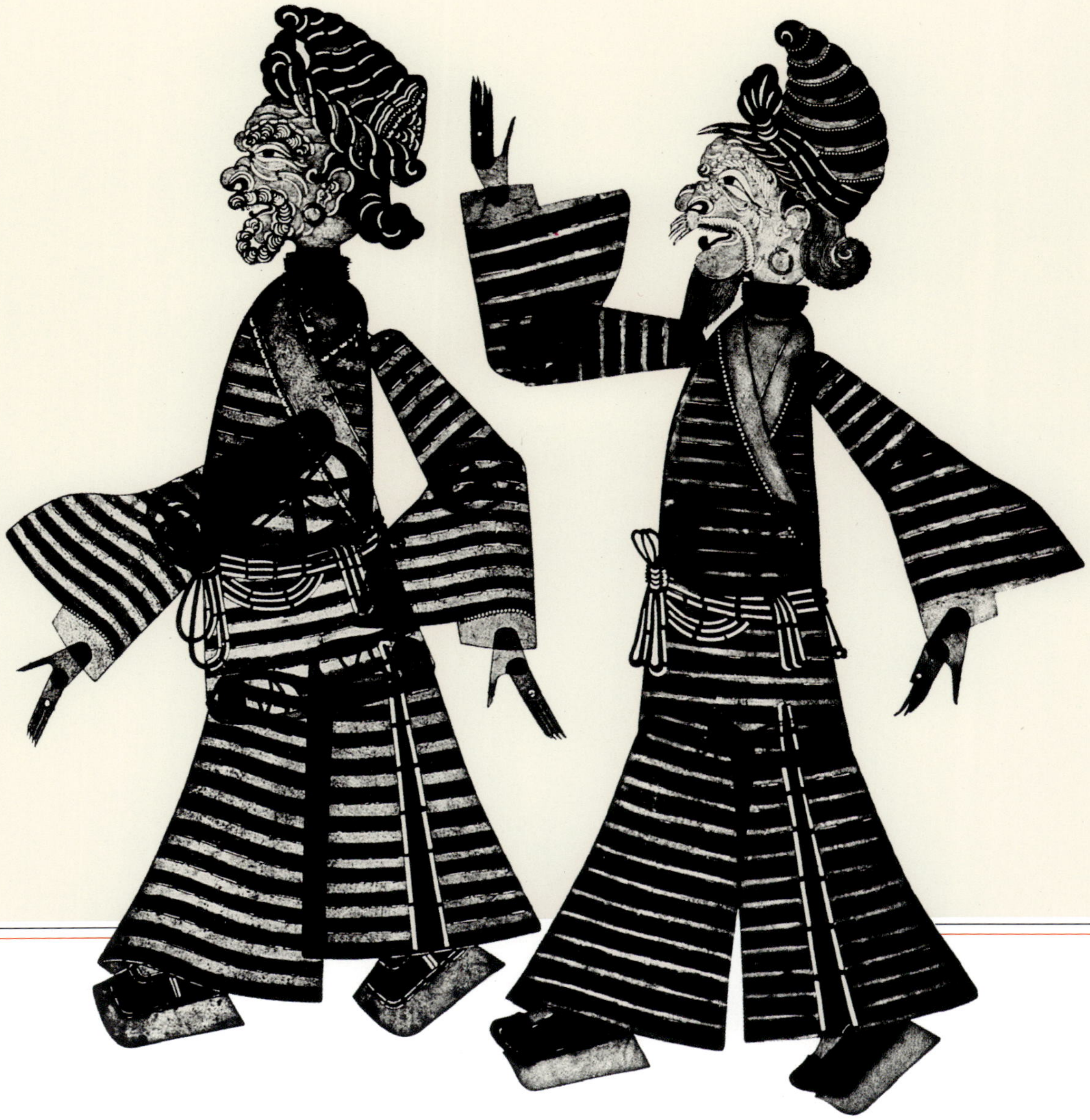

PASTIMES

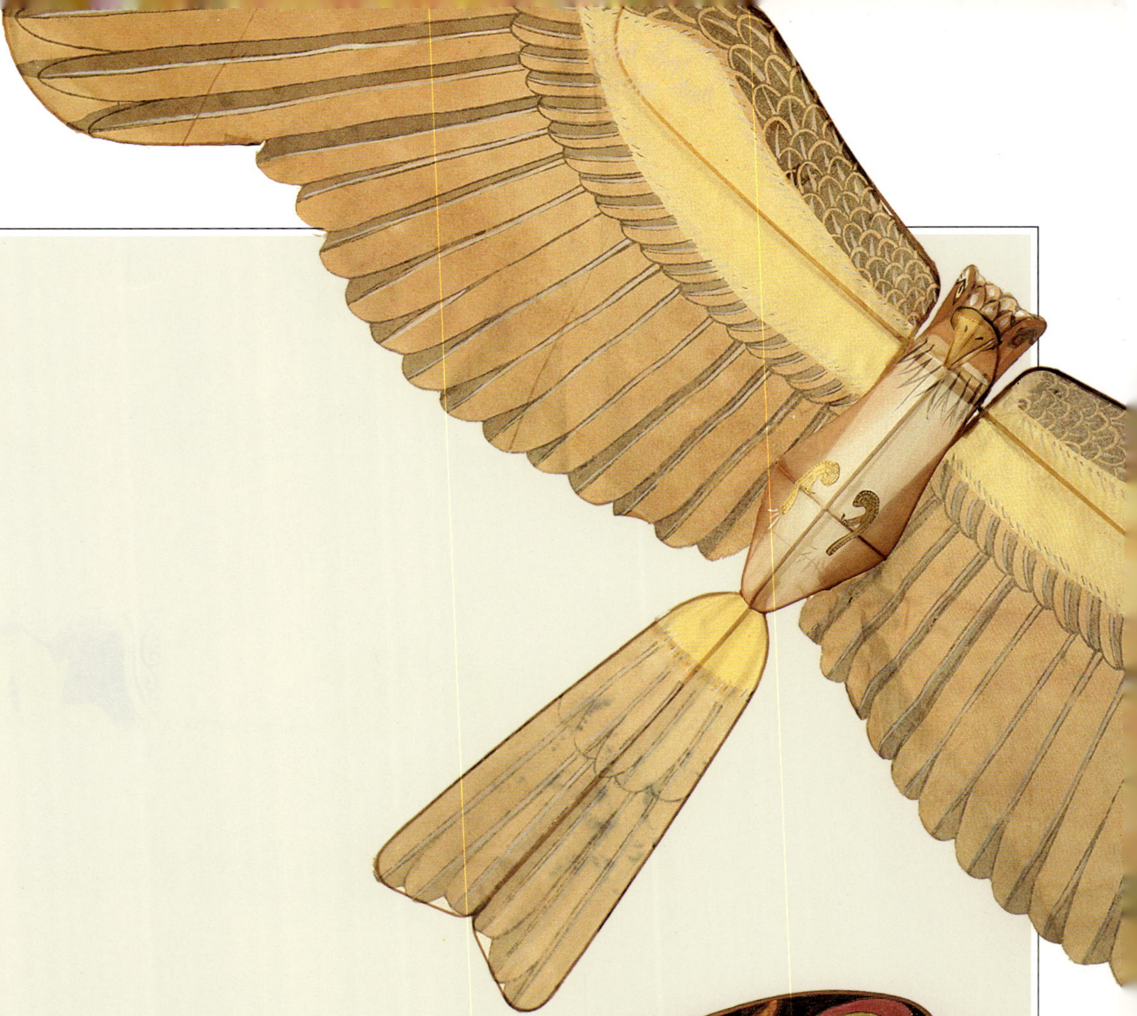

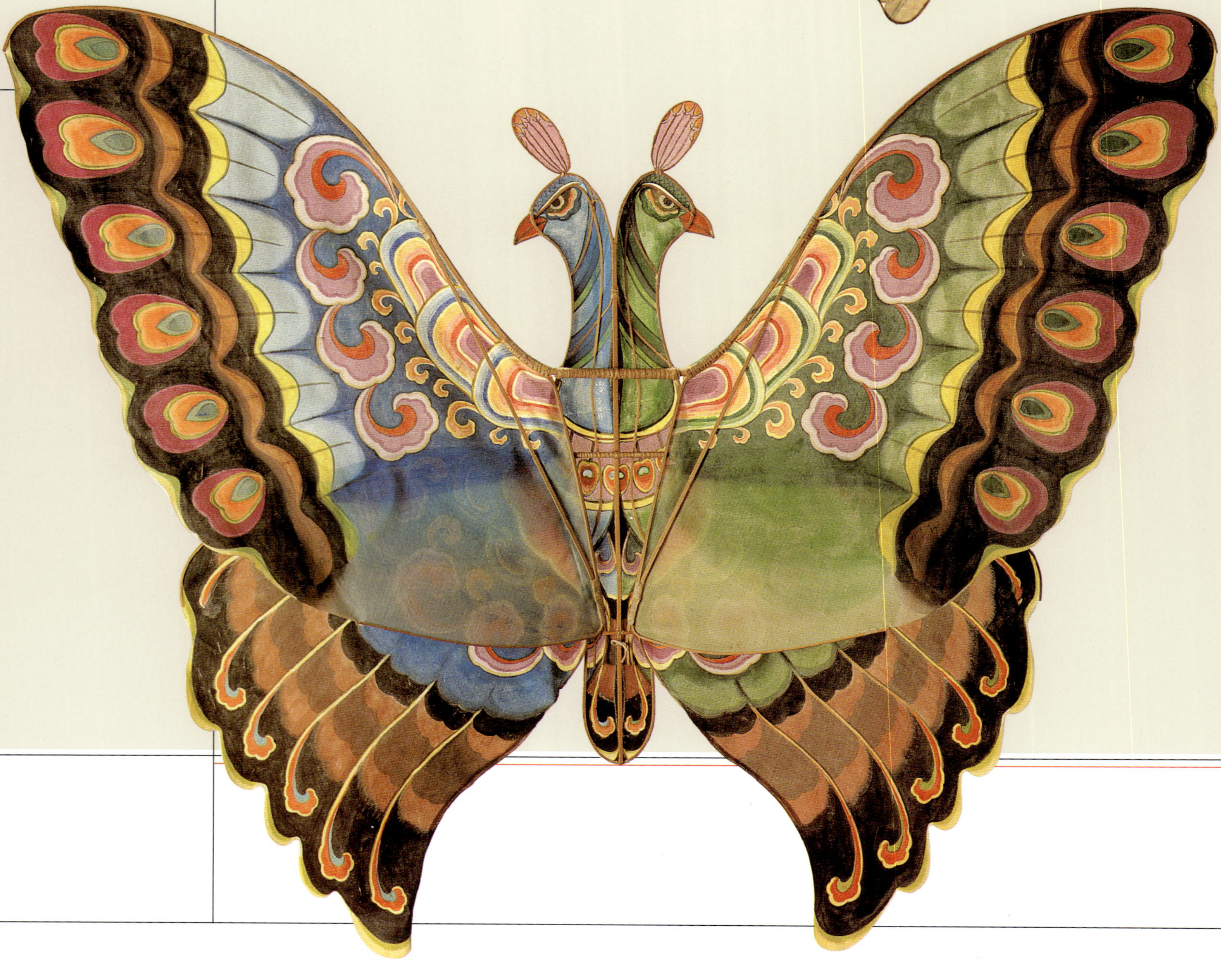

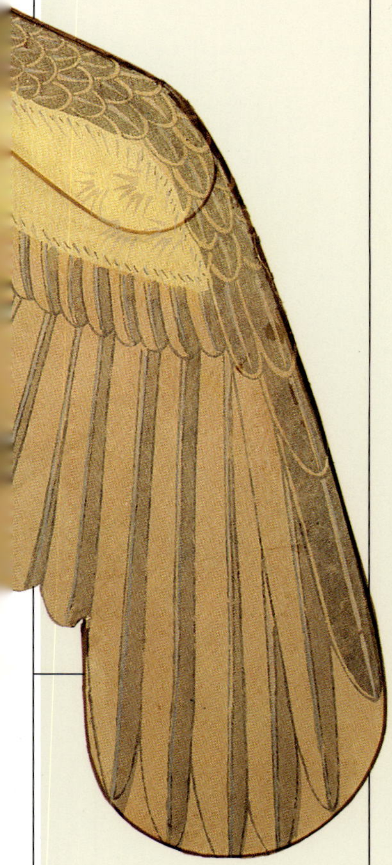

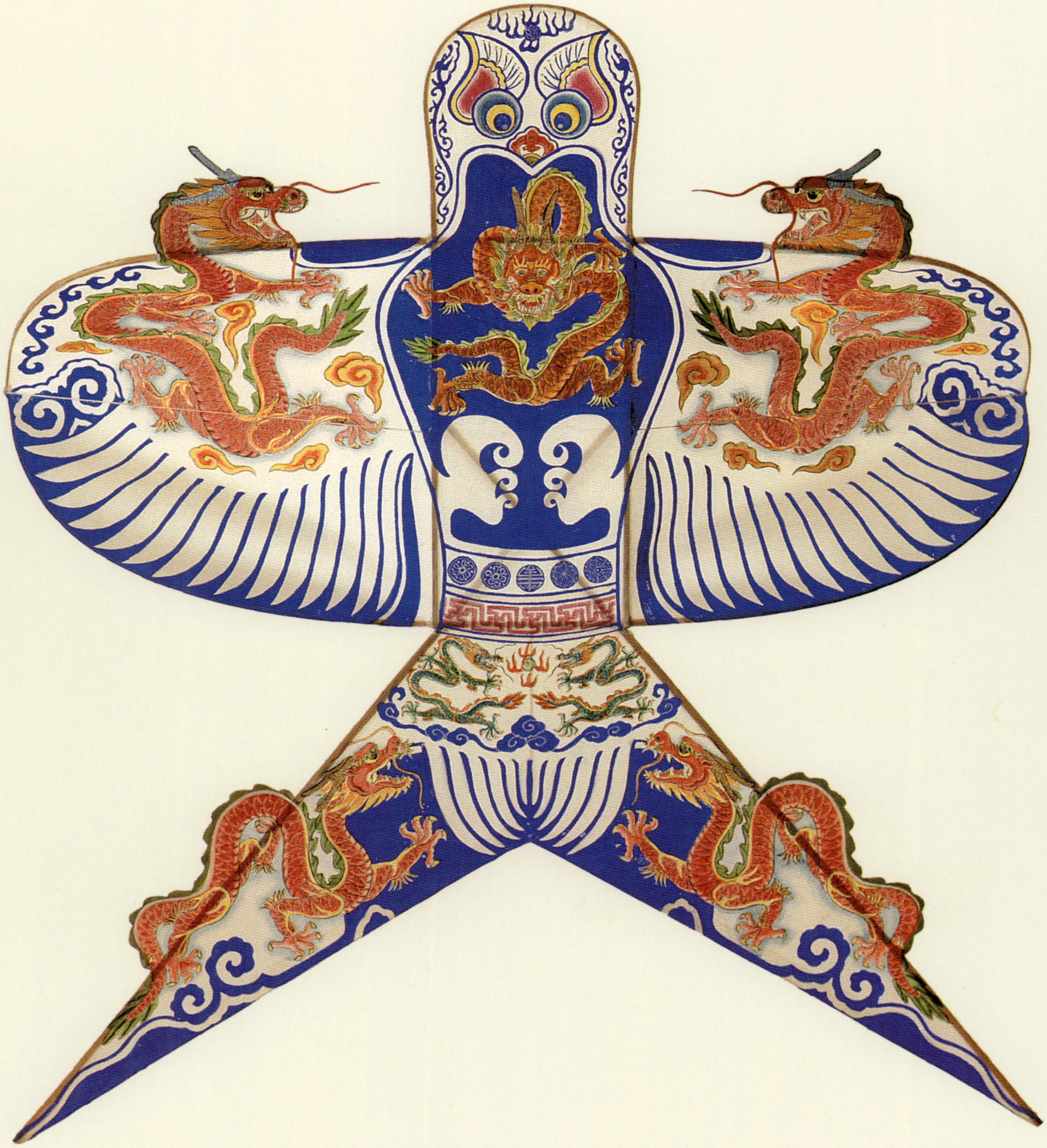

Kites made with bamboo splints and strong paper take numerous shapes of which the sand swallow *(right)* is the most popular and the easiest to fly.

PASTIMES

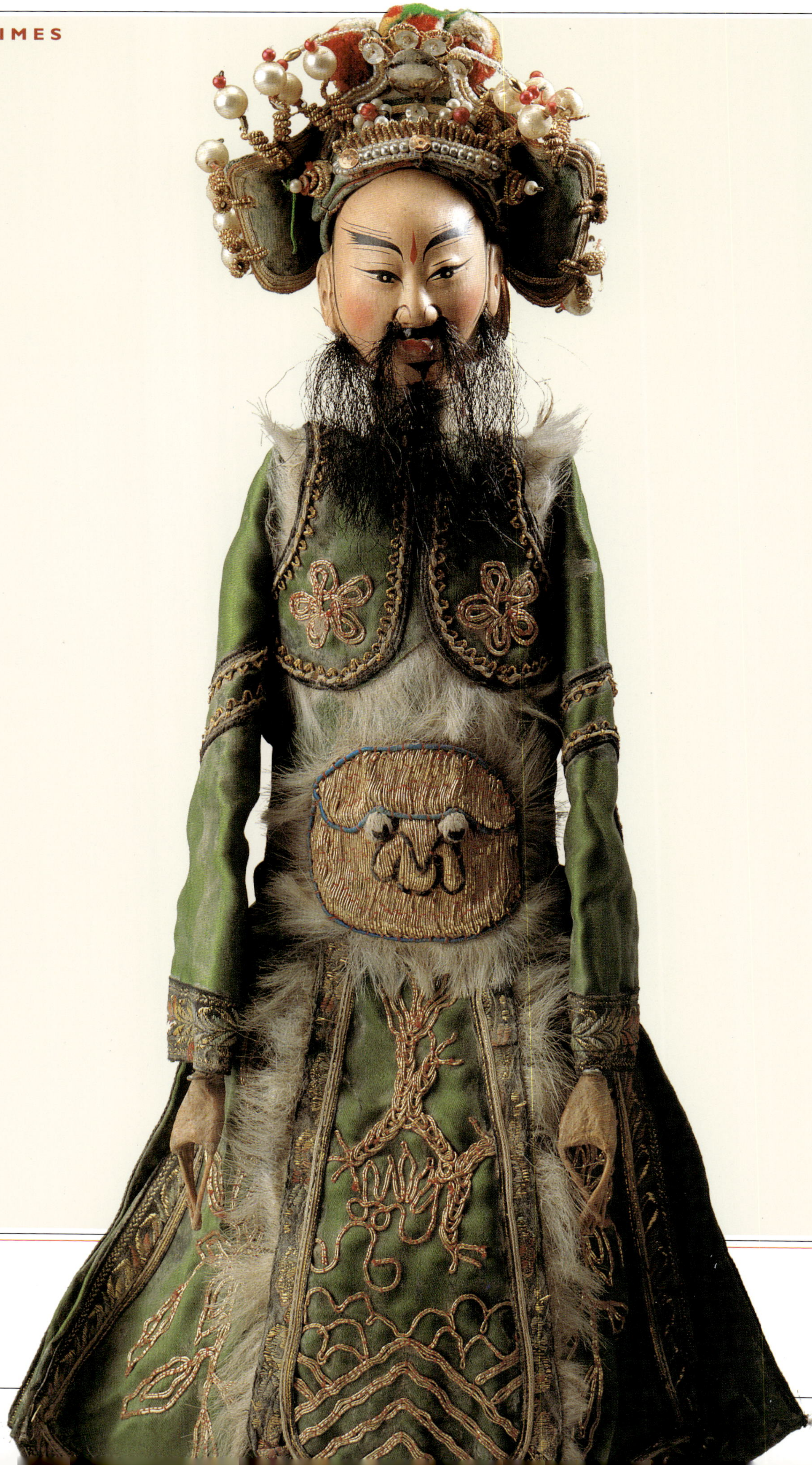

Rod marionette, one of several kinds of puppet theatre performed in streets in China. Puppeteers' repertoire could include plays about spirits and monsters, beautiful ladies, valiant knights, court cases, and stories taken from Chinese history and legend, height 30 cm.

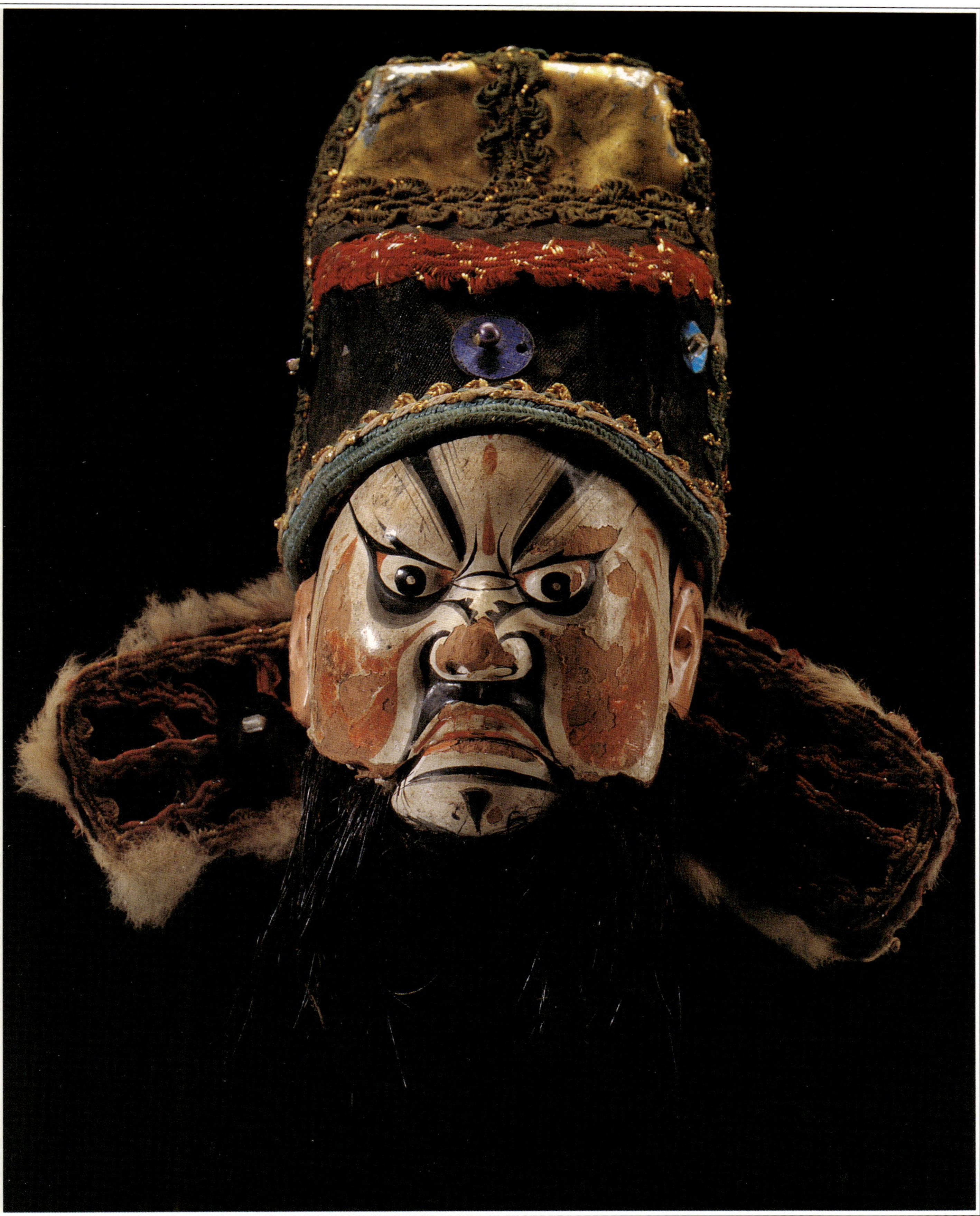

Head of rod puppet carved from wood with painted face reminiscent of the *hualian* of Peking opera, height 8 cm.

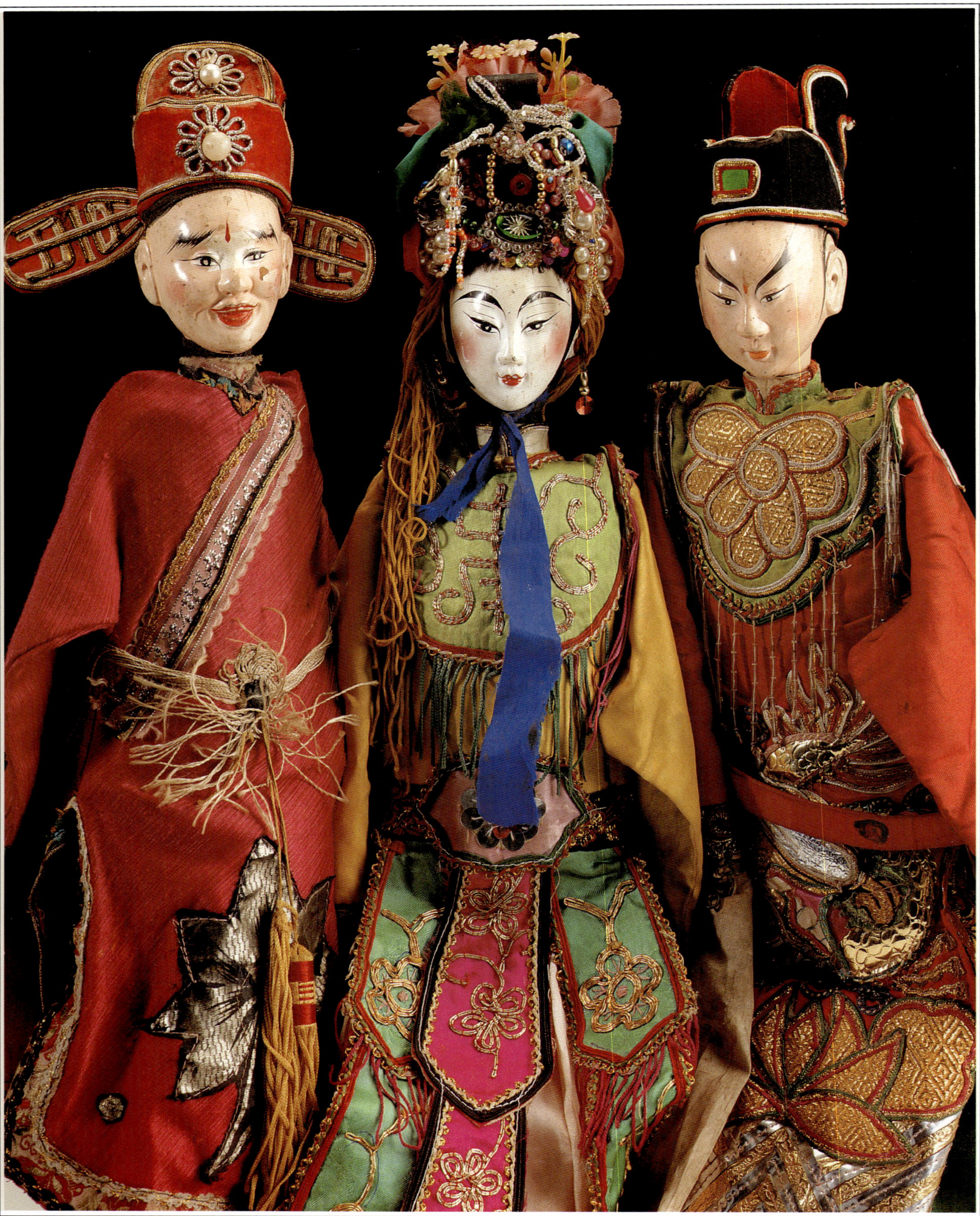

Marionettes in embroidered costumes on rods manipulated from below in puppet theatre popular in Fuzhou, Fujian province, height 30 cm.

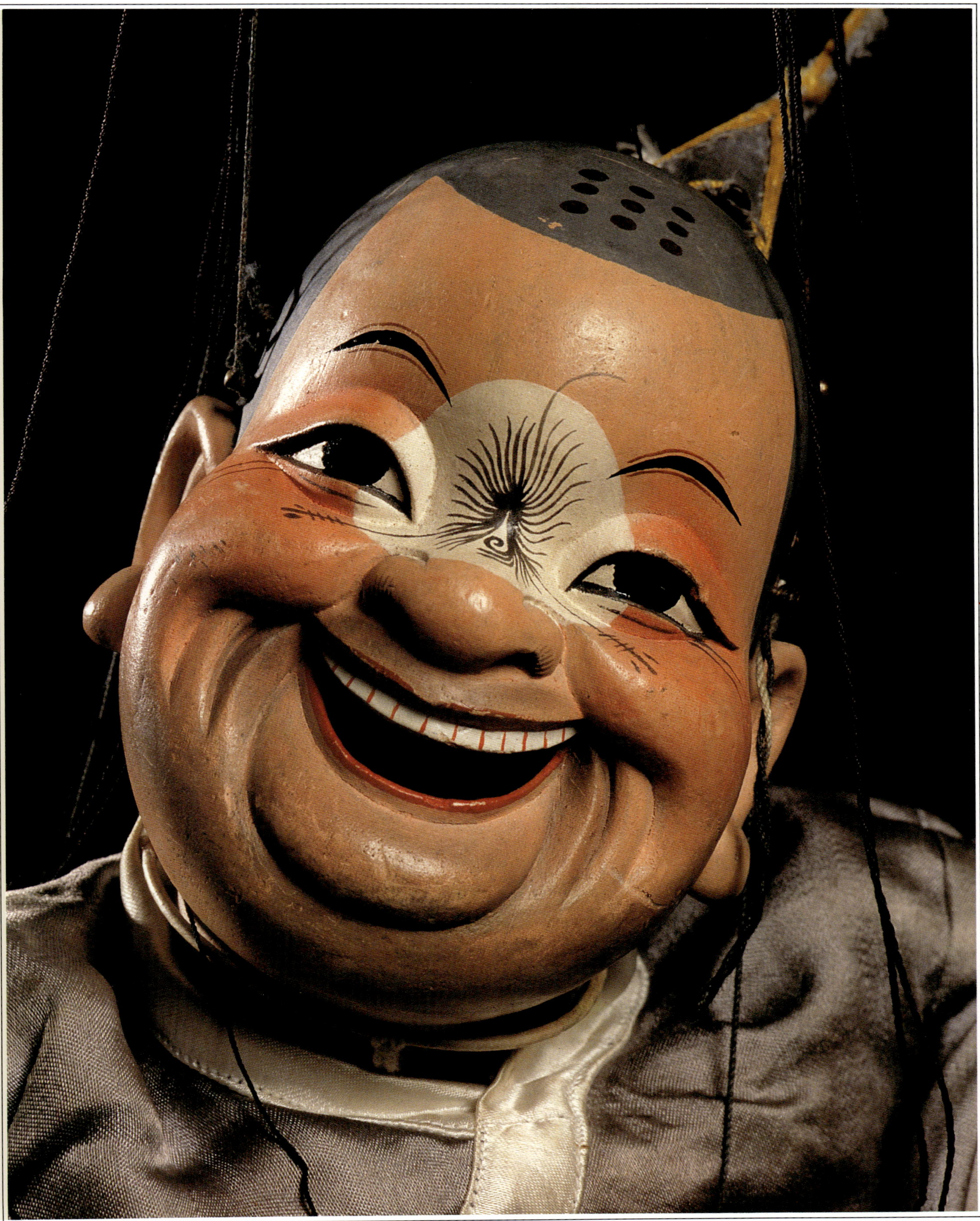

Head of puppet on strings pulled from above, full-length height 60 cm.

WHY TRUE TO FORM?

HOLLYWOOD ROAD, SO TO SPEAK, IS MY BACKYARD. Anyone who has encountered this congested one-way road just above Central in Hong Kong and strolled its length from the top of Ice House Street past the Central Police Station, down towards the green-glazed Man Mo temple, murky with incense, will have been richly rewarded with glimpses of irreplaceable Chinese art on display in the many lively little shops that give the road its distinctive character.

On my daily errands - the bank, a quick sandwich, the cobbler, my laundry - flashes of an amazing variety of Chinese antiques and folk art fleetingly grab my attention from shop windows.

The street never ceases to amaze me as wares on display seem to be replaced on a daily basis. Almost as if strolling through a hands-on-museum. Last week, on a pavement, I swear I saw a life-size camel and two elephants carved in granite chained to a parking meter. Straight from the Ming Tombs, I thought. Two days later they had disappeared.

A friend visiting recently asked if I could help supplement bamboo chairs she had purchased with me on a previous trip. Sure, no problem, I confidently assured her as we dodged angry traffic on our way westward, down Hollywood Road where it becomes more characteristically Hong Kong. Here, almost as if drawn back to another era, bargaining crowds still jostle one another, the spices of instant street-side kitchens mingle sharply with the sound of birdshops and beneath a shop sign in calligraphy— now somewhat discoloured with age— stands a row of traditional shops still selling affordable bamboo. Or so I thought!

In rough Cantonese the shop owner quite bluntly assured me I was living in the past. We haven't stocked those chairs in years! Who in Hong Kong today can afford the rents they're asking by selling bamboo? I am sure I detected him glaring at me in disbelief as I stood there uneasily beneath the propeller fan in his musty shop.

That shock several months ago was the catalyst for this book.

The familiar folk crafts I had so long been accustomed to and almost taken for granted had indeed become irreplaceable over the years.

True To Form is, therefore, with my thanks and appreciation, the outcome of the generous assistance I received from friends who encouraged me to photograph and include in this volume from their private collections worthy examples of the rapidly disappearing art of the Chinese craftsman.

Frank Fischbeck.
FormAsia Books.

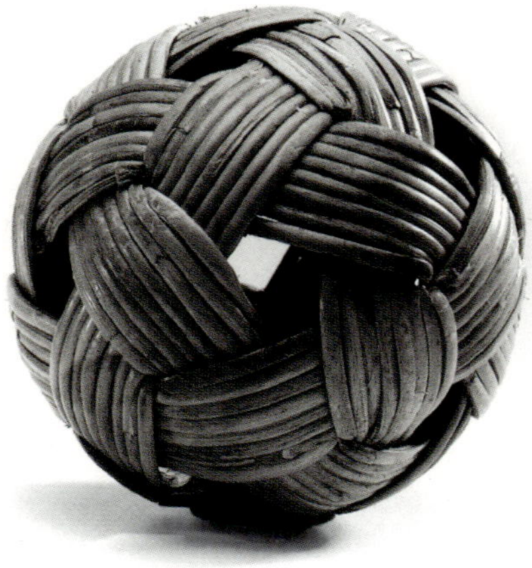

Acknowledgements

James Au,
HK Kite Association:
67,142-143.

Charles and Rosamond Brown:
100-101.

Dr Werner and Lucy Burger,
Asian Research Institute HK:
8,18,36-37,39,72,74,105,110, 116-119,122-125.

Eva Chan:
19,38,40 left,bottom centre, 60,70,77,80,86-87,90-91, 94-95,97-98,108,111,113,115, 129,132-138,147.

Chow Mei Ling,
Yau's Arts Co:
145.

Lai Chu,
Chu Kee Shipyard:
106.

Gerald Godfrey:
Front cover, preface, 12 centre, 15,17,41top,47-55,57,75, 82-83,104,128,130-131.

Keith and Elsie Kerr:
114.

Romy Lit,
Mingei Antiques Limited:
12,16,20-21,24,42-43,58-59, 61- 63,69,96,107,112.

Lo Ting Po,
Jub Tai Choon Limited:
45-46.

Robert and Alice Piccus:
57 bottom,99 top.

Manfred and Wai Yin Schoeni,
Schoeni Fine Oriental Art:
64,144,146.

Agnes Tang,
Mountain Folkcraft:
11top,25,32-33,34 centre,73, 78-79,92-93,102-103,109.

Lilian Tang:
30-31,34-35.

Glenn and Lucille Vessa,
Honeychurch Antiques:
6-7,9,11bottom,13-14,22-23, 26-29,56,88,99 bottom.

John and Arax Warner, London:
10,120-121,126,140-141.

Wong Him Tai,
Wang Yu Cheong Art & Curios:
89.